THE REMINISCENCES OF
Captain Harry A. Jackson
U.S. Navy (Retired)

INTERVIEWED BY
Paul Stillwell

U.S. Naval Institute • Annapolis, Maryland

Copyright © 2002

Preface

Few interviewees have come so often recommended for an oral history as Captain Harry Jackson. When I was working on the oral history of the late Admiral Hal Shear, an experienced submariner, he strongly urged that I interview Captain Jackson because of his breadth of knowledge and many contributions in the field of submarine design. Jackson also had a long teaching career at the Massachusetts Institute of technology. Some of his former students separately suggested that his memories should be captured through the medium of oral history: Casey J. Moton, Mike Bosworth, and Richard Boyle.

Further testimony to the importance of Jackson's contributions in the field of naval architecture and marine engineering is that he is one of only two individuals who have received both the Harold E. Saunders Award and the David W. Taylor Medal for notable achievement in naval architecture. The other person who received both awards was John Niedermair, whose oral history is also in the Naval Institute collection.

Jackson's interest in submarine engineering was evident as far back as the late 1920s when the loss of the submarine S-4 captured the nation's attention. As a youngster, he created a model of the submarine and practiced salvaging it in a pond near his home. After being educated in naval architecture and marine engineering at the University of Michigan, he was recruited into the Construction Corps of the Navy and proceeded to make substantial contributions in his chosen field.

Initially, he got lots of practical hands-on experience during World War II in design, construction, and repair of Navy ships. Soon after war's end he was one of the first officers selected for the Navy's fledgling nuclear power program. In the years that followed he made groundbreaking contributions in the field of submarine design, working on both diesel-powered and nuclear-powered vessels. He played an important role in developing the applications of the teardrop-hull design and the creation of the U.S. Navy's first ballistic missile submarine as part of the nation's strategic deterrent. Class after class bears Jackson's imprint: Albacore, Skipjack, George Washington, Ethan Allen, Thresher, and Sturgeon. And the practical part of working on real ships continued as well, particularly at the Portsmouth Naval Shipyard and Puget Sound Naval Shipyard.

In later years he was involved in trying to find an explanation for the loss of the U.S. submarine Scorpion and in the U.S. effort to recover a lost Soviet submarine. Harry Jackson was an engineering duty officer who particularly welcomed the challenge of confronting problems and solving them. This memoir contains dozens of examples of the finding of solutions. The many students he has taught continue his legacy to the service.

George Van, a retired naval officer, did the initial transcription of the interview tapes. Both Captain Jackson and I have done some editing of the transcript in the interests of accuracy, smoothness, and clarity. In addition, I have inserted footnotes to provide further information for readers who use the volume.

Ms. Ann Hassinger of the Naval Institute's history division has made a significant contribution through her diligence in the overall process of printing, proofreading, and overseeing the binding of the completed volumes.

Finally, the Naval Institute expresses its gratitude to the McMullen Family Foundation of Secaucus, New Jersey, for its generous financial support to facilitate completion of this memoir. Both John J. McMullen and Harry Jackson had substantial achievements in the field of ship design and engineering.

Paul Stillwell
Director, History Division
U.S. Naval Institute
November 2002

CAPTAIN HARRY ALLEN JACKSON, UNITED STATES NAVY (RETIRED)

Personal Data

Born: 7 December 1916, Saginaw, Michigan

Married: 15 April 1944 at Tiburon, California, to Mary Rebecca McElroy

Children: Harry A. Jackson, Jr., born 11 May 1947
Lisle Ann Jackson, born 25 July 1949

Education and Training

Bay City Junior College, Bay City, Michigan, Associate of Science (Engineering), June 1938

University of Michigan, Ann Arbor, Michigan, Bachelor of Science (Naval Architecture and Marine Engineering), February 1941

General Electric Corporation, Advanced Engineering Course in Nuclear Engineering, September 1946 to June 1950

Dates of Rank

Ensign: February 1941
Lieutenant (junior grade): June 1942
Lieutenant: November 1942
Lieutenant Commander: July 1945
Commander: July 1951
Captain: April 1960

Chronological Transcript of Service

December 1935-February 1941	Various duties as enlisted reservist
February 1941-December 1941	Boston Navy Yard Docking officer and ship superintendent
December 1941-September 1943	Bureau of Ships, Washington, D.C. Assistant to type desk officer

September 1943-December 1945	USS ABSD #3, Service Force PacFlt Docking and repair officer
January 1946-October 1946	USS Wharton (AP-7), Joint Task Force One
October 1946-February 1951	Atomic Energy Commission, Schenectady, NY Special assistant to operations manager
February 1951 to August 1954	Portsmouth Naval Shipyard, Kittery, Maine Ship superintendent, assistant design superintendent, Design superintendent
September 1954-June 1956	Office of the Chief of Naval Operations Nuclear Power Section Head
June 1956-June 1958	Bureau of Ships, Washington, D.C. Project officer, FBM submarines
June 1958-August 1962	Portsmouth Naval Shipyard, Kittery, Maine Design Superintendent
September 1962-July 1964	Puget Sound Naval Shipyard, Bremerton, Washington FBM project officer, planning officer
August 1964-December 1968	Superintendent of shipbuilding, Groton, Connecticut Supervisor of shipbuilding, conversion, and repair
November 1968-December 1968	Temporary Additional duty from Groton as supervisor of shipbuilding at Quincy, Massachusetts
January 1969-September 1969	Technical director, Operation Scorpion Search, Phase II
October 1969	Retired from active duty.

Awards

Legion of Merit plus gold star in lieu of second award
Navy Commendation Ribbon
American Defense Medal
American Theater Medal
World War II Victory Medal
Asiatic Pacific Theater Medal
Korean Service Medal with star
Naval Reserve Medal

Authorization

The U.S. Naval Institute is hereby authorized to make available to individuals, libraries, and other repositories of its choosing the tapes and/or transcripts of three oral history interviews concerning the life and naval career of the undersigned. The Naval Institute may also, at its discretion, use the material in electronic/digital format, including posting on the Internet. The interviews were recorded on 1 September 1998, 2 September 1998, and 3 September 1998, in collaboration with Paul Stillwell for the U.S. Naval Institute.

The undersigned does hereby release and assign to the U.S. Naval Institute the rights and title to these interviews, with the exception that the undersigned retains the right to use the material for his own purposes, as he sees fit. The copyright in both the oral and transcribed versions shall be the sole property of the U.S. Naval Institute. The tape recordings of the interviews are and will remain the property of the U.S. Naval Institute.

Signed and sealed this 3rd day of May 2000.

Harry Jackson
Captain, U.S. Navy (Retired)

Interview Number 1 with Captain Harry A. Jackson, U.S. Navy (Retired)

Place: Captain Jackson's home, Groton, Connecticut

Date: Tuesday, 1 September 1998

Interviewer: Paul Stillwell

Paul Stillwell: Well, it's a delight to see you in this beautiful setting not far from the Navy's submarine headquarters and the site where many of them were built. Could you start laying the groundwork for your naval career, please, by talking about when and where you were born and some of your early childhood?

Captain Jackson: Yes, I was born in Saginaw, Michigan, on December 7, 1916. My father was Alan D. Jackson, and my mother was Ina Ruth Lorimer Jackson. I have one older brother who died in 1984. The hope was that the second child would be a girl, and I think my parents were disappointed that I turned out to be a boy.

Paul Stillwell: But you've managed to deal with it nevertheless.

Captain Jackson: Yes, I did. I recovered from that, although there are number of reasons that I developed a severe inferiority complex, which turned out to be good because it caused me to work harder and try to excel in later life.

Paul Stillwell: Was that disappointment to your parents one of the causes of that complex?

Captain Jackson: That and others. When my mother and father married, he was a rather successful businessman who made electric automobiles. When the gasoline engines took over from the electrics, he started another company, making trailers to be towed by automobiles and was called auto-camp trailer. The Depression came along, and he lost everything in the Depression.* The banks foreclosed on the mortgage of our house, and so we had to move. This made a big impact on me. It was quite a struggle to just survive in those days.

Paul Stillwell: Where did you wind up living after you lost the house?

Captain Jackson: Well, in the same city, Saginaw, but in the outskirts of it known as South Saginaw. My brother was real smart. He excelled in school without much study, and as I was going to school two years behind him everybody said, "Why don't you be like your brother?"

When they'd say that, I'd say, "In no way am I going to be like him." So I really didn't study very hard. In the early days my grades were very good, but in high school they were on the low end.

Paul Stillwell: Well, I can imagine psychologically you could feel that if you didn't compete, there was no way you can lose the competition.

Captain Jackson: [Chuckle] Well, that could have been. But it turns out that I learned a lot more than I was given credit for.

Paul Stillwell: And how did you do that?

Captain Jackson: By listening to what the teachers said, and the teachers of that era were superb. They were teachers not for the money, but because that's what they wanted to do. They were great. The only one that I had a little difficulty with was Mr. Klutz. All the students called him Automatic Klutz. He would make me stay after school frequently, and his idea of punishment was to add up and subtract large columns of large numbers. I did it so often that I could do that like lightning. It was no problem to add them up.

---

* Following the crash of the New York Stock Exchange in late October 1929, the United States was plunged into the Great Depression, from which it did not recover until the nation geared up for World War II at the beginning of the 1940s. The Depression was marked by high unemployment and many business failures.

Paul Stillwell: It must have been very frustrating to him.

Captain Jackson: It was.

Paul Stillwell: What did your parents instill in the way of discipline and values?

Captain Jackson: Well, my mother was very, very good about that. She had high moral standards, and she ensured that both my brother and I learned what was right and what was wrong. My father had lots of his own problems, and he really didn't believe in going on to college. He thought it was a waste of time. He had two brothers. He was the oldest one. He decided not to go to college, and the two brothers did, and they were very successful. And that also had a big impact on me.

Paul Stillwell: In what way?

Captain Jackson: Well, my grandfather was a rector of a several Episcopal churches. He encouraged both my brother and me to go to college, and he was an excellent mathematician. When he retired from the ministry he became a professor at Case College Western Reserve, teaching classical math. He was always after me to study Euclid. I wasn't quite sure who Euclid was, and it wasn't until long after he had passed away that I started reading Euclid, and I found out that it was just the basis for all the math that I had learned. It was very interesting.

Paul Stillwell: You told me last night that things were so desperate in the Depression that you didn't eat well at times.

Captain Jackson: That's right. My mother and father had good friends who owned a farm, and I spent a lot of time on the farm, mostly because I enjoyed it, but also that was one place you could always get something to eat and that was good.

Paul Stillwell: I would think that your father would not be in a good frame of mind, their losing a house and being unable to provide for the family well.

Captain Jackson: Yes, it was pretty bad.

Paul Stillwell: Please tell me about the interest you had in the S-4 and its sinking.*

Captain Jackson: Well, I think I was 11 or 12 when the S-4 sank, and, of course, the local newspapers were filled with reports of not only the loss of the submarine but the efforts to rescue the people that were alive in the ship. That rescue turned out to be a failure, because they didn't have the equipment ready in time to get them out.

At that age I was interested in making models. Didn't have many toys, and I substituted by making my own. I made a model of the S-4 and some of the rescue ships and the pontoons to raise it. Then I took it to a pond and actually played around raising the submarine. I learned a great deal from doing that, but the biggest thing I learned was how really difficult it was to undertake that project. I was operating in only three or four feet of water, and the S-4 was at something like 150 feet, and their problems were just magnified many times.

Paul Stillwell: What did you use for making the models?

Captain Jackson: Wood because, one, it was cheap and, secondly, it was easy to work with.

Paul Stillwell: How would you keep your submarine from just floating to the surface?

---

* On 17 December 1927, as the submarine S-4 (SS-109) was surfacing from a submerged run over the measured mile off Provincetown, Cape Cod, Massachusetts, she was accidentally rammed and sunk by the Coast Guard destroyer Paulding. The Navy tried unsuccessfully to rescue six survivors who sent a series of signals to divers by tapping from inside the hull. The S-4 was eventually raised on 17 March 1928.

Captain Jackson: Well, I had to ballast it. Along the way I got a little mold to make lead soldiers, and I got a little ladle. I made hundreds of lead soldiers, and so I got pretty good at casting things, and I cast lead ballast for the submarine.

Paul Stillwell: How did you fill the pontoons with air to bring the submarine up?

Captain Jackson: With a bicycle pump. It was pretty crude, but it taught me a lot of lessons, and I still use those lessons.

Paul Stillwell: What lessons did you get from that?

Captain Jackson: Well, if you want something, set about doing it, and you'll find a way. That's a big lesson that I try to pass on to all my students.

Another thing that went on shortly after that is that I went to junior high school, and there was a woodworking teacher in the manual training part of the school who was a boat builder. He was very much interested in boat design and construction. I didn't realize it till later, but he had a purpose in establishing what he called The Model Boat Club, in which he would enroll many of the students. They were practically all boys because girls didn't do that kind of thing in those days.

He would design a boat and then get one of the students to make a model of it. We built sometimes just display models and sometimes actually sailing models. And he would study these models with great interest. I can see him yet holding the model up in the light so he could see the shadows and so forth. Later on, he started to build what he knew was to be the last boat that he would build. In that boat you could see all the models that had been made over a number of years, and it turned out to be a beautiful cutter. It really was. The workmanship on it was superb, and it was beautiful.

Paul Stillwell: Did you have any interest in sailing?

Captain Jackson: Oh, yes. As a matter of fact, he built a little sailing dinghy that he had designed. I was working in the little shipyard where he was building it, so I did a lot of the work on this little dinghy. Later on I bought it from him, and I still have it. It was finished in 1937, so that's 61 years old.

Paul Stillwell: Built to last.

Captain Jackson: Yes, it was.

Paul Stillwell: Well, I take it from what you say that you must have a high degree of manual dexterity as well.

Captain Jackson: Yes, I can do carpenter work or machinist work.

Paul Stillwell: Well, as we were walking in, you said you built this entire building we're in, which is an office and workshop out in your back yard.

Captain Jackson: Yes, that's right. I can tell you some other stories.

Paul Stillwell: Well, please do.

Captain Jackson: It sort of jumps ahead, but on the Thresher we were on sea trials, and we had a failure in one of the strainers for the high-pressure air system.* We wanted to continue running, but we had to do something about repairing that piece. The simplest way was just to make a new pipe, and so I made a sketch and said, "We'll make a pipe." The word came back that they didn't have anybody that could do it. I said, "Well, I'll do it." I went down to the lathe and got a big piece of bar stock and started working on it. I just started on it pretty good, and I could see this chief machinist's mate watching me. He was getting more antsy all the time.

I could just imagine him saying, "Hey, I'm not going to stand here and watch some dumb captain make something that I should be making."

---

* USS Thresher (SSN-593) was a nuclear attack submarine commissioned 3 August 1961. She was later lost in an accident at sea in April 1963.

Paul Stillwell: Did he eventually take it over?

Captain Jackson: Yes, he did, and he did a good job. We repaired the valve and went on with the trials.

Paul Stillwell: Was this on a lathe?

Captain Jackson: Yes, it was a lathe job all the way, but we had to cut threads on it and drill a big hole to carry the flow of air.

Paul Stillwell: I never realized there'd be a lathe in a submarine.

Captain Jackson: Oh, sure. All submarines have lathes, as well as destroyers and other ships.

Paul Stillwell: That's part of my education then.

Captain Jackson: Yes.

Paul Stillwell: Well, back about the same time as the S-4, Lindbergh was flying the Atlantic.* Did aviation capture your attention at all?

Captain Jackson: Yes, a little bit, but not enough to make we want to follow that. I actually saw Lindbergh fly. He came to our town, which had an airport. Actually, he didn't land. He just flew over, and we were all standing there waiting to see him. Somebody said, "Gee, he's late. Maybe he got lost."

Another guy said, "Hell, if he could find Paris he can find Saginaw." I remember that very clearly.

---

* Charles A. Lindbergh became a national hero when he made the first solo flight across the Atlantic Ocean in May 1927. The light cruiser Memphis (CL-13) brought Lindbergh and his plane back to the United States, arriving at the Washington Navy Yard on 11 June.

Paul Stillwell: What was it about submarines that so captured your imagination at that age?

Captain Jackson: I really don't know except that they were complex things. But that's when I decided I wanted to be a submarine naval constructor eventually. As I told you last night, John Niedermair played a big part in both the S-4 and the S-51, and I wanted to do what he did.*

Paul Stillwell: And you read Ellsberg's book, On the Bottom.†

Captain Jackson: Oh, yes. Yes, I sure did, many times. So that decided that. But there appeared to be no hope for me to go on to college. There was just no way. So I didn't really exert myself in school. As a matter of fact, my Latin teacher said that she understood that everybody didn't like Latin, but she thought that there were other things that I could do that I was very good at. So she was inferring I ought to be a manual trades student instead of a college preparatory.

Paul Stillwell: Well, you said that you'd had this lesson imparted to you—to find a way to achieve what you wanted to achieve. How then did you go about getting to college?

Captain Jackson: Well, I have to give my brother a lot of credit, too, because there was no doubt in his mind he was going to go to college somehow. When I graduated from high school, there weren't very many jobs available. I worked in a little boatyard for a while until that work ran out.

Paul Stillwell: What year was that?

---

* John Niedermair was a civilian engineer for the Navy for many, many years. His oral history is in the Naval Institute collection.
† On the night of 25 September 1925, the USS S-51 (SS-162) was rammed and sunk off Block Island, New York, by the merchant steamer City of Rome. Of the 36 men on board the submarine, only three survived. For a compelling account by the principal salvage officer, see Edward Ellsberg, On the Bottom (New York: Literary Guild of America, Inc., 1929).

Captain Jackson: I graduated in '34. There was a factory that built stepladders. I got a job there at 20 cents an hour. That too folded after a while. But while I was there I accumulated enough money so that I could finance one year at Bay City Junior College. But my brother wanted to go, so I gave him the money to go first, with the idea that when he graduated he would help me. So I got a job working at Sears & Roebuck in the maintenance part of the store, and also I was the setup man for the appliances. I would go out and set them up. I did that while I was going to school, so, in effect, I was earning my own way through school. I got good grades. As a matter of fact, I graduated from Bay City Junior College with honors.

Paul Stillwell: What course did you major in?

Captain Jackson: Engineering. It was the same course one took at Michigan. They used the same textbooks and so forth, so it was a good education. When I graduated from there, I decided that I could support myself and go to school in Ann Arbor, which I did. When I went there, I had enough money to pay the first semester's tuition and not much else, so the first thing I had to do was to get a job for my board. I worked in a sorority house washing dishes for my meals. Then I had to get a place to live, so I got a place where they would give me free room if I would rake the leaves and shovel the walks and do a little maintenance around the house.

Then that left books to pay for, and you could get books at a fairly reasonable price in those days if you'd buy used books, so that I was marginally making it. But then I got a job with the department of engineering research, where I got 25 cents an hour. That was good pay. I was able to work 30-40 hours a week, so I was getting enough money to live on and save a little bit too. But I had to send money home to help my mother. She was working in a department store, and I remember very clearly she got $12.00 a week, which was not enough to really run the household on.

Paul Stillwell: Was your dad not working at all at that point?

Captain Jackson: No, he didn't do much to support the family. So, anyway, because I was working so much, I had to take an extra semester at Michigan to finish up.

Paul Stillwell: That was a pretty demanding regimen you imposed on yourself.

Captain Jackson: Yes, it was. And I had enlisted in the Naval Reserve in 1935, and I stayed in the Naval Reserve while I was going to school. I got one day's pay a week, which turned out to be about $18.00 a month, and that helped pay for the books. So it was a lot of hard work, but I learned a lot, too, by doing it.

Paul Stillwell: Before the tape started this morning, we were talking about the Squalus, which sank during your time as an undergraduate. Please tell me about your awareness and perceptions on that.[*]

Captain Jackson: Well, the loss of the Squalus was a real tragedy that need not have happened. At that time the training was to dive the submarine as quickly as possible so that one would go from the surface condition to periscope depth in 30 seconds. That was the objective. When you consider all the things that have to be done in order to dive a submarine, that's a remarkably short time.

There are number of things about that. Since the purpose of the trial run they were on was to make timed dives, they had decided to take certain shortcuts. In the air supply lines to the engine room there are two valves that should be closed when the ship is submerged, and they are open when the ship is on the surface. One is an outboard valve, and the other one is called an inboard valve. In order to make the dive quickly, they decided that they would only close the outboard valve. They would close it first, and as soon as that was shut they would close the inboards. But the inboards were big gate

---

[*] USS Squalus (SS-192), commanded by Lieutenant Oliver F. Naquin, USN, sank in 243 feet of water while conducting exercise dives on 23 May 1939 off Portsmouth, New Hampshire. Twenty-six men died, but 33, including Naquin, were recovered through the use of the McCann rescue chamber. The submarine later was salvaged, refurbished, and renamed the Sailfish. For details, see Carl La VO, Back from the Deep (Annapolis; Naval Institute Press, 1994).

valves. They had a big flywheel on them, and they had to reach up over the engine and close it.

For people that have seen movies of fleet submarines diving, they generally showed a view of someone closing those inboard valves with the handle so you can recognize what it was. The other thing is a big air induction valve in the superstructure above the pressure hull. This is 36 inches in diameter, and it goes into a pipe that was about 18 inches in diameter. The valve on the top could be opened and closed with hydraulic power. The other valve, the hull valve, could be closed by an operator in the control room.

They prepared the ship to make the first dive, and they started down. Everything apparently worked all right, and they leveled off at periscope depth. And it is customary to vent the main ballast tanks to ensure that you get all the air out of the tanks. There are levers in the control room that can control the hydraulic oil to the operator on the vent valve. Normally this vent valve manifold is manned by the chief of the boat, but on the day of the trials, the chief of the boat had a medical problem and stayed in to go to the hospital. A trainee, a first class petty officer, was substituting for him.

It's thought, and I have to put the thought underlined because there's no proof in any way whether it happened or not, but at least it's thought that the trainee opened up the vent valves one at time going aft, and so he bled off the air in all the tanks. But there was one more lever that operated the main induction valve, so it's thought that he opened that, and the water started flooding into the engine rooms.

The first thing the control room knew about that, somebody ran up from the engine room and said, "Flooding in the engine room." By that time the ship was so heavy that she was doomed to at least sink and go to the bottom. There were 33 people alive in the ship in the forward end, and that was unique in submarines to have so many. But as a result of the S-4 and S-51 the Navy had prepared for this contingency under the leadership of Admiral Momsen, who was later captain of the South Dakota when I docked her in Guam.*

The Navy had developed a rescue chamber and it was on several of the submarine rescue ships. Tringa had one, and it was called the McCann Chamber, and it took it out there and a diver went down and hooked it on. It could pull itself down on the hatch and

---

* At the time of the Squalus incident, Charles B. Momsen was a lieutenant commander, noted for his development of a submarine escape breathing device known as the Momsen lung. As a captain he commanded the battleship South Dakota (BB-57) from 3 December 1944 to 29 July 1945.

de-water the chamber, so the hatch into the submarine could be opened, as well as the hatch into the chamber. So people could go from the submarine into the chamber, and as a result in about four trips they were able to rescue all 33 people that were alive in the Squalus.[*]

This was a real achievement, and certainly those 33 people were very grateful that the Navy had made that provision. There was some controversy about whether it was a mechanical failure or was a human failure in the operation of the main induction valve. It was never proved for certain one way or the other, and that's the reason that the word "thought" is in quotation marks. It's not sure.

Paul Stillwell: What is your source for that supposition?

Captain Jackson: Well, I had a chance to interview Bob Evans, who was ship superintendent during the whole construction period on that ship.[†] So that's one source. Over the years I had met some of the survivors of the crew and also the yard inspection person, and I put a lot of bits and pieces together to come up with that scenario. There are so many things that could have happened that we don't know about. It's very difficult to say for sure exactly what it is.

Paul Stillwell: I thought I heard one hypothesis that a piece of wood or something had gotten stuck and jammed the main induction valve in an open position.

Captain Jackson: That I'll have to say is a rumor because no one knows. When the ship was raised, there was no evidence of that, but that doesn't mean it wasn't there at one time and it came out during the salvage.

Paul Stillwell: And there's no way of knowing what would have happened had that chief been on board instead of at sick bay that day.

---

[*] See the Naval Institute oral history of Chief Machinist's Mate William Badders, USN (Ret.), who was one of the rescuers.
[†] See the Naval Institute oral history of Captain Robert L. Evans, USN (Ret.).

Captain Jackson: In all these tragedies a great many things have to happen, and they all have to happen in the right sequence, because if they don't all happen or if they don't happen in the right sequence, why, all you have is a near miss.

Paul Stillwell: You break the chain.

Captain Jackson: And that's reason why it's so hard to pinpoint what happened.

Paul Stillwell: What can you say about the substance of the courses you took at Michigan?

Captain Jackson: Well, they were pretty standard for the naval architecture schools at that time. Michigan had the reputation of being one of the preeminent schools along with MIT and Webb.[*] And certainly the quality and the quantity of the education were very good.

Paul Stillwell: Was the Navy sending some of its postgraduate students to the University of Michigan at that time?

Captain Jackson: No, not at that time. They started a naval ROTC when I was a senior.[†] I applied to go to it, but I got turned down because I only had a year to go.

Paul Stillwell: Had you had any interest in going to the Naval Academy?

Captain Jackson: Oh, yes. Sure. But I couldn't see. Couldn't pass the eye exam. That was another thing that gave me an inferiority complex. I don't know why it should, but it did.

Paul Stillwell: Something you had no control over.

---

[*] MIT—Massachusetts Institute of Technology, Cambridge, Massachusetts; Webb Institute of Naval Architecture, Glen Cove, New York
[†] ROTC--reserve officers' training corps.

Captain Jackson: But I graduated near the top of the group that I was in, and while I was there the war was coming on. Among the things that they needed were young naval officers; in those days they called them naval constructors. So they sent officers from the Bureau of Construction and Repair up to give lectures, and I took those lectures. There were two lieutenant commanders, one Pyne and the other one Kniskern, that gave the lectures.*

Paul Stillwell: Schuyler Pyne?

Captain Jackson: Schuyler Pyne, right. You've probably interviewed him.

Paul Stillwell: Well, my predecessor did. I remember seeing Admiral Pyne around Annapolis before he died.†

Captain Jackson: Yes, he was a good guy, and whenever we would get together he would tell the other people that he'd recruited me into the Construction Corps, which is true. He did.

Paul Stillwell: Was it always your intention to fulfill this career in uniform, as opposed to being a civilian?

Captain Jackson: No, but particularly after I joined the Naval Reserve I wanted to be in uniform.

Paul Stillwell: I take it you gave no consideration to being a line officer.

Captain Jackson: Oh, I did. Yes, I did, but I was caught. When we were commissioned, we knew we were getting into war. We knew that the German submarine menace was our biggest obstacle, but we didn't have much of an ASW fleet, and they needed people, young

---

* Lieutenant Commander Schuyler N. Pyne, USN; the oral history of Pyne, who retired as a rear admiral, is in the Naval Institute collection. Lieutenant Commander Leslie A. Kniskern, USN.
† Admiral Pyne died 13 June 1987.

people, to step in and do the work.* That's why Pyne and Kniskern came up and, in effect, recruited us. But because we were recruited, we were programmed to go as naval constructors.

Paul Stillwell: So you really didn't get into talking to recruiters about a seagoing type job.

Captain Jackson: No, but I wanted to. I had a lot of sea duty in the Naval Reserve, and I was an ardent small-boat sailor. When I was going to college, summer times I would work on big yachts, and there I learned a great deal more. I learned how to navigate, how to pilot, how to maintain ships, how to fix engines, all that kind of stuff.

Paul Stillwell: What was included in your sea duty while you were in the Naval Reserve?

Captain Jackson: Well, most of it was on an old gunboat, the Dubuque, which wasn't too large.† It was only 1,800 tons, but she had iron sides and a wooden bottom. I couldn't for the life of me figure out why they had a wooden bottom on the ship. It wasn't until I read a history of the Construction Corps that they discussed it. They said when they first started using iron ships they would put copper on the outside to keep down the marine growth. But then they had a good battery, and iron just eroded away. So to solve that problem on the later ships—and the Dubuque was one of the later ships—they put about six inches of teak planking on the bottom, and then they could nail the copper sheathing to the wood. That way there wasn't a battery, and both the wood and the copper lasted much longer. But that was a good little ship. It had two little reciprocating steam engines, and by the time I got on it, it had oil fuel, but she was built to be coal-fired.

Paul Stillwell: Where did she operate while you were on board?

---

* ASW—antisubmarine warfare.
† USS Dubuque (gunboat number 17) was commissioned 3 June 1905. She had a standard displacement of 1,084 tons, was 200 feet long, and 35 feet in the beam. Her top speed was 13 knots. She was fitted out as a mine training ship in 1915. The ship was assigned hull numbers as follows: AG-6 in 1919; IX-9 in 1922, and PG-17 in 1940.

Captain Jackson: Oh, out on the Great Lakes.

Paul Stillwell: Was it a reserve training ship?

Captain Jackson: Yes, that's what she did. When the war started, she went back to saltwater and was homeported in Portsmouth Naval Shipyard and operated on the East Coast, training gun crews for the merchant marine.

Paul Stillwell: I think she'd been on duty in World War I as well.

Captain Jackson: Oh, she was.

Paul Stillwell: Any specific incidents or anecdotes you remember from being on board the Dubuque?

Captain Jackson: Oh, a lot of them. The first cruise I made on it was my first time on a big ship like that, and so that made a big impression on me.

Paul Stillwell: In what ways?

Captain Jackson: Well, just the routine and organization. Because I was interested in both the hull construction and operating the engines, I got assignments both on deck and in the engine room. I was an oiler on the engines. One summer we went on the Wilmette, which was a converted passenger ship. She had bigger engines on that, and I was an oiler on that one too.

Paul Stillwell: What do you remember about working with those reciprocating engines?

Captain Jackson: Well, when you'd go into suicide alley to feel the bearings it was frightening.

Paul Stillwell: Well, trying to hit one of those oil cups when it's moving up and down would also be a challenge.

Captain Jackson: Yes. Well, it was a lot of fun to get the vertical slides for the connecting rods with a big squirt gun. You squirted up there, and most of time you'd hit it.

Paul Stillwell: Were you rated as a petty officer during that time?

Captain Jackson: No, never did get to be a petty officer because promotion in those days was pretty slow, particularly in the reserves, because nobody was getting transferred and out. But there were lots of seamen with two hash marks.* I only got one hash mark.

Paul Stillwell: Well, you said your brother was going to help you in the college venture. How was that?

Captain Jackson: Oh, that turned out he never did help me. He was supposed to.

Paul Stillwell: Oh, I see. You helped him.

Captain Jackson: Yes, I helped him, but he went off and went to work for General Electric Company, and he forgot about the fact that he was supposed to help me.

Paul Stillwell: Well, it sounds as if you felt sort of a sense of obligation to get out of the house so that your parents wouldn't have to support you as well.

Captain Jackson: Yes, yes, I did. I was on my own off and on.

Paul Stillwell: What transpired after you were recruited by Kniskern and Pyne into the Construction Corps?

---

* Hash mark is a slang term for the service mark worn on the sleeves of the uniforms of Navy enlisted personnel to denote length of service. Each stripe denotes four years.

Captain Jackson: Well, they had a program which was good. I was sent to Boston Navy Yard to really get some practical experience in the construction of ships, particularly destroyers. I reported for duty on March 1, 1941. The first assignment I had was as an assistant ship superintendent on the Mayrant, which was one of the destroyers being repaired. My real duty was was to observe the process of building the ship and get to know the people and so forth.

I wasn't on that very long when there were two trawlers sent there to be converted into minesweepers. Lo and behold, I got to be ship superintendent in charge. And that was real good experience because the stability of the trawlers was insufficient for a minesweeper, so we had to put big blisters on it. Because most of the old-timers were working on the bigger ships, I got to run that thing pretty much by myself, which was really good experience, because it was sink or swim. We turned out a good job.

Paul Stillwell: So you had to do the design work as well as supervising the implementation.

Captain Jackson: Well, there wasn't much design work on it. That was one of the problems. The design people were busy.

Paul Stillwell: Well, somebody had to design the blisters.

Captain Jackson: Yes, they did, but when we started to put them on they didn't fit. You know, typical. So we had to make them fit.

Paul Stillwell: And how did you do that?

Captain Jackson: Well, remembering my work in the boatyard, I got a bunch of big 2x4s and used them like splines. I put them around the ship and then put the floors in to match that. Then we put the plates on the outside of that. When that job was done, I got two new assignments. The Rodney came in for overhaul, and I was assistant ship superintendent on the Rodney.[*]

Paul Stillwell: Well, please tell me about that. What work did she need?

Captain Jackson: Oh, man. She needed everything.

Paul Stillwell: Was this still before the United States got into the war?

Captain Jackson: That's right. She came into the yard directly from her battle with the Bismarck.[†] The biggest thing that I saw was that she was firing her guns right dead ahead, and the blast from the guns deformed the deck. Just sank it down. Also that they had carried oil in their oil tanks, and a lot of those were damaged.

Paul Stillwell: Just by the blast effect?

Captain Jackson: No. Old age. Operating. One of the impressions maybe is the bilges were chock-a-block full with waste fuel oil. I don't think they'd ever pumped them out.

Paul Stillwell: And that ship was probably at least 15 years old by that point.[‡] She came in the wake of the Washington Disarmament Conference, so she had that odd arrangement with the turrets.[§]

Captain Jackson: That's right. Absolutely correct. So that was 1922.

---

[*] HMS Rodney was a British battleship.
[†] In May 1941, the German battleship Bismarck, accompanied by the cruiser Prinz Eugen, entered the Atlantic to operate as a surface raider. In a gun duel on 24 May against the British, she sank HMS Hood and damaged HMS Prince of Wales. The Bismarck herself was damaged on the 26th by British torpedo planes and sunk on the 27th by gunfire from the British battleships Rodney and King George V.
[‡] HMS Rodney was laid down in 1922, launched in 1925, and completed in 1927.
[§] To save weight of armor, all three turrets for the 16-inch guns were forward of the superstructure.

Paul Stillwell: So you got all the oil out of the bilges for them?

Captain Jackson: Yes, we did that. Actually, as I was touring the ship I went into a compartment that was absolutely beautiful. It was spotlessly clean. All the pipes that were copper or brass were polished, and so I talked to the petty officer in charge of that, and I said, "Hey, what is this stuff?"

He said, "This is the hydraulic plant." They supplied the hydraulic pressure for all the machinery throughout the ship.

I said, "Gee, that's beautiful."

He said, "Yeah, we're real proud of that. That came out of the old Rodney."[*] And you could tell that he was real proud of it, and this compartment was head and shoulders above any other.

Paul Stillwell: The impression I've gotten is that wouldn't have taken much because typically the British ships were not nearly as clean as American ones.

Captain Jackson: Boy, that's for sure. And there was a four-stack destroyer in there, and one of my reserve assignments was on a four-stack destroyer. It was out in San Diego, and so we never saw it much, but that was our mobilization billet, the USS Welles, DD-257. It was one of the 50 that were given to the British.[†]

Paul Stillwell: Had you spent time on her?

Captain Jackson: No.

Paul Stillwell: Just that's where you would have gone had you been mobilized.

---

[*] It could be that the individual was referring to a planned British battle cruiser, sister of HMS Hood, which was built during World War II. Construction of that Rodney was cancelled in 1918 because battle cruisers as a type had been largely discredited in the 1916 Battle of Jutland.

[†] In September 1940 President Franklin D. Roosevelt concluded a deal with Prime Minister Winston Churchill of Great Britain whereby the United States transferred 50 destroyers to the Royal Navy for use against German submarines. In return the United States received 99-year leases to British bases in the West Indies, Bermuda, and Newfoundland. On 9 September 1941 the USS Welles became HMS Cameron.

Captain Jackson: But we did an awful lot of study on it, you know, with the theory that if we looked at all the plans and the history of the ship and everything that we'd be better prepared to put it in commission.

Paul Stillwell: Well, it would be of some help, I would think.

Captain Jackson: Yes, yes, sure. Yes, it would.

Paul Stillwell: What do you remember about your dealings with the British officers and enlisted men, other than the hydraulic man?

Captain Jackson: Well, the two guys that I was impressed with—there was a British Naval Constructor, Sammy Davis, who later came to Canada and became their Chief Naval Constructor as a Canadian. Another guy was Taffy Evans, and I lost track of him after the war, but since they had similar education to mine we had a lot to talk about.

Another thing, those two guys developed in me a lifelong interest in the British naval constructors, and later on I became an honorary member of the Corps of Naval Constructors. So I remember those things. Another thing is that without fail they would secure at 1600 and have tea. It was always a problem to make the tea, the toast and the jam come out even. Sometimes the tea lasted a long time. I remember that.

Paul Stillwell: Were you finally making enough money that you could just do your job without all the extracurricular work?

Captain Jackson: I was in the Navy then, and so I had plenty of money.

Captain Jackson: Great. Where did you wind up living?

Captain Jackson: I lived at 346 Beacon Street in Boston. I had a college classmate who also was recruited, Bob Wheeler, and he worked at the shipyard too.[*]

---

[*] Ensign Robert J. Wheeler, USNR.

Paul Stillwell: How busy was the pace of activity in the shipyard at that point?

Captain Jackson: Very busy, and in general their guys worked pretty hard. There were some slackers, but I have to say that the majority of the guys worked hard.

Paul Stillwell: How much connection was there with the yard at Quincy? The yard there must have been doing new construction at that point.

Captain Jackson: Well, there was not much because Quincy was a commercial yard, and we were a Navy yard, although all of us young naval constructors were invited to go over and watch the launching of the Massachusetts to develop our knowledge of how things worked, and that was good.*

Paul Stillwell: What specifics do you remember about that?

Captain Jackson: Well, I was down underneath the ship or right beside the ship when she started to move, and I can still in my mind's eye see the ship going down the ways, and I was amazed at how fast it went.

Paul Stillwell: It builds up considerable momentum.

Captain Jackson: It does that. Sure does.

Paul Stillwell: I was here about 1976 for the launching of the submarine Groton, and I remember it was really an emotional thrill to see the ship going down the ways.† It's as if she'd been inert all this time, and now there's some life in her.

---

* The battleship Massachusetts (BB-59) was built by the Bethlehem Steel Company yard at Quincy, Massachusetts. The hull was launched on 23 September 1941.
† The submarine Groton (SSN-694) was launched 9 October 1976 at the General Dynamics shipyard in Groton, Connecticut.

Captain Jackson: Yes. When we talk about the Thresher, I'll talk about the launch of her. Very interesting.

Paul Stillwell: Well, one thing about the Quincy yard, they had to build ships that would fit through that drawbridge.

Captain Jackson: Right.

Paul Stillwell: There was not much clearance there, I think, for something like the Massachusetts.

Captain Jackson: No. Jumping ahead of the story, I was later the supervisor of shipbuilding at Quincy, and we built three big range instrumentation ships up there. Also a submarine tender and a supply ship.

Paul Stillwell: You mentioned before the recorder was running that you were the custodian of the great pontoons at Boston Navy Yard.

Captain Jackson: That's right, for a while, in Boston when I was there.

Paul Stillwell: When had they been constructed?

Captain Jackson: Oh, they were constructed for the salvage of S-51 in the 1920s.

Paul Stillwell: How big where they?

Captain Jackson: Oh, they were 20 feet in diameter and about 40 feet long. They were big.

Paul Stillwell: They'd hold a lot of water.

Captain Jackson: They sure did. The cables that they used to lift the submarine with were humongous, and then the clamps to hold them were real ingenious. A lot of Niedermair and McKee was in that.*

Paul Stillwell: What happened to them in between salvage jobs? They just sat around?

Captain Jackson: Yes, that's why you had an officer-in-charge at the shipyard, to be sure that somebody went down and looked at them once in a while.

Paul Stillwell: What were they made out of?

Captain Jackson: Oh, they were steel with wooden covering, and the wood was so that they would bang up against the ships and so forth and not be damaged. Easier to repair the wood than it was the steel.

Paul Stillwell: And so you'd blow them up just by blowing in compressed air.

Captain Jackson: Yes. That was a tricky business. You had to be very, very careful, and they were compartmented so you could blow one end without the other, and then they would upend, and so you had to very careful to be sure that you blew them level.

Paul Stillwell: If you had multiple pontoons on the same ship, you'd want to keep them going up at the same rate.

Captain Jackson: Yes, and once you start up the air expands, and they blow themselves. You just have to put a bubble in and then as soon as she gets a little lift it keeps on going.

Paul Stillwell: I didn't realize that.

---

* In the 1920s Andrew I. McKee was a lieutenant commander in the Navy's Construction Corps. He was a noted submarine designer. For details on his remarkable career, see John D. Alden, "Andrew Irwin McKee, Naval Constructor," U.S. Naval Institute Proceedings, June 1979, pages 49-57.

Captain Jackson: Yes.

Paul Stillwell: I think those same pontoons were later used when the Missouri ran aground in 1950.*

Captain Jackson: That's what I heard. I don't know that for a fact.

Paul Stillwell: Any more specifics you remember from the time at Boston?

Captain Jackson: Well, I was only there nine months. but after I had finished up the Catbird and Curlew, which were the two minesweepers, I was given assignment to build a sludge barge.† Once again, because most of the people were working on what were considered to be more important ships, I got to do that all by myself. It was my first experience in building something, and that instilled in me if you want to learn something, do it. Don't read a book about it or something. Go do it, and then you learn probably what not to do more than what to do. But that was interesting.

Paul Stillwell: Was the supply of raw materials a problem at all?

Captain Jackson: Yep. I got in trouble because I needed some I-beams, and the supply department didn't have any. I was walking past the boiler shop, and there were a lot of I-beams the right size, so I just called up transportation and said, "Bring those things down to the sludge barge." It wasn't long before the shop master was down there wanting to know what I was doing with his I-beams.

Paul Stillwell: And what was your response?

---

* The battleship Missouri (BB-63) ran aground near Norfolk, Virginia, on 17 January 1950. She was not refloated until 1 February. See Dr. Malcolm Muir, Jr., "Hard Aground on Thimble Shoal," Naval History, Fall 1991, pages 30-35.
† The Navy purchased the Catbird (AM-68) on 12 August 1940 and commissioned her 27 November 1940; the Navy purchased the Curlew (AM-69) on 6 August 1940 and commissioned her 7 November 1940.

Captain Jackson: Well, I had to get the job done.

Paul Stillwell: Had you already incorporated them in the vessel by that time?

Captain Jackson: Some of them before he got there.

Paul Stillwell: How large a crew did you have working on the project?

Captain Jackson: Well, that was another thing. Because it was low on the totem pole some days we didn't have many, and other days we would have more than we could use. It was a flywheel. But I was transferred out of there before that job was finished.

Paul Stillwell: You were getting some early management experience too.

Captain Jackson: Right, it was good experience.

Paul Stillwell: You probably left that job just about the time the war started.

Captain Jackson: Yes, I had been detached from Boston and was en route to Washington when the war started.

Paul Stillwell: You celebrated your 25th birthday on the day of the Japanese attack.*

Captain Jackson: Yes.

Captain Jackson: How had the orders come about moving you to Washington?

---

* In late November 1941, the Imperial Japanese Navy dispatched from the Kurile Islands in the North Pacific a task force built around six aircraft carriers. A force of some 350 fighters, dive-bombers, and torpedo planes attacked U.S. military installations on the island of Oahu, Hawaii, on Sunday, 7 December 1941. The principal focus of attack was the collection of American warships at the naval base at Pearl Harbor. The U.S. Congress declared war on Japan the following day.

Captain Jackson: Oh, because they needed people down there, and it was decided that I had had enough training and had done a sufficiently good job that they'd send me down to work on the design of new ASW ships.

Paul Stillwell: Please tell me about that.

Captain Jackson: Well, actually I reported in on Monday. When I heard that the war had started, I immediately beat it down there, and I reported in. I was disappointed, because I expected to see everybody working like mad. But all they were doing was standing around talking about the start of the war, and this didn't seem to make sense. I thought they should all be working at what they were supposed to be working at.

Paul Stillwell: Well, I think probably there was a lot of professional curiosity. How could something like this have happened?

Captain Jackson: Yes, that was true.

Paul Stillwell: Was housing a problem in Washington at that time?

Captain Jackson: Yes. As a matter of fact, it was very difficult, but I had a college classmate who had gone to work for the Maritime Commission, and he already had been established and he had a room over the garage of a woman's boarding house. It was an old embassy, and the rooms above the garage had been built to provide a place for the help to live, the chauffeur and the mechanics and people like that. It was acceptable, but it was not the first order. I stayed there all the 18 months that I was there. That also turned out to be a good job, because I not only was able to, but it was expected that I would use my education. And I was given the opportunity to do that.

Paul Stillwell: In what ways?

Captain Jackson: Well, making decisions on designs and so forth. Reviewing plans that were coming in from the shipyards that were building our destroyers, and so I was checking them to be sure that they were satisfactory.

Paul Stillwell: What specific projects were you on during that period?

Captain Jackson: Well, I worked on the design of the various classes of DEs, the British DEs first and then the other DEs.[*] I worked on the design of the <u>Fletcher</u>, and I made the shakedown cruise on the <u>Fletcher</u>.[†]

The Navy was given the plans for the British frigates, ASW ships, and they set up a separate type desk for that and put me in charge of that type desk. I was given a pretty free hand on it. As a matter of fact, my immediate boss was a commander, naval constructor, then converted to ED.[‡] He wrote me a little note and said that he'd opened a package of stuff that came from the Maritime Commission, which was going to build the ships, and he put on there questions, "Are you starting a Navy office at these yards?"

My answer was, "Yes."

"Did you tell the Maritime Commission?"

And the answer was, "Yes."

"And did they agree?"

"Yes."

Then he said, "If so, you're performing miracles." I have a copy of that in all this stuff. I saved that because he was a hard taskmaster.

Paul Stillwell: Who was he?

Captain Jackson: Bob Sutherland.[§]

---

[*] DEs—destroyer escorts.
[†] USS <u>Fletcher</u> (DD-445) and her sisters comprised the largest class of destroyers ever built for the U.S. Navy. All told, there were 175 ships of the class, commissioned 1942-44. Characteristics as originally built: standard displacement of 2,050 tons, 376 feet long, and 40 feet in the beam; top speed of 37 knots. Each ship was armed with five 5-inch guns, ten 40-millimeter guns, and ten 21-inch torpedo tubes. USS <u>Fletcher</u> was commissioned 30 June 1942.
[‡] ED—engineering duty.
[§] Lieutenant Commander Robert T. Sutherland, Jr., USN.

Paul Stillwell: I don't know that name.

Captain Jackson: He was in the class of '30 at the Naval Academy.

Paul Stillwell: How had you accomplished these miracles?

Captain Jackson: By doing it. The agreement was that the Maritime Commission would build these ships, and they would have no Navy involvement at all. But that agreement was made by people who didn't understand shipbuilding. They didn't realize that they were going to have beaucoup government-furnished material coming in. And whom do you send it to? Who looks after it? So in a big conference we talked about that, and I started asking these questions and saying, "We're not going to tell you how to build ships, but what we've got to do is have somebody looking after the Navy's interests." The sea trial on the first ship was a disaster. Absolutely a disaster. The ship was not ready to go.

Paul Stillwell: What ship was that? Do you recall?

Captain Jackson: No, I don't recall.

Captain Jackson: Was this a frigate?

Captain Jackson: Yes, it was a frigate.

Paul Stillwell: Where was it being built?

Captain Jackson: It was being built in Providence, Rhode Island. When it started out, the first thing they got was a whole bunch of people coming on board to ride the ship. Everybody wanted their breakfast, and so the cook said, "Where's the fresh water?"

The yard people sort of looked blank. "Fresh water? You guys want more water?" So the only water they had on board was feed water for the boilers, but it had been treated, so the coffee was terrible.

Paul Stillwell: This is the way lessons get learned.

Captain Jackson: Yes. We got one of the big cables out to one of the islands that were carrying power and communications. We had to test the anchor, and we tested it. Found out it had picked the cable up.

Paul Stillwell: Where was this island?

Captain Jackson: Right in Providence harbor. Then they had trouble with the steering engine all day, and on the way up in the nighttime it failed and the ship ran aground.

Paul Stillwell: Did this lead to a change in procedures after that?

Captain Jackson: Well, yes. It led to the point where everybody agreed that the Navy would come and look at the ships before they made their sea trials. Before that the Navy couldn't look at them.

Paul Stillwell: Was this just arrogance on the part of the Maritime Commission?

Captain Jackson: Oh, no, I can't say that. The decisions were made by people who didn't understand.

Paul Stillwell: I see. A bureaucratic problem.

Captain Jackson: Yes. The shipyard people didn't understand. The Maritime Commission didn't understand.

Paul Stillwell: You'd think they would understand something like the need for a fresh water supply on board.

Captain Jackson: Well, yes, you would think so, but in times of stress when you're trying to do everything all at once, something falls through the cracks.

Paul Stillwell: Were you then able to establish Navy ship superintendents in these yards?

Captain Jackson: No, no, but we did get more influence.

Paul Stillwell: The <u>Fletcher</u> class is widely praised among destroyermen. What do you remember about working on that project and going on the trials?

Paul Stillwell: Well, I thought it was a pretty damn good design because I worked on the design.

Captain Jackson: What contributions did you make to it?

Paul Stillwell: Well, I had a lot to do with the arrangements. I did a little work on the structures. At that time there was still division between the power-plant people and the hull people, but I worked on the integration of machinery plants. BuOrd was in on the action, and we had to work out the details on supporting the guns and feeding the ammunition and storing the ammunition.* So all those were problems that come up from day to day, and you have to sit down and debate the pros and cons and come to a decision. "Hey, we're going to do it this way."

Paul Stillwell: Any specific problems that you remember?

Captain Jackson: Oh, the big debate about the stability of the ship due to the big fire control director that was up on top of the pilothouse.

---

* BuOrd—Bureau of Ordnance.

Paul Stillwell: Mark 37.

Captain Jackson: Yes, I think that's the number of it. But they were good ships. Gibbs & Cox did all the detail design work on it, and we had to review that.[*] That's another aspect of this. Wartime is bad, it's terrible, but there's also some good things about it.

Paul Stillwell: It expedites things.

Captain Jackson: Yes, it expedites things and it gives the young people an opportunity to do something, make a contribution.

Paul Stillwell: I interviewed the first executive officer of Fletcher, Admiral Wylie.[†] He was an impressive gentleman.

Captain Jackson: He sure was.

Paul Stillwell: What memories do you have of him?

Captain Jackson: Just that, that he was a great guy and a good ship handler. As a matter of fact, he was a much better ship handler than the captain, Cole, who was a good guy.[‡] I don't belittle him. He was a good ship handler, too, but he couldn't match Wylie.

Paul Stillwell: Admiral Wylie told me he was also involved in setting up the CIC concept, which was really brand new at that time.[§]

---

[*] Gibbs & Cox, Inc., is a naval architecture and marine engineering firm. It was founded in 1929 as an outgrowth of the Gibbs Brothers organization, which had been established in 1922. An early Gibbs Brothers task was the conversion of the German ocean liner Vaterland to the Leviathan, a transport in World War I and later a U.S.-flag commercial liner. During World War II, more than 70% of the tonnage launched to support the U.S. war effort was built to Gibbs & Cox designs.

[†] Rear Admiral Joseph C. Wylie, Jr., USN (Ret.). He was a lieutenant when he reported to the Fletcher in 1942 and was promoted to lieutenant commander while serving on board.

[‡] Lieutenant Commander William M. Cole, USN, was the first commanding officer when the Fletcher was commissioned.

[§] CIC—combat information center. By using ranges and bearings taken from a radarscope, the CIC team can develop fixes and plot the ship's course, either as a backup to the visual navigation or as a replacement for it. CIC personnel also track air and surface contacts and can play a role in a ship's gunnery.

Captain Jackson: Right. He sure did.

Paul Stillwell: How much accommodation did you have to make for radar since the hull presumably had been designed without that in mind?

Captain Jackson: Oh, plenty. Once again, topside weight was a booger with the big radar. They had provisions for a little radar. This is probably good place to tell it. In the late '30s great things were happening. Even though they were getting much more horsepower, the machinery plants themselves were getting lighter.

Paul Stillwell: Is this because of going to higher steam pressure?

Captain Jackson: Higher steam pressure is one part of it. But also better design. They weren't quite so over-designed, and so they'd taken a lot of weight out of it. But that weight was all low. At the same time BuOrd was making great strides in fire control, and they got the big directors which they were putting way up high. The ships were designed to go fast, which generally means that they were narrow, which reduced the stability.[*] Then when they went to sea there were lots of complaints about them being unstable or top-heavy, and they got to be known as the top-heavy destroyers, the Farraguts. Later on three of those ships were caught in a typhoon, and the seas were large enough, and the course was maintained that made them roll and they capsized. Three of them capsized, including one from the Fletcher class.[†]

Paul Stillwell: Spence, I think, was in the Fletcher class.

Captain Jackson: That's right. That's affirmative. But that's a good example how things gradually deteriorate, and there were so many people who were involved in that that you

---
[*] A ship's stability, the capacity to come back upright from a roll, is adversely affected by topside weight.
[†] While operating off the Philippines, ships of the Third Fleet ran into a ferocious typhoon on 18 December 1944. In all, three destroyers—Hull (DD-350), Spence (DD-512), and Monaghan (DD-354)—sank, and a number of other ships were damaged. For details, see C. Raymond Calhoun, Typhoon: The Other Enemy: The Third Fleet and the Pacific Storm of December 1944 (Annapolis: Naval Institute Press, 1981).

couldn't point your finger at any one person or one group to say, "Hey, it's your fault." One of the things I like very much is that the ship that rescued most of the survivors was a DE.

Paul Stillwell: Tabberer.*

Captain Jackson: Right. That's right. And there are two things about it. One, it was a good ship. And, two, the seamanship by reserve officers was outstanding. And those points, I think, get lost.

Paul Stillwell: Well, might a lesson be drawn that there might have usefully been more margins for growth in the original design?

Captain Jackson: Oh, yes, but you've got to put yourself back at that time in history. They didn't worry that much about growth, because progress was not being made at that time in great strides. And so instead of trying to make an old ship better, you would make a new one.

Paul Stillwell: And these were the 2,200-tonners.†

Captain Jackson: Yes, right, which were good ships.

Paul Stillwell: And some still said they liked the Fletchers better, but it's a matter of taste there.

Captain Jackson: Well, yes. The reason that the Fletcher class capsized in the typhoon was not that she was tender but because they didn't compensate the fuel tanks. Nobody likes to put water in oil tanks, but if you want to be safe that's what you've got to do.

---

* The destroyer escort Tabberer (DE-418) gained a measure of fame in December 1944 when she rescued 55 men from U.S. destroyers sunk in a typhoon off the Philippine Islands.
† The 2,200-ton destroyers were those of the Allen M. Sumner (DD-692) and Gearing (DD-710) classes, both built during World War II. They entered the fleet after the Fletcher class.

Paul Stillwell: Well, I think the problem also is that the ballast was pumped out in anticipation of a fueling that was not able to take place.

Captain Jackson: Right. Well, I don't think on that ship they ever had water in it. The engineer just didn't do it. I'm not sure of those details, but that's the way I remember it. But also the task force commander, who was in a big battleship, as far as they were concerned it was just a rough day, but the poor little old destroyers out there, you know it was a humongous day.* So the task force maintained course and speed, which put them on probably the most unfavorable relationship between the ship and the waves. Then they needed fuel, and they didn't have fuel. They were rolling 45 to 50 degrees. A couple of the captains broke off and said, "Hey, we can't keep up." That's what all of those ships should have done, but they're not trained to do that. They're trained to, "Hey, maintain course and speed," we do it.

Paul Stillwell: "Aye, aye, sir."

Captain Jackson: Yes.

Paul Stillwell: Did you make more of a relative contribution on the DEs than on the destroyer itself.

Captain Jackson: Yes. I was really supposed to work on the DEs, but there was plenty of opportunity to work on anything that came along.

Paul Stillwell: What specifically do you remember doing on the DEs?

Captain Jackson: Oh. I remember working on the fairing of the lines just because I wanted to. I like to draw lines. Doc Ferris was the civilian in charge of doing that, and a

---

* Admiral William F. Halsey, Jr., USN, served as Commander Third Fleet from 15 March 1943 to 22 November 1945. He was embarked in the USS New Jersey (BB-62) at the time of the December 1944 typhoon.

great guy, and I could talk to him and say, "Hey, why do you do it this way?" And he'd take the time to tell me.

Paul Stillwell: Where is the intersection between preliminary design and detail design?

Captain Jackson: Well, in those days you had preliminary design and then contract design, and that had to apply both to the naval shipyards and the commercial yards. It was the basis for a contract to build the ship. Then the detail design was generally done by the shipyard or a naval architecture firm like Gibbs & Cox. Most of the work that we were doing, the detail work, was with Gibbs & Cox. I had an opportunity to get to know the Gibbs people quite well. As a matter of fact, William Francis Gibbs, who was a patron of the opera, used to give me opera tickets. When I'd go to New York, he'd give me a ticket and I'd go to the opera.

Paul Stillwell: Please tell me about his personality.

Captain Jackson: Unique.

Paul Stillwell: Can you go beyond that?

Captain Jackson: Yes. He was a good guy, and if you did a good job, or if he thought you did a good job he'd treat you pretty fairly. But if you didn't do a good job, he had no use for you. He had the ability and he exercised it. He could run several conferences all at the same time. He would vibrate from one to the other, back and forth. He would give a few talks and say, "Now, you guys look at this." Then he would go at the other one and do the same thing. Then he'd come back and say, "What did you do?" And he was meticulous in keeping files and records. Very, very meticulous. He was also an excellent naval architect in his own right, so you couldn't put anything over on him at all.

Paul Stillwell: Well, I mentioned to you I'd interviewed Fred Edwards.[*] He was the first chief engineer in the Mahan, and he had not much use for Gibbs & Cox in the design of the plant in that ship.

Captain Jackson: Well, I'm not sure that that's all Gibbs & Cox fault, because as far as layout and so forth, the major decisions were made by the Bureau of Engineering, and Gibbs was just to do the detail design. So that may not have been a good criticism.

Paul Stillwell: Would strong-willed be a good descriptor of Gibbs?

Captain Jackson: Gibbs? As I understood the organization Cox was the businessman. He looked after all the contractual things and the monies and so forth.

Paul Stillwell: From talking to Admiral Mumma I gathered that Gibbs had sort of an imperial air about him.[†]

Captain Jackson: Oh, he tried to, yes. But—like Rickover—if you did a good job, he'd be civil to you.[‡]

Captain Jackson: Was civil the best you could hope for?

Captain Jackson: Yes, I think so. He wasn't uncivil anyway. But if you goofed up he would ride pretty hard.

Paul Stillwell: Jumping back at something you told me before the tape recorder started is that you had some interaction with Rickover when you were working on the DEs. What was that?

---

[*] See the Naval Institute oral history of Captain Frederick A. Edwards, Sr., USN (Ret.).
[†] See the Naval Institute oral history of Rear Admiral Albert G. Mumma, USN (Ret.).
[‡] Hyman G. Rickover was considered the father of the nuclear Navy. He ran the U.S. Navy's nuclear-power program for many years, from 1948 until he eventually left active duty in 1982 with the rank of four-star admiral on the retired list. Rickover Hall at the Naval Academy is named in his honor, as is the nuclear-powered attack submarine Hyman G. Rickover (SSN-709), which was commissioned 21 July 1984.

Captain Jackson: Oh, well, he was head of the electrical section in BuShips, and he had to provide all the electric motors and so forth for the DEs.* I was working on the design of the ships, and so I had to take his motors and be sure that they'd fit in the ships.

Paul Stillwell: Any personal interchanges with him in that period?

Captain Jackson: Well, we talked.

Paul Stillwell: Was he reasonable?

Captain Jackson: To me he was, but not to everybody. My boss hated him.

Paul Stillwell: Who was your boss?

Captain Jackson: Well, Harry Burris was two years behind him at the Naval Academy.† And I got along with him all right until the end.

Paul Stillwell: By the end you mean much later than World War II?

Captain Jackson: Oh, yes.

Paul Stillwell: What was the cause of the friction between Burris and Rickover?

Captain Jackson: Personalities, I guess. It was the cause of the friction. Rickover used the anti-Semitic thing incorrectly. In that same class there was a fellow by the name of Kaplan.‡

---

* BuShips—Bureau of Ships.
† Commander Harry Burris, USN, later a captain.
‡ Midshipman Jerauld L. Olmstead, USN, had the top standing at the graduation of the Naval Academy's class of 1922. Midshipman Leonard Kaplan, USN, finished second in the class and was the victim of prejudice and mistreatment because he was Jewish. His entry in the 1922 yearbook was printed on a perforated page so it could be removed from the book by those who so desired. For more on the Olmstead-Kaplan rivalry, see Norman Polmar and Thomas B. Allen, Rickover: Controversy and Genius: a Biography (New York: Simon & Schuster, 1982), pages 53-58.

Paul Stillwell: He stood number two.

Captain Jackson: Yes, and between the number-one guy and the number-two guy there was real jealousy and real animosity. Kaplan was Jewish, and so the animosity and so forth was really directed at the Jewish religion more than the individual. As a result, as you know, Kaplan didn't stand number one, which probably he should have. But he didn't, and therefore he applied to go to the Construction Corps, which means that he would rank on the same level as the number-one guy.

Paul Stillwell: I interviewed an officer who put the USS Fresno into commission in New York near the end of the war, and Kaplan was there, and he said he was an extremely capable officer.[*]

Captain Jackson: He was that. I never got to know him very well, but I did know him, and I had an opportunity to meet him on occasions.

Paul Stillwell: Any observations at all on him from those?

Captain Jackson: Just as the same as the other guy. He seemed like a real nice gent. I certainly could see nothing to be jealous of him or anything like that. He was most capable, and so I could only say good things about him.

Paul Stillwell: How did Rickover misuse the anti-Semitism?

Captain Jackson: Oh, when he was struggling for power, he said, "You guys are against me just because I'm Jewish." That's not true. In no way is it true. He played that up wherever it was to his advantage, and if it was not to his advantage he'd downplay it.

Paul Stillwell: So he threw it out as a red herring?

---

[*] This is in the Naval Institute oral history of Rear Admiral Elliott B. Strauss, USN (Ret.).

Captain Jackson: Right. That's just a fact of life, I guess. Rickover always treated me pretty good. Where I got real annoyed with him was at the commissioning of the Hyman G. Rickover.* He took Lewis to task something fierce in his acceptance speech.† I guess that's what you'd call it.

Paul Stillwell: He could turn graciousness on and off.

Captain Jackson: He did that. Boy, he turned it off, and it made me mad. Not so much that it was Rickover, but here was a naval officer degrading the profession. There was one other time he annoyed me. I went to introduce my wife to him. We were at an affair, and so we walked up there, and I said, "Admiral, this is my wife," and he turned around and walked away. He could do things like that.

Paul Stillwell: There's no excuse for that.

Captain Jackson: No, none whatsoever.

Paul Stillwell: Well, back to BuShips. In the DEs how did you go about designing them to accommodate a variety of power plants?

Captain Jackson: Actually that was fun, and it was necessary because of the limited capability to produce that kind of material during the war. As you know, we had diesels, we had steam-turbine direct drive, we had turboelectric drive. We had practically anything that people could dream up, and I like to think that those DEs played a real big part in defeating the German submarines.

Paul Stillwell: You have company in that assessment certainly.

---

* The nuclear-powered attack submarine Hyman G. Rickover (SSN-709) was commissioned 21 July 1984 at the General Dynamics shipyard in Groton, Connecticut.
† David S. Lewis, Jr., was then the chairman and CEO of the General Dynamics Corporation.

Captain Jackson: Yes, and the other part of that, though, was the jeep carriers. The preeminent example of that is Dan Gallery's capture of the 505.*

Paul Stillwell: We're coming out with a new book on Gallery, and certainly that's a prominent chapter in it.†

What accommodations did you have to make in the designs for these different plants?

Captain Jackson: Well, actually since they were all new designs the accommodations came very easily. We didn't have to change the basic dimensions of the ship at all. It was just mostly the foundations for the different kinds of machinery, and so it was not hard. If we had tried to take something that had been already designed, then it would be a major alteration. But since we were starting out with a clean sheet of paper it was not difficult.

Paul Stillwell: How did you solve the matter of having more than one shipyard building a class and ensuring some degree of uniformity?

Captain Jackson: With once again great difficulty. The one yard we had trouble with was the one down in Orange, Texas. They were used to building oilrigs and stuff like that, and the mechanics would do whatever they wanted to do and make improvements. But that's one reason that they had Navy inspectors there—to ensure that they made them like the plans.

Paul Stillwell: Did you get involved with the LSTs at all?‡

Captain Jackson: No. No, I didn't have any connection with that other than what John

---
* Captain Daniel V. Gallery, Jr., USN. While in command of the USS Guadalcanal (CVE-60) in June 1944, his forces captured the German submarine U-505. Gallery eventually became a rear admiral and wrote a number of popular books about the Navy. His oral history is in the Naval Institute collection.
† C. Herbert Gilliland and Robert Shenk, Admiral Dan Gallery: the Life and Wit of a Navy Original (Annapolis: Naval Institute Press, 1999).
‡ LST–tank landing ship, an amphibious warfare ship capable of putting her bow directly onto a beach, opening bow doors, and lowering a bow ramp to permit vehicles to exit.

Niedermair fed me.

Paul Stillwell: Well, he said he essentially sketched it out on the back of the envelope one day.

Captain Jackson: Well, there's a lot of uncertainty about that. Rollie Baker, who was a British naval constructor, claims credit for development of the LST. From some of things that Rollie showed me I tend to believe that the basic concept was given to our Navy by the Brits, and all we did was refine them. Now, I may be wrong on that, but I don't think so.

Paul Stillwell: While you were in BuShips did you have any opportunity to work with or observe Admiral Cochrane?*

Captain Jackson: Oh, very much so. I'll tell you a sea story about him. He was very much interested in all of the young naval architects there, and to drive his points home he would ask questions. One day he was walking in a different direction from me in the passageway, and he stopped me. With no preamble he said, "What is a good prismatic coefficient for a destroyer?" And so I guessed at it at .54. He said, "You go find out what it is and come down to my office and report to me and tell me what's the proper coefficient." The only guy I knew that I knew would know the answer was Doc Ferris, so I ran down to see him and he said, "Well, a good one is about .535."

Paul Stillwell: You were pretty close.

Captain Jackson: Yes, and not without reason. I had looked at things like that. Anyway, I went down to his office and I told his secretary that I was there to see Admiral Cochrane.
    She said, "What about?"
    I said, "Well, he told me to come and report to him."

---

* Rear Admiral/Vice Admiral Edward L. Cochrane, USN, served as Chief of the Bureau of Ships from 1942 to 1946.

So she went in, and he said, "Come right in." So I went in there and I told him, and he said, "Ah, that was a good guess, wasn't it?"

After reflecting on that, I said, "Gee whiz. Here's the Chief of the Bureau of Ships in wartime, who's probably the busiest man in Washington, takes the trouble to recognize one of his younger officers and teach him a lesson." That made an impression on me until this day. It still does, to think that he had enough interest in his young people to do that. And he did it with everybody that he knew. Sometimes he didn't. If he'd see a strange face, he'd stop and introduce himself.

Paul Stillwell: What other contacts did you have with him?

Captain Jackson: Oh, I had a lot of opportunities to brief him on things that we were doing, because he was very much interested in all design work. Generally they were very short, because he didn't have much time to spend.

Paul Stillwell: But he had time to have an interchange like that with a young officer.

Captain Jackson: Yes. I got to know him quite well when he was at MIT.[*]

Paul Stillwell: Well, just for those of us who don't know, what's a prismatic coefficient?

Captain Jackson: A prismatic coefficient is the ratio of the ship's displacement volume to a prism whose area is the same as the cross-sectional area at the maximum section times the length. It's a very useful term in that it puts you in the ballpark of the shape of the ship. There are lots of useful terms like that.

Paul Stillwell: Well, he had to be a very broad-scoped individual just because of the vast array of programs he was managing.

---

[*] MIT—Massachusetts Institute of Technology.

Captain Jackson: Right. Oh, he was. He was terrific. And Admiral Mills was equally good.*

Paul Stillwell: What do you remember about him specifically?

Captain Jackson: The first time I met him was at a meeting of the Society of Naval Architects and I was a young officer. I think I was a jaygee by that time.† I saw him in the hall, and he came over to me and put his hand out and said, "My name's Mills. What's yours?" Obviously I knew him immediately just by looking at him. I knew who he was. But he also had an interest in the young people.

Paul Stillwell: When you were first commissioned did you wear the sleeve device of the Construction Corps?

Captain Jackson: Yes, for a short time. About three months.‡

Paul Stillwell: I understand there was a disappointment in a number of people that they lost that distinctive badge.

Captain Jackson: Yes, there was. But there are a lot of people who thought it was good. I would have preferred to stay a naval constructor, but—

Paul Stillwell: Why did people think it was good to get the same insignia as the line?

Captain Jackson: Oh, it made them feel a closer part of the Navy. You know, when you'd go to an affair you couldn't tell who was an unrestricted line officer and a restricted line

---

* Rear Admiral Earle W. Mills, USN, served as Assistant Chief of the Bureau of Ships from November 1942 to November 1945.
† Jaygee—lieutenant (junior grade).
‡ The Bureau of Steam Engineering merged with the Bureau of Construction and Repair on 20 June 1940 to form the new Bureau of Ships. Naval constructors no longer wore a distinctive sleeve device; instead they wore a star, indicating they were restricted line officers. The star was the same device worn by the unrestricted line officers who operated ships and aircraft.

officer. The uniforms were the same, so they liked that.

Paul Stillwell: Did you observe divisions between the constructors and the engineers?

Captain Jackson: Yes, sometimes they were bitter.

Paul Stillwell: What manifestations did you see of that?

Captain Jackson: Well, at the time of amalgamation, the constructors were really in the driver's seat.

Paul Stillwell: An elite corps.

Captain Jackson: An elite corps, right, and with an excellent reputation. And the engineers were guys that had made their mark by being good engineers on ships.

Paul Stillwell: The greasy-hands type guys.

Captain Jackson: That's right. But they had a lot of well-educated people, too, that contributed much to the development of steam engineering for ships. So there shouldn't have been this friction, but there was. That lasted till several years after the end of the war when all the engineers and the naval constructors retired, and then it sort of disappeared because now everybody was together. They first started calling them "congineers," combined naval constructors and engineers, but it developed in to being the engineering duty community. Now I see really no conflict for guys that work in engineering and in the rest of the ship. If there is any conflict at all, it's those fellows in the nuclear power section as compared to the rest of the Navy. The nuclear people think they're sort of the elite these days.

Paul Stillwell: Do you think ultimately that amalgamation was good for the Navy?

Captain Jackson: Yes, probably, probably.

Paul Stillwell: Anything else on Admiral Cochrane to mention?

Captain Jackson: Oh, just that he was one my real heroes, and I tried to emulate him as much as I could.

Paul Stillwell: What qualities about him did you want to emulate?

Captain Jackson: Oh, his technical knowledge and his interest in young people, both of those which I tried to excel in. Another one of my heroes was old Andy McKee, and I think he's been interviewed, too, several times.

Paul Stillwell: Going back to Admiral Cochrane, somebody was telling me about a bureaucratic technique that he used. Cochrane had an in-box, an out-box and a "too hard" box. The last one was sort of a percolation box, and he put things in there that he wasn't ready to deal with at the moment. Then he'd sift through them periodically, and some things would have solved themselves. Others then he would be forced to deal with.

Paul Stillwell: Yes, that's a fact.

Captain Jackson: You saw evidence of that also?

Captain Jackson: Yes. Well, I still do it.

Paul Stillwell: I think we all do that or the "I can keep putting this one off indefinitely" box. Anything else about Admiral Cochrane's bureaucratic style or personality?

Captain Jackson: Well, he was in my opinion a true gentleman. He had all the attributes of a true gentleman, and he lived it.

Paul Stillwell: What do you mean by that?

Captain Jackson: Well, you know, a lot of people say they're faithful, but they don't live it. They don't practice their religion. They just take credit for going to church. And some people who never go to church live their religion but don't tell anybody. They just do it. Beck's that way.* She goes to church and she works in the altar guild, but she doesn't try to force her religion on other people. She just lives it. By example, you know, she influences people.

    Well, that's digressing.

Paul Stillwell: Yes, but it's interesting. Could you tell me about meeting and marrying your wife?

Captain Jackson: Well, I met her when I was in BuShips, and we got well acquainted, but I went off to the West Coast to join the dry dock, and she went off to Texas to work in the arsenal out there.

Captain Jackson: Was she working in Washington?

Captain Jackson: Yes, she was working in Washington. She worked for a colonel in the Army, and he got to be commanding officer of an arsenal in Kentucky, where her home was. So he asked her if she would come and be his personal secretary, and she said, "Sure." It was near her home, so she liked that. But she was only there about a year when he got transferred to Texas, to the San Antonio Arsenal, as commanding officer and so he asked her if she wanted to go along and be his secretary in Texas. And she said, "Yes." It was an experience. So she was in Texas and I was on the West Coast, and I got to see her when she was at home before she went out to Texas. I called her up on the telephone when I got back from a trip to Espiritu Santo and said, "Hey, why don't you come on out and visit me?" I never thought she would. I really didn't. But she did, and we decided then

---

* This is a reference to Captain Jackson's wife, whose maiden name was Mary Rebecca McElroy.

that we would get married. So that's human interest. Two months later I departed for Guam on the USS ASBD-3.

Paul Stillwell: When were you married?

Captain Jackson: On the 15th of April, which is payday, in 1944.

Paul Stillwell: So you get to celebrate your anniversary on income tax day.

Captain Jackson: Right.

Paul Stillwell: What were the circumstances of your first meeting? How did you become acquainted?

Captain Jackson: Oh, she lived in the big mansion, and I lived in the garage, the servants' quarters, and we were paying our rent at the same time. That's when we met.

Paul Stillwell: What else do you remember about that tour in BuShips? What other projects were you involved in?

Captain Jackson: Well, I was only there 18 months, and looking back at it, I accomplished quite a bit in that 18 months. But all the time I was there I felt unhappy, because there I was in Washington, perfectly sound and safe, and so many people were out doing great things for the war effort. It took me a long time to realize that the things I was doing were important for those guys that were out there fighting, and if we hadn't done that well—but I kept chafing at the bit to go to sea. And by this time I was caught up in the naval constructor or ED organization, and the only way I could get to sea would be to go and be a docking officer on one of the big floating dry docks. So I requested to go and was assigned to the ABSD-3.*

---

* In the Navy's nomenclature of ship types, ABSD stood for advance base sectional dock; it was a floating dry dock comprised of sections fastened together.

Paul Stillwell: There was no chance to be engineer in a combatant ship?

Captain Jackson: No, no, because they were still talking about constructors.

Paul Stillwell: I see.

Captain Jackson: They had force constructors, but they were all very senior officers. But that was not a bad job, and it turns out that it was a wonderful experience.

Paul Stillwell: Where was the dry dock located?

Captain Jackson: Well, I went to two of them. I went to the ABSD-1 really for indoctrination, and I was down there in Espiritu Santo. Then we came back to the ABSD-3. The war was moving so fast that we had a base change almost every week. Not quite that often, but it seemed very rapid. We finally ended up in Guam, and we were in there for a little over a year. The best part of that job was it was 7,000 miles from Washington.

Paul Stillwell: Why do you say that was the best part of it?

Captain Jackson: We didn't have all the interference. We didn't have to be reporting to them all the time. The base that we were partially attached to was the Naval Repair Activity at Guam, and Captain Pyne was in charge of that.* The captain of the dry dock was a passed-over commander. Had actually been retired and was called back to active duty. He hated Pyne because Pyne and I had a good relationship, and it sort of bypassed the captain of the dry dock.

Paul Stillwell: Did Pyne view you as a protégé?

---

* Captain Schuyler N. Pyne, USN, served as industrial manager for Naval Operating Base Guam from January 1945 to September 1946.

Captain Jackson: I think so. I never talked to him about that, but I think so.

Paul Stillwell: Well, and the fact that he had recruited you was a factor.

Captain Jackson: Yes, and he certainly looked after me while I was on the dry dock.

Paul Stillwell: What do you remember about Captain Pyne, the rank he was then?

Captain Jackson: Oh, he was a good engineer, a good naval architect, and he gave me a pretty free hand. I guess that was partly because he had so much to do over on the base, and he felt responsibility for all the dry docks out there, and we had a number of them. He would come out and look at what we were doing. He didn't force it on there, but he would make suggestions and say, "Oh, gee, I would have a bracket in there," and stuff like that. And generally he was right, so we did it.

Paul Stillwell: What duties are involved for a docking officer?

Captain Jackson: Well, one, you're in charge of bringing the ship in and setting it on the blocks and pumping it up. That's the docking part. But then the repair officer is like the industrial manager of a big naval shipyard.

Paul Stillwell: Well, are you also responsible for getting those blocks set before the ship comes in?

Captain Jackson: Oh, sure. When we started out, I was the only guy on the ship that had ever done it before, and so I had to train all the shipwrights and other people on how to set blocks.

Paul Stillwell: Did you learn that at Boston?

Captain Jackson: Yes. That's one reason I went to Boston, to learn things like that.

Paul Stillwell: What are some of the secrets or tricks of the trade in preparing to accommodate a ship in dry dock?

Captain Jackson: Well, first of all, you've got to be sure that you set the blocks such that a ship won't turn over when you pump it up.

Paul Stillwell: That would be number one.

Captain Jackson: Yes. And also you have to ensure that the dock won't tip over with that heavy weight sitting on deck. Those are problems of concern particularly in a floating dry dock. One of the reasons I got to go down to the ABSD-1 in Espiritu Santo is that they tipped a section over endwise, which is pretty hard to do. One has to work at it. But they did it. They had started out with a tremendous amount of longitudinal stability, and then step by step they reduced it till finally they had zero, and it tipped over. I think they killed seven people on it. That happened just before I got orders to go down there, and so I was there during all the work of finally assembling the dock and the investigations that were going on.

Paul Stillwell: What had been the cause of it?

Captain Jackson: Well, as a sectional dry dock, it came in sections which had to be assembled together to make a big dry dock out of it. There was an awful lot of movement from one section to another, and it was convenient to submerge the dock or lower the dock down so the freeboard of the dock matched that of the small boats that they had coming alongside all the time. Then they were doing some work in the tanks, so they took the covers off of all the accesses to the tanks. Then the wing walls were loosened up in preparation for erecting in a vertical position.

It was decided that they would pump the dock up, and so they went below and opened up all the piping from the pumps to the tanks, which were all cross-connected. So now there was a free surface effect that was almost the same as a water-plane area, which resulted in no stability.* They started pumping, and—as always happens—one tank will pump a little faster than the others, so that end goes up. Instead of correcting it, they just started to pump harder. They put all the pumps on, so they were pumping from the high end all the time. So the other end of was going down, and finally the deck went under the water and all those access covers were open, flooding those tanks. The situation was that water was flooding in one end and being pumped out the other. They just kept on pumping until it went over endways and sank.

Paul Stillwell: Did this one section break off from the rest of the dock,?

Captain Jackson: No, this was before it was connected.

Paul Stillwell: I see.

Captain Jackson: I use that as an example of in my course on stability—that just because you have quote lots of GM, it doesn't mean anything, because it can be destroyed very rapidly.† When they started out they had 257 feet of GM, and when it went over endways they had zero.

Paul Stillwell: It's a textbook example of what not to do.

Captain Jackson: Yep, that's why I use it. The Coast Guard had a seminar on ship stability, and they asked me if I would talk to them at lunchtime. So I told them that story, and I wrote a paper on it. The sponsors liked the paper so much they put it in the Proceedings. So it's a good example.

---

* Free surface effect comes about when a ship's tank or other compartment is partially filled with liquid so that the liquid is free to move from side to side of the ship. Because the liquid goes to the low side of the compartment, a large amount of free surface can be dangerous to the ship's stability.
† GM—metacentric height, which is the distance between a ship's metacenter and her center of gravity; the greater the metacentric height, the greater the ship's stability.

Paul Stillwell: What ships do you remember bringing into your dry dock at Guam?

Captain Jackson: Oh, we had lots of them. We had the Idaho, New Mexico, South Dakota. With the South Dakota we also had two 1,800-ton net tenders on at the same time. Another time we had 26 ships from destroyer size down to LSTs and LSMs.* That was a nightmare. Took us all day long.

Paul Stillwell: Why, just because there were so many?

Captain Jackson: Yes, so many, and trying to keep them all in position at the same time.

Paul Stillwell: How did you do it? You didn't tie them down, did you?

Captain Jackson: Well, we tried to, but we had so many of them we had lines going every which way. There were people on the ships that didn't understand what they were doing. You tell them to ease off, and they let the lines go.

Paul Stillwell: I've seen a picture of that one with the South Dakota docking, and she pretty well filled it up.

Captain Jackson: Oh, we still had two 1,800-ton net tenders. That was another very interesting thing. She came in because she'd wrapped a wire rope around one of her propellers. I've forgotten the numbers, but it was probably the number-one propeller. It was on the starboard side. The wire had wound around there and broken the bearing, so it rotated the bearing, and it wore it and got it smooth. So we got it in dock. We looked at it, and we pulled the shaft and looked at the bearing. The wood was all gone, and we had to re-wood it. But also the bearing shell was worn smaller.

So the question, "How is it going to be repaired?" Some spares were available, but they were all back in the States. But the war was going on, and the ship was needed to

---

* LSM—medium landing ship, a type of craft used for amphibious landings, generally used to carry troops to an invasion beachhead and put them ashore on ramps at the bow of the vessel.

operate with the task force.* So we said, "We'll have to make a new one." Well, that's a pretty hard thing to do, because it is a big bronze casting that weighs several thousand pounds, and there was no foundry around big enough to cast that. The tenders had some casting capability but not that big. So, well, got to fix it. We scrounged up some big round bronze bars, put them in the shaper and squared them up, bent a ring around, and brazed them on to the casting.

Well, first of all, we prepared the casting so that we could do this, and we brazed them on. Next it was put it in the lathe, but the lathe wasn't big enough, so we had to raise the head stock and the tail stock up and they put an extension on the end, to put the tail stock on the bed. We were pretty shaky, but we did it. We turned it down and got satisfied that we were in the tolerances. By that time we had some lignum vitae, so we cut the new barrel staves and put them in. Took it down and put it in the ship and, boy, what do you know, it fit. That was a great day of elation.

So we quickly buttoned it up, put the shaft back in, and put the seal in. Put the propeller on and the fool's cap, and she went off to sea and went and joined the task force and made the next raid. We all felt pretty good about that, and we'd done something for the war effort. But that was another example of "If you want to do something, do it." Don't stand around and wring your hands and say, "I can't do it because I don't have this or that." Figure out a way to do it.

Paul Stillwell: And that bearing was probably still in the ship when she was scrapped 15 or so years later.

Captain Jackson: Probably. Yes.

Paul Stillwell: What jobs did you do on those other battleships that you mentioned?

Captain Jackson: Idaho, we really didn't do anything in this area, because she came in to get her bottom painted, which we did, and they got a good job. But the captain said that no matter what happened that she always wanted to turn to port. Well, we looked at the ship

---

* The dry-docking of the South Dakota (BB-57) took place in June of 1945.

and looked at the rudder. We checked the rudder to be sure that the alignment was correct. You know, put it on the zero on the bridge and then the rudder would go to zero. There could have been an error in there to make it do that. Somebody said, "Well, maybe the ship is bent." So we looked by eye and said, "You know, that bow looks like it's over to portside a little bit," which if it were would cause the ship to turn to the port.

So we got out the transits and we took all kinds of measurements of everything, and we couldn't see anything out of line. The centerline was just as straight as an arrow. So we went to the captain and said, "Hey, Captain, we've come to a conclusion. One, there's nothing wrong with this ship. And if you let her coast, it'll turn to port. What we suggest is that if you want to go in a straight line, give it about a one-degree starboard rudder.

Paul Stillwell: Which, of course, he'd been doing all along.

Paul Stillwell: Right. We had a little difficulty with the chief engineer on that, too, because he thought his shafts were bent. And they may have been. You know, she was an old ship, and she'd been working awful hard.*

Let's see, what was the other? Oh, the Pennsylvania.† Oh, boy. She was up at Buckner Bay, and she was torpedoed in the area of the propellers and the rudder. They towed her back to Guam, and we put her in our dry dock and they said, "Fix it." I looked at the job, and I said, "Holy mackerel." Three propellers were gone. One of them was still hanging down from the bracket. The fourth one was misaligned—badly misaligned—and a huge great big hole back in the aft end. You could look right into the steering machinery room.

They had something like 19 sailors missing. There'd been a dice game being run back there when the explosion came. Well, the first thing we had to do was look for those bodies, and we found them all, all but one. We didn't find one. It was, oh, several days later after they had filed a report and said that they couldn't find this guy, and they

---

* USS Idaho (BB-42) was commissioned 24 March 1919.
† On 12 August 1945, a Japanese aircraft torpedoed the battleship Pennsylvania (BB-38) while she was anchored in Buckner Bay, Okinawa. The battleship, which was hit well aft, suffered extensive damage. Twenty men were killed and ten injured. After preliminary salvage work, she left Buckner Bay under tow on 18 August and arrived in Apra Harbor, Guam on 6 September for dry-docking.

assumed that he was washed out. But we had to cut a hole through a longitudinal bulkhead to do some repair work in there, and I was the first one through the hole. Then I saw something white laying down way down in the corner.

I went down and looked at it, and it was a body. So I went up to the captain, and I said, "Hey, I found your missing sailor." He gave his people a real riot act because they were the ones that couldn't find him, and so I interceded for them. I said, "Hey, Captain, don't blame them. If we hadn't cut that hole in there, you wouldn't have found it until you got it back in a shipyard." I said, "It's my fault as much as anybody." But we did find him.

Paul Stillwell: That was not in the curriculum they taught at Michigan.

Captain Jackson: No, that wasn't in there. So at any rate we got him out, and they prepared his body to ship back to the United States. But we repaired the damage. We made a big truss that went from the bulkhead at the forward end of the steering machinery all the way out to the stern and put enough longitudinal strength in there.

We decided that we wouldn't try to give her new propellers. We would take number-four shaft and realign it, so we had to cut the brackets, which we did, and reweld them. But we had to align them up, and that was a pretty difficult job for us, because none of us had ever really tackled a task like that. We found one thing—that we could control the alignment by where we put the welding, and so we'd weld on one side and pull it one way and then weld on the other side and pull it back, and it did a pretty good job. She went off to sea on that propeller.

Paul Stillwell: Just one?

Captain Jackson: Just that one propeller but she had escorts. And almost made it to Bremerton, not quite, when the alignment we had on her apparently was not good enough, and there was enough flexing in the shaft so that the shaft broke. But it almost got there.

Paul Stillwell: And then she got towed the rest of the way, I take it?

Captain Jackson: Yes. They had the ship's reunion here when they launched the submarine Pennsylvania, and there were a number of people that were on the battleship Pennsylvania when we did that.* I talked to them, and I was amazed that very few of them had the slightest idea what we did. They just said, "Well, they did something down on the propellers, and we weren't sure what it was."

Paul Stillwell: That's typical of ship's crews. They take that part of it for granted.

Captain Jackson: Yes. So that was one of the bigger jobs we did.

Paul Stillwell: Did you get any aircraft carriers?

Captain Jackson: Oh, yes. Had the Wake Island in there.† She was a jeep carrier. She was dive-bombed. A bomb went through the ship, and we had to put a big patch on the side. The bomb also went through a deck, so we had to cut the deck out. And it hit a freeze box, so we had to rebuild the freeze box. That turned out good, because they got a new compressor, and I said, "What are you going to do with the old one?"

"Well, we don't know. They're going to trash it I guess."

I said, "Well, I'll take it." So I air-conditioned my room.

Paul Stillwell: Did you get any of the big carriers in the dry dock? Would they fit?

Captain Jackson: Yes, they'd fit, but the Wake Island was the biggest one. We had the big cruiser that lost her bow.

Paul Stillwell: Pittsburgh.

---

* The nuclear-powered ballistic missile submarine Pennsylvania (SSBN-735) was launched 23 April 1988 at the General Dynamics shipyard in Groton, Connecticut.
† USS Wake Island (CVE-65), a Casablanca-class escort carrier, was commissioned 7 November 1943.

Captain Jackson: Yes, had the Pittsburgh in there, and so we had to put a temporary bow on it, which we did in a very short time, and there was only one problem.* We didn't make it as strong as we should have, and it bent up pretty badly on the way home. They got in some heavy seas, and it wouldn't take it. But that was a case of driving the ship too hard for the sea conditions and maintaining speed.

We had the Duluth in another dry dock at the same time, and they were both in the same storm. The Duluth's bow was just bent up 18 degrees, but Pittsburgh's came all the way off. The reason that it came off is that there was what's known as a slug weld in the flat plate keel. A slug weld is one in which the welder lays a welding rod in and deposits metal around it, a very poor practice. People probably thought he was doing a good job, because he welded fast, but it cost them 120 feet of the ship. Also, I was sent out to salvage the bow, and the officer in charge of salvaging it was Commodore Sullivan, who was the one who cleaned up the Red Sea after the war.† A great guy. I liked him. We went on a Coast Guard ship to salvage the bow, and it was just a lot of fun being on there and being with him.

Paul Stillwell: In what ways?

Captain Jackson: Well, he had obviously a tremendous amount of experience in salvage work, and I observed all the things he was doing and saying, and so I learned a lot from him. It was just enjoyable to sit in the wardroom at mealtimes and so forth and listen to him talk about his philosophy of life and so forth.

Paul Stillwell: Any examples of things you learned from him?

Captain Jackson: Well, I learned how to tip a bow over endwise

---

* The heavy cruiser Pittsburgh (CA-72) was caught in a violent typhoon on 4 June 1945 while operating with the Third Fleet. Her second deck buckled in the storm, and her bow structure, 104 feet long, was torn loose. After the storm subsided, the ship proceeded to Guam. Her bow was later salvaged by the tug Munsee (AT-107) and towed to Guam.
† Commodore William A. Sullivan, USN.

Paul Stillwell: Well, how do you actually go about that? Do you go out with a lasso or what?

Captain Jackson: No. It was towed in to shallow water, about 100 feet, so you could dive with a facemask.

Paul Stillwell: Well, someone had to get a line on it initially, just to be able to tow it.

Captain Jackson: Yes, that's right, they did. It was floating with the bow partly out of the water. We sank it first so that it wouldn't be bouncing around. When we got all the preparations done we blew air in the tanks to blow the water out. Then it tipped over just the way it should have. And then we took that, and it was towed in, and it was hauled up on the beach. They were going to send it back to the States, but by that time the war was essentially over, and they said, "Let's stop." I guess they eventually scrapped it and cut it up in little pieces.

Paul Stillwell: So you were essentially getting it out of the way as a menace to navigation.

Captain Jackson: Yes. Well, it was a salvage job. It could have been used again. In other words it could have been put back on the Pittsburgh.

Paul Stillwell: So presumably the shipyard at Bremerton fabricated a new one for it.

Captain Jackson: Yes. Right. That's exactly what happened. And, you know, if you have time to sit down and rationalize things, we probably wouldn't have salvaged it. We would have sunk it with gunfire. But they had lots of booze on it, and it was up in the forepeak, and so all the divers thought, gee, they had a good thing.

Paul Stillwell: Did you get any of the loot?

Captain Jackson: No. The corks all leaked. The biggest disappointment.

Paul Stillwell: Well, I can imagine it was kind of a professional challenge, though, to figure out how to do this with a detached part of the ship.

Captain Jackson: Oh, it was. And that's where Commodore Sullivan used his expertise, because he'd done a lot of things like that.

Paul Stillwell: Well, there was kind of a gibe that the Pittsburgh was the longest ship in the Navy because there was so much distance between the bow and the rest of the ship.

Captain Jackson: Yes, but we can do better than that because we had different sections of the dry dock. As a matter of fact, I was shipmates with guys on the ABSD-3 for a whole year before I met them.

Paul Stillwell: How did that come about?

Captain Jackson: Well, several sections were built in Pittsburgh. Some were built in Everett, Washington. Some were built in California. And the guys in Pittsburgh had to go down the Mississippi River to New Orleans, through the canal, and out to Guam. And we left San Francisco in our section to go to Guam and we met up in Guam.

Paul Stillwell: How well did the sections mate up?

Captain Jackson: Excellent. They were very good. They were originally made to be bolted together, so you could disassemble it, but we worked out a way to weld in up. Then if we had to move it we would cut through the welds and then reweld them again.

Paul Stillwell: Well, and you have to connect up the piping and so forth as well.

Captain Jackson: Sure, all that. But each section could be operated independently.

Paul Stillwell: Did you observe anything of the professional rivalry between Ellsberg and Sullivan or hear about it?*

Captain Jackson: No, no. We talked about Ellsberg because of my interest with him and the submarines, but I presume there was some rivalry there. I never met Ellsberg, but Sullivan never said anything, and I was with him for, oh gee, it was close to two weeks on board the ship. I don't remember him ever even mentioning Ellsberg's name, which might be an indicator.

Paul Stillwell: It might be. Well, I got the impression there was some kind of a feud regarding jobs over in Europe and the Middle East and what have you. I'd have to look at John Alden's book again for details on that.

Captain Jackson: I think that's right. I think that's correct.

Paul Stillwell: So you were the docking officer, but it sounds as if you had duties much broader than just getting ships docked and undocked.

Captain Jackson: Well, I was the docking and repair officer. I had both jobs.

The New Mexico came in our dry dock, and we had some work to do on it. It was customary to put a long brow from the ship in the dock off to the wing wall of the dry dock for access. It was being installed, and one of the young sailors didn't wait to get permission to leave the ship. He ran out on the gangway, which wasn't securely fastened yet. He fell over the side, and he dropped maybe 60 feet and hit the dock floor. He was injured so badly that in about two hours he died.

We all felt pretty bad about that, because both the dry dock personnel and the ship's personnel were involved. The dry dock people should have taken the precautions to ensure that nobody got out there until it was properly secured. The same thing was it should have been the responsibility of the officer of the deck on the battleship saying,

---

* Captain Edward Ellsberg, USNR, was one of the Navy's principal salvage specialists. For a biography, see John D. Alden, Salvage Man : Edward Ellsberg and the U.S. Navy (Annapolis: Naval Institute Press, 1998).

"Hey, you don't get out there until it's all ready for you." In this case you can say, "Hey, people didn't do their job, and the young fellow got killed." It's a real tragedy. And so what you learn about that is, hey, you've got to be cautious. You've got to be sure that things are safe for people to do.

That's one lesson. Another one was when we had the Wake Island in there. It had been damaged by a kamikaze aerial bomber, but she had a big crane on her. It was the same crane as on another ship which had been damaged, and so it was decided we'd pull that crane off of the Wake Island and transfer it over to the other ship. We dismantled the crane and got ready to life it off, and it was time for lunch. The captain had said not to lift it until he could come. But since everybody was at lunch except the crane operator and the chief boatswain and a couple of other sailors, we said we would lift it during lunchtime because nobody was around. It was an interesting thing that previous to that time there'd been a whole bunch of people around.

The concept of doing it at lunchtime was probably pretty good, but the fact that the captain had said don't do it was bad. Anyway, we picked it up, and a pinion and shaft which were supposed to come out didn't come, and we did everything we could. We had jacks pushing on it and everything and couldn't budge it. So we said, well, we'll pick it up, and it got almost to the apex of the path that we had to take to move it, and this big gear fell out, just fell out. The chief boatswain and I were pretty close down there, and we saw it coming. We both dove out of the way and it missed us. But we could have been killed very easily there.

The moral for that story is first of all we should have taken precautions to ensure that that gear wouldn't come out while it was in the air, either that or insist on it getting loose and taking it out where it was. The other thing was that we ought to follow the captain's orders, and if he says don't lift it we shouldn't have lifted it, but we did. He chastised us mildly, but eventually he forgave us.

Paul Stillwell: But he knew that you had already learned your lesson very well before he said anything.

Captain Jackson: Oh, yes, learned in a very dramatic way.

Paul Stillwell: Anything else on the dry dock?

Captain Jackson: Well, material accumulated on it. The dry docks were configured such that you could break them down into components and tow them to wherever you're going and then reassemble. But we had to take all the gear we needed, in effect, to run a shipyard, so each one of the sections was loaded up with all kinds of stuff. And when we were assembling it we had to transfer all this material from one section to another so that we could do the work on the assembly of the sections.

Among the big things we had to transfer were the two big cranes that we put up on the top of the wing walls. They were carried out under way with the cranes sitting on the main deck, and we had to put them up on the walls. The way we did that was to raise the wing walls on one section, then submerge it to the level of the deck of the other section where they had the crane. Then we put some temporary lengths of railroad track, and we rolled it across. This was a very ticklish job because you're transferring big heavy weights from one side of the ship to the other. Then you're taking the weight off of one ship and putting it on another one, so there's lots of adjustment of ballasting on that. It's a tricky maneuver.

Fortunately that one had been well planned out. We followed the procedure exactly. Everything that had been planned we did. We had no problem. So we learned that lesson. And I told you the story about ABSD-1. When the pontoon capsized they lost one of their cranes. So ABSD-3 was still back in the United States, and they took one of our cranes, and then they needed a pontoon to transfer it down so that we lost one of our pontoons as well. The crane was not too difficult because it was a standard shipyard crane, and we got a new crane long before we left. Those are couple of things that are interesting.

Another one. When we were in Angel Island or Tiburon we nested the sections and had a big float in between them to keep them separated.[*]

Paul Stillwell: Was this before you went to the Pacific?

---

[*] Tiburon, California, is on San Francisco Bay.

Captain Jackson: Yes, just before we went. The gunnery officer was officer in charge of one of the sections, and he was going to move this big float back. And the wind was blowing such that I could see that two ships were holding the big thing pretty darned tight. But he put a snatch block down there to the big float, and he was going to move it by the crane, and I looked at it and I said, "Hey, that block's pretty small, and you're going to break it."

He said, "Oh, no. That's great. That's good enough."

I said, "Hey, you're going to break it."

He said, "No, I'll move it."

So I said, "Wait a minute." And there were a lot of people standing around looking at it, and I got them all away, and I said, "You guys get on the other side of the ship. On both sections get over there."

He started hauling it, and sure enough the snatch block broke. It went sailing through the air, and the path was right where these guys had been standing, so if I hadn't made them move somebody would have been hurt badly. So that was another lesson to learn.

Paul Stillwell: Any other notable jobs that spring to mind?

Captain Jackson: Well, it's not notable, but at that time Liberty ships were having trouble with tail shafts cracking, breaking.* They all carried spares, and they also carried spare propellers. We attracted those ships because it was the only place they could get their new propellers put on. We got so good on that one day we docked one ship beginning at 4:00 o'clock in the morning and we got her dry. Pulled out the old shaft, put in a new tail shaft. Put on a propeller, had her back in the water at noontime.

Paul Stillwell: Wow!

---

* The Liberty ship was a mass-produced cargo ship designed by the U.S. Maritime Commission for use by the Allies in World War II. All told, American shipyards built 2,770 Liberties. The standard Liberty was 442 feet long, 57 feet in the beam, and had a light displacement of 3,337 tons. It had a cargo capacity of 10,920 deadweight tons. Maximum speed for a Liberty was about 12 knots.

Harry A. Jackson, Interview #1 (9/1/98) – Page 65

Captain Jackson: We docked another one at 1:00 o'clock and had that out at 6:00.

Paul Stillwell: Sounds like an assembly line.

Captain Jackson: It was. Boy, we had that one down cold. We had all the gear we needed, all the little jigs and fixtures that we'd need. The crew was trained. It makes you feel good when you do things like that.

Paul Stillwell: Did you have other cases of battle damage besides the <u>Pennsylvania</u> and the <u>Wake Island</u>?

Captain Jackson: The real damage that we saw out there in Guam was when the picket destroyers that were supposed to intercept the kamikazes coming in, and it didn't take the Japs long to figure out that their first target should be the picket ships.[*] Some of those destroyers really got beat up, because sterns would be blown off, or a bow would be blown off, or amidships would be blown out. One destroyer came in, and it didn't have either a bow or a stern. And they were really wrecks. We had little docks called the ARDs that could take those, so they all went to there and we didn't have to worry about those ships.

But another story on the dry dock. We had an LST in dock, and we had to put in a new shaft, and we needed a tapered reamer to put the bolts in the flanges of the shaft. We didn't have one the right size. So I went over to the tender and talked to the repair officer over there and said, "Hey, I need a tapered reamer. Would you let me borrow one?"

He was a mustang, and he said, "We don't lend tools here."[†]

I said, "But I need one. Where am I going to get it?"

He said, "I'll tell you, Sonny. If I was in your shoes, I'd go make one."

So I went back, and I got the chief machinist's mate, and I said, "Hey, Chief.

---

[*] Kamikazes were Japanese suicide aircraft that began showing up in the Philippines campaign in the autumn of 1944. The pilots attempted to crash their bomb-armed aircraft directly into American warships. Hundreds of them successfully hit their targets and inflicted great damage. The kamikazes hit the picket ships particularly hard during the Okinawa operation in the spring of 1945.

[†] "Mustang" is Navy slang for a former enlisted man who has risen through the ranks to become an officer.

We're going to make a tapered reamer." We got out some books that gave us the dimensions and so forth, so we made it, heat-treated it, and it worked.

Paul Stillwell: And from then on you had one.

Captain Jackson: Yes, and that was a great lesson to me.

Paul Stillwell: Well, it sounds like a reinforcement of what you'd already had: "Find a way to do it."

Captain Jackson: Yes. So that was good.

Paul Stillwell: We have the oral history of Admiral Bauernschmidt, who was involved in the supply depot at Guam, and I got the impression there was just scads of everything.* Did you find that to be the case in most of the material needs you had?

Captain Jackson: Yes, I can't complain too much. If we didn't have the precise thing that we needed, we could always find an adequate substitute.

Paul Stillwell: As in the case of the bearing for the South Dakota.

Captain Jackson: A little ingenuity.

Paul Stillwell: I've heard about these units like the Lions and Acorns and Cubs. What was their role?

Captain Jackson: Well, they were generally the advanced groups to go there and prepare for the bases to be established. They would clear the jungles, provide some kind of pier spaces. They would make primitive roads and if they had an airfield they would also clear

---
* Rear Admiral George W. Bauernschmidt, Supply Corps, USN (Ret.).

the jungle and make the runways for the planes. They did a tremendous job and most of them were civil engineers.

Paul Stillwell: So by the time you got there they had essentially done their work?

Captain Jackson: They were all done.

Paul Stillwell: There's a book about Lion Six, and as I remember it has a picture in it of the bow of the Pittsburgh, so maybe they were using that as an example of what comes along after they'd done their job.[*]

Captain Jackson: Yes. As far as I know, those guys didn't have anything to do with us. When they set it up on the dock they may have done that. I didn't have anything to do with that, to put it on the pier over there. So the Seabees might have done that.[†]

Paul Stillwell: What were living conditions like for you in the forward area?

Captain Jackson: Oh, we lived pretty well. We were on a ship, and they had good accommodations.

Paul Stillwell: Was this a tender?

Captain Jackson: No, on the dry dock.

Paul Stillwell: Oh, the dock itself was called a ship?

Captain Jackson: Yes, it was a fully commissioned ship, the USS ASBD-3.

Paul Stillwell: What kind of quarters did you have on board?

---
[*] David Harry Hammer, Lion Six (Annapolis: U.S. Naval Institute, 1947).
[†] Seabees is the nickname applied to members of the Navy's mobile construction battalions (CBs).

Captain Jackson: Well, in the big wing walls they had rooms in there. The officers had staterooms. The crew had what I thought were adequate accommodations.

Paul Stillwell: I had no idea you lived on board.

Captain Jackson: Yes.

Paul Stillwell: Did you have messing facilities also?

Captain Jackson: Oh, sure, it was a commissioned ship. It flew a commission pennant.

Paul Stillwell: Did you have an officer-of-the-deck rotation?

Captain Jackson: Oh, sure. Oh, absolutely.

Paul Stillwell: What would the officer of the deck do? How did he spend his watch?

Captain Jackson: Well, we had a gangway, people coming off and on and he was the guy that they reported to.

Paul Stillwell: Just like an in-port watch?

Captain Jackson: Yes, just exactly like it. Right.

Paul Stillwell: And your room had air-conditioning because you got that compressor.

Captain Jackson: Well, actually we had gotten some compressors, and all the wing wall staterooms had air-conditioning, but it was inadequate. So when I got a new compressor, a bigger one, why, it was a big deal.

Paul Stillwell: Was there a machine shop actually in the dry dock?

Captain Jackson: No, we had a barge and a carpenter's barge too. And it turned out that the chief carpenter, a warrant officer that was in charge of the carpenter barge, had been warrant carpenter on the Dubuque when I was a seaman.

Paul Stillwell: That's a great thing about the Navy. You keep running across former shipmates.

Captain Jackson: Yes.

Paul Stillwell: Well, were you the officer-in-charge or was there somebody else?

Captain Jackson: No, we had a captain and an executive officer. And then the engineer officer and the first lieutenant were senior to me. But I got to be senior to them because I got promoted to lieutenant commander just before I left. One of the few advantages of wartime is that I went from ensign to lieutenant commander in four years.

Paul Stillwell: That's fast.

Captain Jackson: Yes, that's fast.

Paul Stillwell: Did this dry dock have any means of propulsion?

Captain Jackson: No, each section was towed by big ATFs.* But on the section I went out on, we were towed by a Liberty ship. Went eight knots. That was a pretty good voyage. The sections rolled fairly heavily; an average roll was about 15 degrees and a period around about 25 seconds, something like that.

Paul Stillwell: Could you lessen that by ballasting down partway?

---

* ATFs—oceangoing fleet tugboats.

Captain Jackson: Well, we could have, but it would slow us down and wasn't worth the trouble. I ran some experiments. I had lots of time going out there because speed was slow. Some days we made negative mileage. But I made a spring balance so I could measure the accelerations. I was interested in what makes people get seasick. From experience I reasoned that you're more apt to get seasick if you're going up and down vertically, so it's the vertical accelerations. The first thing I did was go around on the ship and find out what the accelerations were at various points. Then I started out by taking guys that I knew were susceptible to seasickness. I'd put them where the accelerations were high, and I'd time them to see how long it took for them to get sick with that acceleration.

Paul Stillwell: I'll bet they loved that job.

Captain Jackson: But one day it was pretty rough. We were getting accelerations about 10 to 12 feet per second squared, which is high. There was an old chief on there that had been in the Navy for about 30 years, and so I said, "Hey, Chief, you're good and salty, aren't you?"

He said, "Oh, yeah, I've never been seasick in my life."

I said, "I've got just the place for you." So I took him out where the maximum acceleration was, and he stood out there. I started my stopwatch. In about ten minutes he said, "That's about enough, isn't it? You get all you want?"

"No, Chief. Time is very important." I said, "You've got to stay at least another ten minutes."

So after about five more minutes he said, "Don't you think you've got enough?"

"No, Chief. Another ten minutes." And before the ten minutes were up, he said, "Hey, I've got to come off there."

I told that story to somebody, and there was a doctor making some investigations on getting seasick. He said, "Hey, you still have that data?"

I said, "Yeah. I've got some."

He said, "Could you send me a copy?" and I sent him the whole thing. But I concluded that if you get a vertical acceleration of about ten feet per second squared, that most everybody will get sick.

Paul Stillwell: So the chief did a good job of holding out.

Captain Jackson: He did that. Oh, his pride was at stake.

Paul Stillwell: He wanted to keep his record unblemished.

Captain Jackson: Right. And so I said, "Well, that's all right, Chief. This is the first dry dock you've been on."

Paul Stillwell: What else do you remember about the dry dock duty?

Captain Jackson: Oh, there were all kinds of incidents. Typhoons were always a problem. The time we had the 26 boats in there a typhoon came along, and we had to button them up and flood down to get the boats out of there. That was a couple of days of intense activity, so I remember that one real good.

Paul Stillwell: Would there be any chance of the dock itself capsizing?

Captain Jackson: No, she was well moored. Actually, it ended up in Portland, Maine. The Navy gave it to Bath Iron Works, and they used it up there. About ten years ago the crew members started an annual reunion, and we had it on the dry dock one time.

Paul Stillwell: How large a crew did you have?

Captain Jackson: We had 880 people at one time. That was our crew. That was a shipyard. So it was a big crew.

Paul Stillwell: So did that include the people on the barge with the machine shop?

Captain Jackson: Yes, and they had their own quarters on the barge.

Paul Stillwell: So that was sort of a sub-command from the dry dock?

Captain Jackson: No, it came under the dry dock captain, but they had an officer in charge, you know, like a division officer. The officer in charge of the carpenter barge was this chief warrant officer who had been on the Dubuque with me. Also, our ship's writer had been at the University of Michigan ROTC when I was commissioned there. And they had a warrant machinist in the machine shop.

Paul Stillwell: Were you there till the end of the war?

Captain Jackson: Yes.

Paul Stillwell: What do you remember about the coming of peace? What was the reaction when the end of the war came and you were on board the dry dock.

Captain Jackson: That's very difficult to either explain or understand, but to me it was like a letdown. There was no urgent need to do things anymore. In other words, if it didn't get done today it'd get done tomorrow and nobody would care. That was sort of a letdown to me.

Paul Stillwell: Especially after such a frantic pace as you had done.

Captain Jackson: Yes. Right.

Paul Stillwell: When we were talking earlier, you quoted the captain. What did he say?

Captain Jackson: Oh, what he said, and I'm sure he was just trying to maintain morale, he got us all at quarters and said, "Hey, the war's over, but our work is not done. We've got to work twice as hard." If you think about it, they had all this mass of men and material and stuff to take back. Everybody wanted to go, and they had to have ships to do it, and if they needed a repair the dry dock would be called on to do it. So there was some justification in what he said, even though nobody really thought we were going to work harder.

Paul Stillwell: Admiral Bauernschmidt said there was a lot of stuff that was not allowed to be salvaged because the production plants would have been out of business for a considerable period.

Captain Jackson: Yes. Took brand-new Jeeps out on a barge and just pushed them off the edge.

Paul Stillwell: A lot of aircraft destroyed.

Captain Jackson: Yes, for the same reasons. War doesn't make any sense.

Paul Stillwell: It's the most wasteful thing ever devised by human beings.

Captain Jackson: Now we'll just burn everything up.

Paul Stillwell: You mentioned leaving BuShips because you wanted to get out to the war zone and make a contribution.

Captain Jackson: Right.

Paul Stillwell: After having done that, did you feel satisfaction at having made that venture? Did it live up to your expectations?

Captain Jackson: Well, I came away from my tour of duty in the Pacific feeling that I had contributed to the war effort and that I fully realized that I was not the only guy that could have done it. There were plenty of others that did it.

Paul Stillwell: But obviously it was a lot different from staying at a desk or a drawing board.

Captain Jackson: Oh, yes. Well, that's what hurt me. There were a lot of people out there fighting, but there were also a lot of people in Washington just because they had a safe job, and I didn't want to be counted with those guys, even though I was making a contribution.

Paul Stillwell: Where did you go from Guam?

Captain Jackson: Well, big question, what happens now? I always wanted to stay in the Navy, but there was lots of confusion. You know, everybody wanted to go home.

Paul Stillwell: Did you have a regular commission?

Captain Jackson: Not then. Well, I had lots of leave coming because I didn't take any during the war, and so I came back to the States. I wanted to go to Japan with the group of people that went over there to make an assessment of their technical capabilities and what they did for the war and so forth. Bob Evans was in charge of that, but the communications between Guam and back home and so forth were difficult, so I never did make that grade, but that's really what I wanted to do.*

So I came back, and I took some leave. I didn't know what I wanted to do. Like everybody else. It was a period of uncertainty. So I went down to American Shipbuilding Company in Lorain, Ohio. I talked to the guys, and they offered me a job. I went there,

---

* Evans discussed the technical mission to Japan in his Naval Institute oral history.

and Steinbrenner was running the place the way his son runs the Yankees.* I just decided I didn't want any part of that.

After that I went back to see my friend, Admiral Lee. I said, "Admiral, I don't know what I want to do, but I see that we're entering into a new world with atomic energy. We've demonstrated that it can be useful. Somehow, I would like to get connected with that."†

He said, "Oh, we're going to start a program, and if you'd like to do that, why don't you go see Al Mumma?"‡

So I went back to see him, and he said, "Oh, sure. That's going to be good, and we'd like to have you. But the trouble is you're going to have to get an AEC clearance, and it'll take a while. And so we'll send you out to Bikini, where they're going to test the weapons." He said, "You'll be gone all summer, and when you come back we'll have a place for you."§

Paul Stillwell: That was the summer of 1946.

Captain Jackson: Right. So I went out there, and Louie Roddis and I went on the Wharton, the two of us, and we had similar jobs.** That's when I got to know him real well, on that trip. He grew up in Hawaii, and so we stopped in Hawaii for a couple of weeks and he took me all over the islands there.

Paul Stillwell: What kind of a gent was he?

---

* Henry G. Steinbrenner was head of the American Shipbuilding Company; his son, George M. Steinbrenner III, has been the principal owner of the New York Yankees baseball team since 1973. He is noted for his arbitrary manner.
† Commodore Paul F. Lee, USN, served from 1944 to 1946 as chief of the Construction Branch, Shipbuilding Division, Bureau of Ships. In November 1946, as a rear admiral, he became the first Chief of Naval Research. He held that job until his retirement on 1 July 1948.
‡ Mumma was then a captain serving as Deputy Director of Ship Design in charge of the design of machinery in the Bureau of Ships. He became part of the organization established to develop nuclear propulsion for warships.
§ AEC—Atomic Energy Commission. In July 1946 a joint Army-Navy task force conducted tests at Bikini Atoll in the Marshall Islands to determine the effects of atomic bombs on moored warships. Along with an array of U.S. ships were captured German and Japanese warships.
** Lieutenant Commander Louis H. Roddis, Jr., USN (Ret.). As a Naval Academy midshipman, Roddis stood number one in the class of 1939.

Captain Jackson: Oh, I liked him very much. He was real smart, but he didn't exercise his intelligence in a competitive way at all. In other words, he would ask people questions that obviously he knew the answer to. For instance, I remember one time that we were talking about heat transfer, and so he asked me what the equations were for transferring heat. Fortunately, I knew them, and I also knew that he knew them. But he was that kind of guy. He didn't lord it over you because of it.

Paul Stillwell: You have to admire somebody like that.

Captain Jackson: I do. I really do. When we came back he went down to Oak Ridge, and I went to Schenectady.[*]

Paul Stillwell: What do you remember about the period out in Bikini?

Captain Jackson: Well, the most impressive thing, I was assigned to inspect the Saratoga after the bomb attack.[†] So we spent a lot of time beforehand going on the ship and finding our way around and tentatively making a plan for how we were going to inspect the ship. We were on a little net tender, and the net tender was going to take us in and let us off the ship onto the Saratoga. But by the time we got there they had radioactive readings, and the radioactivity was so high that they wouldn't let us go on the ship. So we laid off and watched her sink.[‡]

    Well, I felt it was my duty to make all the kinds of notes that I could on it, and one of the things I estimated was that she was taking on something like 9,000 tons of water a minute. She was going right down. So the bottom must have just been opened up. The next thing I remember is that the radioactivity on all the ships had to be cleared off, and that this was a horrible job. Eventually the whole project was abandoned because everybody had reached their tolerance level.

---

[*] Oak Ridge National Laboratory, Oak Ridge, Tennessee, which has long been involved in research and development in the field of nuclear energy. The General Electric Company was involved in nuclear engineering at its plant near Schenectady, New York.
[†] USS Saratoga (CV-3), a Lexington-class aircraft carrier, was commissioned 16 November 1927.
[‡] The Saratoga sank on 25 July 1946 following an underwater atomic blast that was detonated under a landing craft 500 yards from the carrier.

Paul Stillwell: You were wearing dosimeters?

Captain Jackson: Oh, right. And the ship that survived the best was the submarine. And actually her superstructure was all pretty well damaged but they got her under way and drove it around. So it was just to demonstrate that they could do it.

Paul Stillwell: Dick Laning was out there with Pilotfish.* Was that the one?

Captain Jackson: Yes. And my roommate on the Wharton, the AP-7, was Clay Tucker.† He was a submariner, and before the test we used to go over on the submarine mostly because it was air-conditioned. So that's what I remember there mostly. Oh. Pennsylvania was there.

Paul Stillwell: Your old friend.

Captain Jackson: Yes. And she still had our patch on it, and it survived. So that felt pretty good.

Paul Stillwell: Nevada was there. She got beat up pretty bad topside.

Captain Jackson: Oh, she did that. And the Prinz Eugen, the German ship, the first test she stood up pretty well.‡ The second test she was pretty badly damaged.

Paul Stillwell: What sorts of data were you collecting?

---

* Lieutenant Commander Richard B. Laning, USN. The oral history of Laning, who retired as a captain, is in the Naval Institute collection.
† Lieutenant Commander Houston Clay Tucker, Jr., USN.
‡ The Prinz Eugen, a German heavy cruiser commissioned in 1940, was probably best known for being a part of the ill-fated Bismarck's last cruise in 1941. The cruiser was turned over to the United States as part of the postwar reparations and was later used as a target ship in the Bikini atomic bomb tests in the Marshall Islands in the summer of 1946. For an account by one of the German officers who remained after the ship became part of the U.S. Navy, see Helmut Raumann, "Life As 'Employed Enemy Personnel,'" Naval History, Summer 1989, pages 28-34.

Captain Jackson: Well, fortunately we had a trained fellow to monitor the radioactivity, so we didn't have to worry about that and what we were looking for was structural damage so that later on you could design ships to resist that kind of damage. Like on the Saratoga a lot of the ships we just never got on, so it was very difficult to make any detailed analysis. But every ED that was there was required to write a report on his observations and what he thought the Bureau of Ships or the Navy Department could do to cope with atomic weapons.

Paul Stillwell: Which had suddenly become a big concern.

Captain Jackson: They sure did. Boy, after seeing that. Wiped out a whole damn fleet, just one bomb. It changed warfare forever.

Paul Stillwell: Did you have any contact with Deak Parsons out there at Bikini?[*]

Captain Jackson: No, but when I was at the University of Michigan I had a job in the department of research, and also I was student assistant to a fellow called Dr. R. A. Sawyer, who was the chief scientist. And because I'd been his student assistant I had a good in with him, and I used to go over and call on him once in a while, and so I knew a lot of the top scientists.

Paul Stillwell: Did you see the bombs explode while you were out there?

Captain Jackson: Well, I saw them one second after, but nobody would look at them when they detonated.

Paul Stillwell: I see.

---

[*] Captain William S. Parsons, USN, was involved in the development of the atomic bomb in New Mexico. During the mission of 6 August 1945, Parsons was the weaponeer on board the B-29 named "Enola Gay" that dropped the bomb on Hiroshima, Japan. See Al Christman, Target Hiroshima: Deak Parsons and the Creation of the Atomic Bomb (Annapolis: Naval Institute Press, 1998).

Captain Jackson: You didn't want to do that. You'd lose your eyesight.

Paul Stillwell: Did you look through some kind of a blackened glass?

Captain Jackson: No, I made a pinhole camera, a box camera with just a pinhole in it, and I've got a picture of that someplace. And it turned out pretty good. But when the bomb went off on Able, which was dropped, an air bomb, my back was toward the thing so I didn't really see that but I saw all the big cloud. As a matter of fact, I got some pictures of that which I've got out here just because they were in my folder. But the Baker which was underwater, and there was no possibility of getting the strong radiation from the bomb, I watched that, and it sure looked just exactly like the pictures show it. Amazing.

Paul Stillwell: Big base surge?

Captain Jackson: Oh, yes. A base surge and the oil from the oil tanks and the parts of the ships. Unbelievable.

Paul Stillwell: Any other recollections from that experience at Bikini?

Captain Jackson: Yes, a lot of them. When I came home I had a pair of big work boots, and I told my wife and my sister-in-law that they were radioactive and you could see them in the dark. So my sister-in-law went and turned all the lights out, and they didn't glow.

Paul Stillwell: Well, you had been sent out to Bikini while your clearance was being processed. When did that come through?

Captain Jackson: Well, that came through in the summer of 1946. I went up to Schenectady, New York. I think I actually got there on 1 September.

Paul Stillwell: What happened there?

Captain Jackson: Well, I reported in to the engineer for the Manhattan District. It was that early. It was still being run by Manhattan District.* My brother was out there, and he knew the ropes. I signed up to take some General Electric courses, which I could do because they made them available to all government employees. Then I started studying nuclear power.

Paul Stillwell: Who was teaching it?

Captain Jackson: General Electric Company employees. Some of them were very good and some of them were lousy. One guy wrote a great big fourth-order differential equation on the board, and he said, "This is the start of it all. This is where you start."

I said, "There must be some buildup to it like 'What do the terms mean? What do the symbols mean?'" He was a lousy instructor, and practically everybody said that going to his courses was a waste of time. But others were superb. Very good.

Paul Stillwell: Was this still all theoretical at this point? I mean, was there any hardware?

Captain Jackson: Oh, no. No hardware. That's what was going on, trying to develop the hardware. And first of all you had to design the system. And you didn't know whether you could make a reactor that would work. Since GE was working on liquid metal, it was different from the work that Westinghouse was doing. Even the mathematics was different. So we worked on that, and I'd say the naval officers that were up there were moderately qualified when they got through.

Paul Stillwell: Who else was there with you?

Captain Jackson: Well, there was an aviator, Ray Doll, and there was Ed Conrad who was a submarine driver.† Then there was a guy that had a Russian name. We called him Ski

---

* Manhattan Project was the code name for the U.S. effort to create an atomic bomb in World War II.
† Commander Raymond E. Doll, USN; Lieutenant Commander Edward E. Conrad, USN.

because we had trouble pronouncing his name, but Yacthmonov was a good guy, and his wife was a real good person too.

Paul Stillwell: I think you told me last night you were the fourth person in the Navy's nuclear power program?

Captain Jackson: Yes, that's correct, but the qualification was much different now.

Paul Stillwell: Who were those other three ahead of you?

Captain Jackson: Lou Roddis, Jim Dunford and Miles Libbey.[*] The fifth was Gene Wilkinson.[†]

Paul Stillwell: Now, were they at Oak Ridge already?

Captain Jackson: Yes, they went to Oak Ridge, and I went to Schenectady. I spent a lot of TAD down there at Oak Ridge too.[‡]

Paul Stillwell: Ted Rockwell has described that as a pretty primitive place at the time.[§] What are you recollections?

Captain Jackson: I thought it was satisfactory. They all had government quarters that were quite good. When I would go down there, I would stay either with Jim Dunford or Lou Roddis, and if they'd come up to visit me they'd stay with us.

Paul Stillwell: Any perspectives to offer on Dunford or Libbey?

---

[*] Lieutenant Commander Louis H. Roddis, Jr., USN; Lieutenant Commander James M. Dunford, USN; Lieutenant Commander Miles A. Libbey, USN. All three were engineering duty officer specialists.
[†] Lieutenant Commander Eugene P. Wilkinson, USN, a submariner who chose to remain an unrestricted line officer rather than becoming an engineering duty officer. He was later first commanding officer of the USS Nautilus (SSN-571).
[‡] TAD—temporary additional duty.
[§] Theodore Rockwell, The Rickover Effect: How One Man Made a Difference (Annapolis: Naval Institute Press, 1992).

Captain Jackson: Good guys. Dunford particularly was smart. Not as smart as Roddis, but he was very good. Miles Libbey went on to get a Ph.D. in nuclear physics and became a professor, I think, at New York University.

Paul Stillwell: What do you remember about the work at Oak Ridge itself?

Captain Jackson: Well, they had a tremendous foundation from the Manhattan District, so I don't know if they were any smarter than we were, but they'd had a lot more experience, and they were further ahead. So what we were trying to do was extract from them all their experience and see how it would be useful to us in the Navy.

Paul Stillwell: You talk about designing a system. Did you yet have the applications for the system in mind?

Captain Jackson: Oh, sure. We knew we wanted to put it in a submarine, but we thought maybe the route to do that would be to try it in a DE first. The reason we picked a DE is that it was about the right size for a power plant that we needed, and also we could run the DE up to Albany so that it would be close to the GE factory, and they could put it in that. DEs were short-legged because they couldn't carry too much fuel, and so if we could make it for a DE we could make it for practically anything. But the systems were essentially the same, whether for a submarine or a surface ship.

Paul Stillwell: Why did the DE plant not come into being?

Captain Jackson: Well, there were problems with the liquid metal coolant. That had a lot to do with it. But it had progressed to a point where they thought that they could skip the DE and put it in a submarine, which they did, the Seawolf.[*] Dick Laning was very much

---

[*] USS Seawolf (SSN-576) was the Navy's second nuclear-powered submarine. The first, USS Nautilus (SSN-571) had a pressurized water reactor. The Seawolf served as a test bed for a reactor cooled by liquid sodium. The latter was not deemed a success, so the Seawolf was later equipped with the pressurized water type. For the first skipper's view, see Richard B. Laning, "The Seawolf's Sodium-Cooled Power Plant," Naval History, Spring 1992, pages 45-48.

in favor of the liquid metal plant, but there were lots of problems with it.* If you let it cool down, it'd freeze up, and then you have a heck of a job melting all the coolant. Also, it would expand so you had to make it strong enough to withstand the expansion forces, which are large.

Paul Stillwell: Well, corrosion was a problem also, wasn't it?

Captain Jackson: Yes, corrosion, and it was dangerous. If you get a leak of hot sodium in the water, you've got horrible problems. And we demonstrated that. That's sort of an amusing story, but it is important to recognize. We built a liquid metal system in which they had an oil-fired boiler to heat it, but we were looking at developing pumps and valves and control circuits and so forth that would control it, and that was out at Alpaugh. And we recognized that we could get leaks in there, so we had a big pan built underneath all the piping. And it was about a 30- by 40-foot area that was all panned.

There was a big problem between the fire department of General Electric Company and the fire department of Alpaugh. GE said, "We'll take care of this. If there's a fire or something, let us do it."

So Alpaugh said, "Hey, it's in our district, and we put out fires."

"Yeah, but you don't know what you're dealing with."

"Doesn't make any difference. We know how to put out a fire." Well, the inevitable happened, and one snowy day with a lot of snow and the wind was blowing and you couldn't see, we got a leak of hot sodium. Somebody pulled the fire alarm to Alpaugh's Fire Department, and they came running out and said, "Get back, everybody, get back. We're taking charge." They walked into this pan now of liquid sodium, hot sodium, with snow all over their boots, and talk about guys with hot feet. They had them. So then they ran out, you know, and they stomped around in the snow and finally got all the stuff off their boots. They said, "Why didn't you tell us about this?"

"We did and you wouldn't listen. You're the guys that put out fire. Go put it out."

---

* Commander Richard B. Laning, USN. The oral history of Laning, who retired as a captain, is in the Naval Institute collection.

Paul Stillwell: What happened then?

Captain Jackson: Well, they left everything to cool down, and then they had a lot of solid sodium in the pan that they had to break up in pieces. But it could have been real dangerous. We could have killed people easy.

Paul Stillwell: Where's Alpaugh? I've not heard of that.

Captain Jackson: Oh, that's a little town just outside of Schenectady. It's almost a suburb of Schenectady.

Paul Stillwell: Was there a parallel effort going on with Westinghouse at the same time?

Captain Jackson: Oh, sure.

Paul Stillwell: Who was involved in that?

Captain Jackson: Well, that started out to be the same thing as at Schenectady, what eventually became the AEC, but it was still at that time the Manhattan District. Had an office down there. Wilkinson had the same job that I had at Schenectady. He was the Navy rep.

But one the first things we did at Schenectady, and we were commissioned by the Navy, was to look at all the different things we could do. So we looked at three basic differences. One was a liquid metal coolant. Another was pressurized water coolant, and the third one was the gas coolant. We studied this, and I acted just like a GE engineer on that, as a member of the team. The conclusion that we came to was that the pressurized water looked like the safest way to go. The liquid metal had some practical problems, but we thought it could be done. Then we looked at the gas-cooled thing and said, "Well, that needs an awful of research, and it's debatable whether it ever would fit in a ship."

But the government decided that they would fund all three of them, and they gave the liquid metal to General Electric Company, because they'd had lots of experience in liquid metal. They gave the pressurized water to Westinghouse, and they gave the gas-cooled reactor to Allis-Chalmers. After about six months of investigation Allis-Chalmers said, "Hey, we don't think that this is going to work for a ship, and maybe we're wasting our time." I think that was a good decision.

But the other two went forward and they eventually got into ships. As you know, Dick Laning was captain of the Seawolf, and Dennis Wilkinson was captain of the Nautilus, the pressurized water. Dick was very—I won't say outspoken, but he was vocal anyway about the attributes of liquid metal. He thought it was great, and he was very much disappointed when they took it out and replaced it with pressurized water.

Paul Stillwell: Neither Laning nor Wilkinson is a shrinking violet.

Captain Jackson: Oh, no. No. Dick is real good. He thinks a new thought every second.

Paul Stillwell: He's certainly had that reputation.

Captain Jackson: Yes.

Paul Stillwell: And always out ahead: "How can we do something in the future?"

Captain Jackson: Yes.

Paul Stillwell: At what point did Rickover get into this process?

Captain Jackson: Oh, he came along pretty early in the game.

Captain Jackson: But after you.

Captain Jackson: Yes, after I was assigned to it. There was a lot of debate between Mumma and Mills about who should get that job.* Rickover was pretty much in limbo at that time. Finally Mills, I guess, just because he was the senior admiral, outvoted Mumma and said he wanted Rickover.

Paul Stillwell: I think you told me earlier that Mumma's choice was Harry Burris.

Captain Jackson: That's right.

Paul Stillwell: Why did you think Rickover was better?

Captain Jackson: Well, I'm not sure that I thought Rickover was better, but I didn't think that Burris was physically able to handle that job. He came up to Schenectady, and there was a lot of contest between Rickover and Burris, who was running the show at Schenectady. Burris's medical difficulties made it so he was quite ineffective. That's not against him. It was a fact of nature that he just couldn't do it. They had to cut off his leg, and he had horrible stomach trouble.

Paul Stillwell: Well, in the perspective now of more than 50 years afterward, do you think that Rickover was the right man for the job?

Captain Jackson: Well, he certainly was successful, and you can't really fault success. But there are other people who could have done the same job without some of the methods that Rickover used that were not—well, to be nice about it, his methods were unusual.

Paul Stillwell: That is being very nice about it.

Captain Jackson: Yes.

---

* Vice Admiral Earle W. Mills, USN, served as Chief of the Bureau of Ships from November 1946 to February 1949.

Paul Stillwell: Well, some people have suggested that no one except Rickover could have gotten nuclear power to sea as quickly as he. Do you agree with that?

Captain Jackson: No. Red Raborn could have gotten it to sea at the same time.* And Raborn was certainly no technical genius, but he was a leader. People worked for Rickover through fear. Raborn got people to work because they loved him. And to me there's a big difference. I was one of the few guys that worked for both Raborn and Rickover.

Paul Stillwell: That's why it's interesting to get your viewpoint.

Captain Jackson: Yes.

Paul Stillwell: What milestones do you remember in that five-year period as nuclear power progressed toward reality?

Captain Jackson: Oh, actually I left in 1951. I was assigned to Portsmouth for a number of reasons. One, because I asked to go there. It was time of rotation of duty. And they were getting in the nuclear power business, and so one of my assignments was to help them get prepared to do nuclear work. The other thing is that I wanted to get in the submarine design business and I always wanted to do that but I got off on tangents. So I went to Portsmouth in 1951. And so I was only on the fringes of the developments of some of that work.

Paul Stillwell: Well, what happened though between '46 and '51? Can we fill in that period?

---

* Rear Admiral William F. Raborn, Jr., USN, was director of the Special Projects Office, which developed the Polaris submarine-launched ballistic missile system. He held the post from 1955 to 1962, being promoted to vice admiral in 1960. His Polaris oral history is in the Naval Institute collection.

Captain Jackson: Well, in general it was a period of intense study. Bec kept complaining. She says the only time she saw me was when I had my nose in a book, which probably is true. There was not time for anything but work.

One incident. Dr. Kingdon, who was the chief scientist for General Electric Company on the plant asked me what I thought about the diameter of the submarine.[*] The Navy at that time was adamant, mostly due to Admiral Morgan, that the pressure hull had to be 18 feet in diameter.[†] Dr. Kingdon asked me what I thought, and I said, "Well, from what I know now of what the plant's going to be, you can't fit it in 18 feet, and if you could you couldn't float it because you wouldn't get enough buoyancy. So it's going to end up being whatever it has to be to encompass your reactor."

He said, "Are you sure about that?"

I said, "I believe in Archimedes, and he told me that's going to happen." And I remember those words. Sure enough, that's the way it did happen, that the diameter increased to get enough buoyancy to support all that weight.

Captain Jackson: And what did it wind up as?

Captain Jackson: Twenty-seven feet, I think. The Nautilus was 27 feet, and I think the Seawolf was 27 feet too. But the laws of physics drove that, not dictation by any people or anything else. It had to be. That little conversation let Kingdon take a stand and say, "Well, hey, we can't fit it in 18 feet."

Paul Stillwell: Was part of that just the density of the plant per volume that would make it so heavy?

Captain Jackson: Oh, the shielding on it. Shielding's heavy and it's dense, very dense. The water plant was better, because you didn't have that residual radiation in the coolant, and it didn't freeze up, and so it was certainly more practical. It's not as good a coolant, but it was better.

---

[*] Dr. Kenneth H. Kingdon was technical director of the Knolls Laboratory, east of Schenectady, New York.
[†] Captain Armand M. Morgan, USN, later rear admiral.

Paul Stillwell: Well, you spent this time learning. What about spending time applying that knowledge to building the system?

Captain Jackson: Oh, every day—working with the designers and laying it out and making studies. I made lots of layouts of submarines, power plants.

Paul Stillwell: Who was supervising that effort?

Captain Jackson: I guess I was.

Paul Stillwell: And you were working on something that few people had ever seen before because nuclear reactors were so new.

Captain Jackson: Oh, yes, but if you want to see one, go up to the football stadium in Chicago.* That's an interesting insight, too, because the leaders in the Navy would be taken up there and shown this pile of graphite and concrete and so forth and say, "This is a reactor."

So these guys would look around and say, "You mean you're going to put that in a ship? You guys are nuts."

So we would say, "Well, there's going to be some progress, and we'll make it smaller."

And then, "Well, how much smaller?"

"Well, we'll make it small enough so it'll fit in a ship." We'd go around in a circle like that, but they would walk away shaking their heads and saying, "These guys are crazy." As a matter of fact, a couple of my admiral friends said, "You want to get out of that business, because it'll never come to fruition in your lifetime, and what you want to do is go and get a job someplace where you can get some visibility."

---

* During World War II Dr. Enrico Fermi directed a series of experiments in nuclear energy. An atomic pile was built in a modified squash court under the stands of Stagg Field at the University of Chicago. The first controlled release of nuclear energy was in December 1942.

I said, "Well, I don't necessarily agree with you. I think we will produce something."

Paul Stillwell: And indeed you did.

Captain Jackson: Yes. But it was interesting. I've still got some of those early sketches of submarines that I made.

Paul Stillwell: Were you doing a submarine per se or the reactor or both?

Captain Jackson: Both. My real expertise was taking the components that were being developed and fitting them in a confined space like a submarine. But I did contribute a lot, like the layout of the shielding and the piping and so forth. One thing that I did was get some big old pumps so we could pump water through the mockup of a reactor. That was a nice experiment.

Paul Stillwell: Was that at Schenectady?

Captain Jackson: Yes, that was at Schenectady.

Paul Stillwell: At what point did the prototype at Arco take shape?*

Captain Jackson: That took shape about 1950, started out there. They were developing the site by the AEC. By this time it had changed to AEC. And they were testing all kinds of reactors out there.

Paul Stillwell: Do you have memories from being out there at Arco while that was happening?

---

* Arco, Idaho, is the site of an operating nuclear reactor that served as a prototype for the first operational models and has long been used as a training tool for individuals entering the Navy's nuclear power program.

Captain Jackson: Yes, I used to go out there frequently.

Paul Stillwell: Please tell me what you recall.

Captain Jackson: A long ride in an automobile at high speeds. But it was very interesting to see what was going on there and the big water tank that they had a submarine hull going through. The concept was different at Schenectady. We made the big ball and put the reactor compartment inside the ball. We didn't have all the motion and stuff that Arco had.

Paul Stillwell: I would think it would have been just very satisfying to see that take shape after previously just being represented on pieces of paper.

Captain Jackson: Yes, it was. There's no question about that. But it was no different on those ships than other ships. It's just that we had a different power plant. That's all. In fact the Nautilus, except for the reactor, was almost an enlarged copy of the Trigger.* As a matter of fact, that's another bone of contention. They had a standard plan for a submarine door, which is very heavy and lots of mechanical parts on it. They were something like $1,200 per door on the Trigger, and it was $2,400 on the Nautilus. Same door. But it was nuclear power, of course, then it cost more.

Paul Stillwell: What lessons do you remember learning from the operation of the prototype at Arco?

Captain Jackson: I wasn't too much associated with that, but we learned a lot about reactor control, shielding, and all that got passed on to Schenectady, and there was very useful information. I was out there when they first started it up, and that was very thrilling to see the shaft turn, but that's all you could see.

Paul Stillwell: But it was physical movement.

---

* USS Trigger (SS-564) was commissioned 31 March 1952 as one of the new Tang class of fast-attack submarines. They had considerably more speed submerged than did the World War II fleet boats.

Captain Jackson: That's right, the shaft was turning. And it had a tachometer so you could see the counting on the number of turns.

Paul Stillwell: What do you remember about the operation of the one at Schenectady?

Captain Jackson: Well, again I left before they got to that point, so I didn't see that happen. I went to Portsmouth, and I was ship superintendent of the Guppy modifications on the Sea Robin, 407.* Well, to go back, while I was at Schenectady Ed Conrad had gotten command of the Halfbeak, and so I got orders for a two-week tour of duty in the operations on that so that I could start qualifying in submarines. And that was good experience.

Paul Stillwell: I think it would be invaluable just to know how a submarine works.

Captain Jackson: Yes, and I really qualified for submarines on the Sea Robin, because by that time I'd made my notebook so I met all the qualifications.

Paul Stillwell: And, of course, you weren't starting from ground zero either.

Captain Jackson: Oh, no. I was older and more experienced than most of the kids that were trying to get qualified, so I had learned how to apply my knowledge. Let's put it that way.

Paul Stillwell: Any highlights to remember from that time at sea?

Captain Jackson: A lot of hard work. Ed Conrad was good. I went down on board, and my first time on that submarine he said, "You want to get it under way?"
    I said, "Geez. I don't know."

---

* The term "Guppy" grew out of the initials for the postwar modification fitted to World War II fleet boats to give them greater underwater propulsion power (GUPP).

He says, "Oh, go ahead. You can do it." So I got her under way, and I'd only been on the ship about half an hour.

Paul Stillwell: That's line officer work.

Captain Jackson: Yes, but I had done some ship handling. On the <u>Fletcher</u> they let me do a lot of ship handling. And when I was growing up, why, I had lots of experience. Not in big ships like that but—so it turned out all right.

While I was at Portsmouth. I went to a conference on a new submarine, and we had people there from OpNav, people from the various sections of BuShips, and Admiral Morgan was leading the conference. Morgan was a big, tall guy, and a lot of people didn't like him because they thought he was much too arrogant.

Paul Stillwell: I think he stood number one in his class.

Captain Jackson: Yes, he did that.[*] But at the conference he spent most of the time talking about sea stories, all configured to make him look good. Andy McKee was over in the corner, and he had a little 4-inch slide rule he carried in his shirt pocket all the time. So he had a little pad and pencil, and he drew on that. He pulled this out and looked at it, and he'd make some more sketches and stuff like that. Nothing was really accomplished at this conference because they were involved in a lot of talk. It was sort of like a ladies' bridge party. But when they started to break up Andy McKee took these papers in there and his drawing. He said, "Gentlemen, I think that this is what your submarine's going to look like." And, lo and behold, it did. When it was completed, that submarine looked just almost exactly like his preliminary sketches.

Captain Jackson: Do you remember which class that was?

Captain Jackson: Yes, 571.

---

[*] As a midshipman, Morgan finished number one in the final competitive standings for the Naval Academy class of 1924.

Paul Stillwell: The Nautilus. What year would that have been?

Captain Jackson: Let's see. That was about '52 or '53. Anyway, that decided, I looked around at all the people and I said, "I don't want to be like that tall guy. I want to be like that little guy."

Paul Stillwell: So this would be after McKee had already retired and was working for Electric Boat Company?

Captain Jackson: Oh, he was. Affirmative.

Paul Stillwell: He was just universally admired, from everything that I've heard.

Captain Jackson: Yes!

Paul Stillwell: That respect came especially from submarine skippers, because they felt that whatever the prescribed test depth they could probably go beneath that and survive.

Captain Jackson: Yep. But what he used to say was, "If you can't break it, you made it too strong." And it took me a long time to really understand what he was saying. That if you design it to break at a certain stress and then you test it to that and then take it over beyond it and it doesn't break, then you made it too strong. So you can take some weight out, and weight is very, very important. So you learn something from all those guys.

Paul Stillwell: I'll bet the submarine skippers would still rather have it a little stronger.

Captain Jackson: Well, I don't know. I don't know.

Paul Stillwell: Why do you say that?

Captain Jackson: Because you give up something if you made it too strong, and I'm not sure they'd like to give up what they'd have to give up.

Paul Stillwell: What do you give up?

Captain Jackson: Well, it depends. Either you don't have enough room inside the ship, or in order to float it you make it bigger than you need to make it. And if you make it bigger than you need, you slow down, harder to maneuver. So everything's a compromise.

Captain Jackson: You're dealing with a whole collection of tradeoffs.

Captain Jackson: Every step of the way it's a tradeoff. Well, later on I'll tell you about some of things that have transpired, differences of opinion and so forth.

Paul Stillwell: Did you have any involvement in the discussion on whether the Nautilus would carry a weapon system?

Captain Jackson: Yes, and there were lots of debates about what to do. Rickover was really opposed to it, because he didn't want anything interfering with his power plant. I think Wilkinson probably carried the day on that.[*] He said, "Gee, if you're going to have a submarine, you ought to have a submarine. It ought to be able to demonstrate that this is useful." And he's a pretty persuasive guy. So I can give him at least partial if not complete acknowledgement that he convinced Rickover to make it a real submarine. And that, in my opinion, was a submarine that turned out to be good.

Paul Stillwell: Well, and she had a long life span in the fleet after that.[†]

---

[*] Commander Eugene P. Wilkinson, USN, became the first commanding officer of the USS Nautilus (SSN-571), when she was commissioned as the world's first nuclear-powered submarine on 30 September 1954.
[†] The Nautilus was decommissioned 3 March 1980 and has since become a museum ship at the New London, Connecticut, submarine base.

Captain Jackson: That's right. But she was a showboat. She took more congressmen to sea than there are in the House.

Paul Stillwell: And he was very good at that too.

Captain Jackson: Yes, he was superb at that.

Paul Stillwell: Well, one thing I observed about Admiral Wilkinson is he has a real talent for getting his way by whatever it takes.

Captain Jackson: Yes. I later rode the Board of Inspection and Survey trials on the Nautilus as an OpNav representative, and I came to the conclusion from the remarks and stuff that were going on that I was the only one in OpNav who was interested in that ship. Really, that most of the guys that were involved with submarines didn't want to go to sea in that submarine.

Paul Stillwell: Well, Admiral Wilkinson had an interesting story on that. He said that he had requests to put all sorts of people on board, large numbers, and he imposed an upper limit, which I believe was 50. He said he just had to insist on that because he didn't want too many people on board interfering with the crew's work.

Captain Jackson: Well, I'm sure that that's what he wanted to do, but I think he was hard pressed—well, depends on who you're talking about. If you're talking about people from OpNav there were not 50 people who wanted to go.

Paul Stillwell: Well, I suspect these were more from the engineering and AEC side.

Captain Jackson: That's right, from Westinghouse and AEC and so forth.

Paul Stillwell: And BuShips probably.

Captain Jackson: Well, I guess BuShips had some representatives on it. But there were very few bunks available, so Dennis said, "Hey, anytime I'm on watch you can have my bunk." And I thought that was pretty darn nice of him.

Paul Stillwell: We're jumping ahead a little, but what do you remember about those trials for the Nautilus?

Captain Jackson: That they were quite successful. Very good. It was in good shape. Everything ran. We didn't have any problems anywhere. Yes. So I think you could say it was a clean sweep. And the ship's force did an excellent job.

Captain Jackson: I'm sure he had them superbly trained.

Captain Jackson: Yes, he did.

Paul Stillwell: Well, again, this had to be even more satisfying than the mockup out at Arco. You had the real submarine operating that you'd been with it since it was just a concept.

Captain Jackson: Yes. As you probably know, the Albacore was in the same authorization as Nautilus, where Congress authorized the two ships at the same time.* I had a lot of to do with the design and development of the Albacore.

Paul Stillwell: What went into the design of the Albacore? Where did the concepts and ideas come from and then how did you translate that into an actual design?

Captain Jackson: The Albacore was conceived by and in the National Academy of Science at the direction of Admiral Momsen in OP-31.† It was created by a team made up of,

---

* The diesel submarine Albacore (AGSS-569) was commissioned in December 1953 as an experimental vessel to test the feasibility of the teardrop-shaped hull. The test was successful, and the hull shape has since become standard in U.S. nuclear-powered submarines.
† Rear Admiral Charles B. Momsen, USN.

among others, Admiral Paul Lee, Andy McKee, Admiral Cochrane, and Ken Davidson, who was the chairman of the Davidson Laboratory down at Carnegie Tech.* And there were others there. They came to the conclusion that there were many things that not only could be but should be explored. They proposed to make an attack submarine with a streamlined body, with a single propeller, and modified control surfaces.

They proposed this to the Navy, and the Navy said, "Hey, that's too far advanced. We can't make that kind of step."

So under the leadership of Paul Lee they said, "Hey, if you don't like what we're doing, you'd better disband the committee. If you persist in just duplicating what we have, there's no need to have us, and we'll all quit."

Paul Stillwell: To whom was this ultimatum delivered?

Captain Jackson: To the CNO or some staff in CNO. I'm not sure exactly who, but I got this from both Lee and McKee, because I knew them both real well, and I could talk to them. So at any rate there was some debate and controversy, and they said, "Well, we will make an experimental ship. Therefore you guys can go play with it and do what you want, and we won't lose a submarine in our fleet." So it was decided that it would be an experimental ship. Well, the Model Basin then took over, and they really developed the concept design from a hydrodynamic point of view.† Streamlined body of revolution, a sail that had low drag, would go fast. It was made with bow planes up forward, and they considered different configurations of stern control surfaces. They also originally considered a counter-rotation propulsion. The main reason that the <u>Albacore</u> was so fast was her small size.

Paul Stillwell: No planes on the sail at that point?

Captain Jackson: No. They had planes up forward. The Model Basin reps proposed this, and there were some comments by BuShips. BuShips had to get their axe in and they

---
* From 1948 to 1958 Lee, a retired rear admiral, was vice president of Gibbs & Cox.
† The David Taylor Model Basin at Carderock, Maryland, has a long tank in which model ship hulls can be towed to determine their hydrodynamic characteristics.

made some changes to it. But it was approved for construction at the same time Nautilus was approved for construction.

Then Portsmouth was given the job of the contract design and detail design. When I went to Portsmouth, first I was a ship superintendent on the waterfront, and then I went up to the design division, and I was designated design project officer on Albacore. Also, I was the design officer on the new attack submarines, the 563 class, which was very good. I'll tell you some stories about that.*

But we tried all kinds of new things on Albacore. We went to an aircraft-type hydraulic system, and so it was much lighter and faster operating. I can't say it was more reliable, but it was using fly-by-wire electronic-controlled control surfaces and so forth. We didn't have too many problems with that, because we'd had so many problems on the Tang class that we learned how to solve them. When we had the first sea trials, the ship ran real well, and then we started making modifications in the after control surfaces.

When we first designed the ship, we wanted to put the control surfaces forward of the propeller and the general consensus of opinion—actually, Admiral McKee was part of this. He said, "Hey, we tried that once and it didn't work." Well, it was tried on the first Holland. It was also tried on the S-3. But instead of trying to find out why it didn't work and doing something about it, they just said, "Hey, it didn't work. We'll never try it again."†

So the first stern surfaces on the Albacore had to be behind the propeller. In order to support them, we had to have huge big arms out there. The hydrodynamic loads in high-speed turns with vibrations were so high that the factor of safety if all those arms happened at the right time was about .8, and that didn't look very prudent. We did have lots of things. We peened all the welds, and that was to cold-work them so they would be stronger. We ground them all down as smooth as we could, and we had them like billiard balls. But still the maximum stresses if you got them all at once would cause them to crack, and if they cracked they'd probably fall off. So we never did really exercise the ship

---

* USS Tang was SS-563.
† USS Holland (SS-1), the U.S. Navy's first submarine, was commissioned 12 October 1900 at Newport, Rhode Island. She was 54 feet long, 10 feet in the beam, had a maximum draft of 8 feet, 6 inches, and displaced 64 tons. She was armed with three 18-inch torpedo tubes. She was used primarily as an experimental vessel and training submarine. She was struck from the Navy list 21 November 1910 and sold for scrap.

to its maximum. But then we made the next step, where we put the control surfaces forward of the propeller.

Paul Stillwell: With a cruciform tail arrangement.

Captain Jackson: In the cruciform, yes. But we also put a real good high-aspect ratio on them and made them long enough so they got outside the boundary layer to obtain lots of force on the planes. Took it to sea, and it worked fine. No problems at all. We weren't sure whether it was going to work or not, but old Kenny Gummerson, who was the commanding officer at that time, made us pull the ship with tugs into the middle of the river.* Then he started slow ahead because he wasn't sure that you could control it, but it controlled all right. The faster you went the better the control got.

We still had bow planes, but in the trials we wanted to see what it would do if we took the bow planes off. SubLant said, "Hey, you can't do that."†

We said, "Well, we think it's all right. We just want to try it."

After long debate they said, "Okay, you can take it off for one of the sea runs, but they've got to go right back." We took them off, but they never went back because you could control the ship fine. But we only could get away with that on Albacore because she was a high-speed submarine and she ran around at high speed, and she could get enough dynamic lift on the hull that she didn't need the bow planes.

Paul Stillwell: Lift from the stern planes?

Captain Jackson: Well, trim could be changed, and the angle, and drive it up and down with the propeller. Worked fine. So the next step was to put an X-shaped stern plane configuration on it, and that's got lots of merit which people don't understand.‡ The reason they don't understand it is that they can't resolve a vector through 45 degrees. That's beyond their comprehension. I say that because I know it's true. But we finally got

---

* Lieutenant Commander Kenneth C. Gummerson, USN, was the first commanding officer when the Albacore was commissioned on 6 December 1953.
† SubLant—Submarine Force Atlantic Fleet, the type commander for submarines.
‡ This is the cruciform shape referred to earlier.

permission to put X-stern on it, which we did. It turned out fine and the ship behaved marvelously. Most of the foreign submarines have adopted it.

The turning diameter was about one half that of an ASW ship operating with it. The next thing we did we put on counter-rotating propellers, and that increased the speed almost 20%. We tried different kinds of combinations of propellers and number of blades, the pitches and so forth, because we were learning, and we did all that on there.

I was talking to Frank Wadsworth later.[*] He was the division commander, and he said that SubLant called him and said, "Hey, those idiots in the Albacore are doing terrible things in maneuvering. You'd better get up there and straighten them out."

That disturbed me, because they should have said, "Find out why they can do these things," and "Do we need to make other ships like them?"

Well, that really got to me a number of years later when I went to a symposium over in England on submarine design development. I went to a dinner, and all the senior submarine designers from all the different countries were represented there at the table. When they found out that I had known something about the Albacore, that's all they wanted to talk about and the most difficult question to answer was, "Why didn't you guys take advantage of those things you developed on Albacore as we did?"

The only thing I could think of was, and I said, "Because we're smarter than you."

Paul Stillwell: Well, what things were they talking about?

Captain Jackson: Oh, X-sterns, maneuverability. At that time we hadn't used the liquid friction reducers, the long-chain polymers. We're doing it, but that came later. Teardrop shape—the Albacore came the closest to that, but the Barbel was really the first submarine to take advantage of the concepts that were developed on the Albacore, and we didn't go all the way.[†]

Paul Stillwell: Why not?

---

[*] Lieutenant Commander Frank A. Wadsworth, USN.
[†] USS Barbel (SS-580) was commissioned 17 January 1959 as the lead ship of the last class of diesel-electric submarines built for the U.S. Navy.

Captain Jackson: So we could sell the Barbel. We made lots of studies with X-sterns and counter-rotation and all that stuff, but there was too much opposition because it wasn't like the old boats.

Paul Stillwell: So it was too revolutionary to sell?

Captain Jackson: Yes.

Paul Stillwell: Who would be the buyers that wouldn't buy it in that form? Congress?

Captain Jackson: No, operators. Many of the operators.

Paul Stillwell: I see.

Captain Jackson: They didn't like single screws at all. They wanted to have twin screws. But now I don't think they would go back to twin screws.

Paul Stillwell: Why is single screw better?

Captain Jackson: Well, when a submarine is going through the water, it creates a wake and drag behind it. That wake has got energy in it. If you put the propeller on the axis, some of that energy can be recaptured and transferred into thrust. Or if you have two propellers, then they are outside the boundary layer, and there is no opportunity to recover the other. That's the reason that counter-rotation is good. One propeller is behind the other one, and the first one puts rotational energy in the wake, and the second one takes it out, so you recapture that energy that would normally be lost, going downstream. So it's pretty straightforward when you look at the hydrodynamics, but if you're just looking at it through a periscope or from the bridge you don't see all those things.

Paul Stillwell: How much modeling had been done in the Model Basin before the idea came to you?

Captain Jackson: Oh, plenty. The model testing first started out in Ken Davidson's tank up at Stevens Institute, and he did a lot of work up there, and good work. The Model Basin took his data and refined it because they had a bigger tank and better instrumentation. The Model Basin had a lot of good hydrodynamicists at that time who developed all the coefficients for the equations of motion, and that really changed our ability to design submarines with assurance that you could control them. Before that it was sort of like a trial and error.

When they had fleet boats that could only make nine knots for a short time, control was really not very important because as long as you kept your balance of buoyancy and weight, that was the major thing you worried about. Once we got to higher speed submarines, we had to understand the control better. We still haven't solved that problem completely yet. Lots to learn. But the Albacore probably has had more influence on the navies of the world than any submarine since the Holland, and we don't recognize it in this country. A perfect example is the wife of one of the senior naval officers up at Portsmouth, where they have it on exhibit.* She said, "Why do they have that awful old thing sitting out there? It doesn't even have a war record."

Paul Stillwell: Of course not.

Captain Jackson: Well, she completely missed the point of why we built the Albacore.

Paul Stillwell: Now, did I understand correctly that there might have been an even more optimum shape but that you just couldn't sell it?

Captain Jackson: No. At that time they wanted to go fast in a straight line, and so the hull that they came up with, the Skipjack hull, was even better than the Albacore.† But, like

---

* The Albacore is on display at the Portsmouth Naval Shipyard in Kittery, Maine.
† USS Skipjack (SSN-585), commissioned 15 April 1959, was the first ship of her class. She was 252 feet long, 32 feet in the beam, and displaced 3,075 tons surfaced and 3,500 submerged. She had a top speed on the surface around 20 knots and a speed in excess of 30 knots submerged. She was armed with six 21-inch torpedo tubes. She was the first U.S. nuclear-powered submarine with a teardrop-shaped hull. For more on the Skipjack see the Naval Institute oral history of Rear Admiral Albert G. Mumma.

everything else, there's a compromise. If you want to maneuver, then you give up something so that you can maneuver. That is, I think, a small point in the difference between going fast and being able to maneuver. Sometimes, in my opinion, one should give up some speed so you can maneuver fast. And particularly when the distance between the target and a submarine that you can hear, either side can hear, it's getting so short that you've got to be able to maneuver quickly rather go driving in at high speed. So in my opinion, maneuverability is more important than high speed. You've got to make some compromises to get it.

Paul Stillwell: And this is the kind of thing you probably picked up during that period you were qualifying for submarines.

Captain Jackson: Yes, and other places too. Studying at the Model Basin. And I learned a great deal from my students. I talked to them about that kind of stuff. An idea is formed when you're talking, and they contributed a great deal to it. Most of them are experienced submarine drivers so we can talk about cause and effect.

Paul Stillwell: What are your memories of doing the detail design for the Albacore up at Portsmouth?

Captain Jackson: Oh, lots of problems.

Paul Stillwell: Such as?

Captain Jackson: Well, you know everything was new on it. New concepts and so forth. Fortunately, we didn't have any weapon systems to worry about, so that made it pretty easy. But the decisions of whether to have bow planes on the sails or what kind of device you had. And we had cobbled up stowage for the bow planes. They were made on an angle like this, and would just roll around this way, and they went vertical with the trailing edges forward. Frequently they bumped into the piers, and so we finally said, "Why don't we take them off?" As I told you, we got permission to take them off for one run, and they never found their way back. There was always some other thing that took more precedence.

Paul Stillwell: Conveniently.

Captain Jackson: Yes. But it worked, and you could get away with it on <u>Albacore</u> because, one, she always went pretty high speeds. She would make ten knots on dead low power, which was amazing because all the fleet boats had a hard time making ten knots at all out. The Guppies themselves made about 18, but the fleet boats, top speed straight line was ten knots, and that's only for an hour.

Paul Stillwell: What do you remember about working with Commander Gummerson?

Captain Jackson: Oh, he's a good guy. He and I got along pretty well.

Paul Stillwell: Any specific incidents you remember?

Captain Jackson: Yes. We were on sea trials, and it was a beautiful moonlight night, and the bridge was so small we could only put two people on there, so he invited me to come up on the bridge, and he said, "But you've got to be the lookout." So I was the lookout.

He got a message, "Permission to dump garbage?"

He really didn't give it much thought. He said, "Permission granted." Pretty soon we hear a big clatter in the trunk coming up there, and here comes the garbage can up, and the only guys up there to take it were the captain and me. So we reached down and hauled it up and we looked at one another and I said, "I guess we throw it over the side." We dumped it over, and it went all over the sail.

When we sent it down, we said, "Gee, there's got to be a better way," And so the next day we started designing a trash disposal unit.

Paul Stillwell: Well, that's where practical experience can lead to these innovations.

Captain Jackson: Sure did, and that was practical all right.

Paul Stillwell: Well, anything more to say about <u>Albacore</u>?

Captain Jackson: Well, we skipped over the <u>Tang</u>s.

Paul Stillwell: Let's get those in.

Captain Jackson: You know, they were the first postwar full-design submarines, and I still think of them as the new submarines. A lot of things were new on that. First of all, they were deeper diving, went much deeper. The second is that they were streamlined to a point. They weren't as streamlined as much as you could be, but they were not bad. Pretty good.

The first four had the pancake engines, and as I told you it's too bad that they didn't pan out.[*] They were good engines. They came about because during the war, the first part of the war, we were building airplanes at 50,000 at a time, and each one of them needed at least one engine. So the aircraft people developed radial engines, and they had to tremendous capability. But we weren't losing so many airplanes, so we didn't need these 50,000 bundles of airplanes to replace them. The Germans ran out of replacements, but we didn't. We had all the airplanes we could use.

At the same time we were building up the amphibious forces, and we needed engines. And the aircraft people came and said, "Hey, we can make boat engines."

But we said, "We need diesel because we have lots of diesel oil, and we don't want gasoline. We want to use diesel."

So they said, "We can make diesel engines."

We said, "Fine. Make these engines for the landing craft." And they made many of them, and they were more or less successful. But when it came to make submarine engines, the bureau put a limit on the weight and size, and they really specified a weight

---

[*] For more detail on the travails of the pancake diesel engines in the <u>Tang</u> class, see the Naval Institute oral history of Admiral Harold E. Shear, USN (Ret.).

that was about ten tons too light. General Motors made those engines, but in order to meet the weight and space requirements, they had to make them very light, and they had to put in bearings that were really overloaded. They certainly were overloaded by conventional standards at that time. But it made a vast difference in the size of the ship, and at that time we were trying to make ships shorter and bigger in diameter. In other words get a better L over D ratio.[*]

We had a lot of trouble when we first lit the engines off, and we did some stupid things at Portsmouth. We had a shipbuilding superintendent who the only thing he could see is getting those engines running, and he didn't care how he got them running. He was putting hoses in where you should put pipe and all that kind of stuff, but he got them running. But it's the wrong way to do things. We had trouble all along the line with them. The lube oil systems, we had problems. We had problems with the exhaust valves.

Eventually they were corrected to a point where we could keep them running. They had lots of enemies, so there were lots of derogatory comments about these engines not standing up. Three of the ships ran pretty good. They could keep them running. But the motor mechs never got any liberty ashore. As soon as they came in, they had to tear the engines down and rebuild them. Spare parts became a real problem. So it was decided that they would eliminate those engines, and so they cut the ships in two and added 30 feet of length and put in the old Fairbanks-Morse engines. Too bad because had we done it right, the vertical crankshaft engines would have saved an awful lot of room and space in the later ships for auxiliary power.

Paul Stillwell: Now, what do you mean by "doing it right"? How might it have been better?

Captain Jackson: Oh, given enough weight so that they get the bearing load down to a reasonable amount. You didn't have to use exotic materials for the bearings. You wouldn't have to run them at the high speed RPM that we picked. And give it more weight in the foundations and the castings that supported the engine. Maybe allow them a little

---

[*] L over D refers to the length-to-diameter ratio, a very useful term in naval architecture.

more weight in the cooling water system and things like that. Minor details but would make them more rugged, would stand up to submarine service.

Paul Stillwell: Why were they just tossed out rather than being allowed to incorporate those improvements?

Captain Jackson: Oh, they weren't tossed out. The Albacore ended up with 16 spare engines.

Paul Stillwell: Okay. Then why were they replaced in the Tangs?

Captain Jackson: Well, that's a good question, and there were more politics in that than there were engineering judgments. Certain people spoke loud and vociferously how terrible the engines were.

Paul Stillwell: Are there any names you want to mention in that category?

Captain Jackson: No. We'll just say that they were important people. On the Tang class we went to a 3,000 pounds per square inch hydraulic pressure. Electric Boat Company elected to go to 1,500 where the fleet boats were 600. We made a jump of five in the Tangs and EB made a jump of three. We went through the tortures of the damned, but once again our ignorance showed out. It came through. There was both design ignorance, but more importantly there was production ignorance because they didn't realize they had a new strange beast. They thought that they could do the things they did on the old fleet boats, and everything would be all right. It wasn't.

Paul Stillwell: What were some of these things that couldn't be done?

Captain Jackson: Well, the fleet boats had copper lines for the hydraulic system, and that was flexible enough so that if the pipes didn't line up, you could spring them in place mostly by hand. But we used copper-nickel pipe on the Tangs because it was lighter, and that was so stiff they had to use chain falls and hydraulic jacks and so forth to push them in place. What pipefitters did was push them in place and make them up and then let them go, so now you've got a big strain in the piping. Every time they'd move they would open up the O-rings, and pretty soon the O-rings would start leaking, and you had hydraulic leaks all over everywhere.

Another thing is that with the silver brazing, they had to use a new and more flux on the all the joints they silver brazed, and that stayed in the hydraulic pipes. And it would clog up the strainers and get in the valves and so forth. So we had to clean up the system, and the way you did it was actually flush them out with water. When you'd flush them out with water, and then you'd put a hydrotest on them, you'd find that the thing that was making them tight was the flux in the joints, and we'd washed it all out. So now we had all these leaks.

To make a long story short, the next ship we started working on, we used what was known as a bite-tight fitting, and the production shops were adamant that they couldn't make a tight joint with those things. So there was a big confrontation. We finally went back to the silver-brazed joints, which was a mistake, and that all had an impact on the follow boats like the Barbel and the Threshers, which we'll get into later on. So the Tangs had lots of developments. They were the first ones with hydraulic ejection of the weapons, which was a good system, and it worked. Sounded like a freight train when you fired them, but it did its job. It got the weapon out of the tubes in a very short time. The first time we started using it, we didn't have it adjusted right, and we collapsed all the after bodies.

Paul Stillwell: What was it that enabled these boats to go so much faster than the fleet boats?

Captain Jackson: Oh, lots of things. One, had a better L over D ratio, which is very important. And even today people don't understand that. The next thing was they were better streamlined in the details. We were very careful about the size of flooding holes and the shape when we put them in and all the other things like that. But the biggest reason that they would go faster with the same horsepower was the shape of the ship. They were fatter and shorter.

Paul Stillwell: So this was kind of a step toward the <u>Albacore</u> type?

Captain Jackson: Yes. We recognized the advantage of that at that time.

Paul Stillwell: Well, aside from the engineering plants, what can you say about their performance overall?

Captain Jackson: Oh, certainly it was a major step forward from the fleet boats and even the Guppies. It was a major step forward.

Paul Stillwell: And by this time you had snorkels, so that was a plus.

Captain Jackson: Yes, they had a built-in snorkel. And the Guppies had snorkels. It was essentially the same thing with just slight modifications on the fleet ships. Oh, I can tell you some sea stories.

When the <u>Tang</u> went to sea, we had heating problems in the stern diving system, as they had individual pumps and hydraulic systems on each control surface like bow plane, stern plane, and rudder. They were all separate. Stern planes heated up something fierce, and this was really unacceptable because you wear out the oil, and all the seals would deteriorate very rapidly. So we had a big conference, what to do about it. Since I was the design officer the shipyard commander said, "Young man, you don't leave the shipyard until that problem's solved."

"Aye, aye, sir." So here I was. I didn't know how to do it. I knew it had to be done, and there was no help to go figure out what to do.

Paul Stillwell: Find a way.

Captain Jackson: Yes. So I started reviewing everything I knew about the stern planes, and I uncovered something I didn't know. I should have, but I didn't. It was in the specifications that we should be able to back down those ships at full power for four hours. And later on I found out that that was put in there because George Street took his submarine up a river in Japan and sank a big transport alongside the pier.* He told me that the only way he could get out was back out because he didn't have room enough to turn around.† So entered in the specs was that the ship should be able to back down at full power for four hours.

But if you look at the torque curves going ahead, you find that there has to be a balance of the area against the shaft such that if you lose your hydraulic system they'll trail off to neutral. They'll be right in the streamlines. Then it takes much less power to turn the ship, because you've got that area forward of the rudder stop or the plane stop to help you turn it. But if you look at backing down, now you're going the opposite direction, and your axis is way up here. You've got more area back of the shaft, so you need a lot more torque to do it.

Sure enough, the designers on that had done a good job and said that they configured the hydraulic system to be able to control the surface way out backing down at full power. It wasn't up to the 18 knots that she could go forward, but it was reasonably good, like 14 to 15 knots. I reasoned that. I made a whole bunch of little computations, and I drew some curves and I stayed up practically all night on that.

I finally said, "Hey, if I reduce the pressure on that stern plane, the heating problem will go away." Because what you're doing is taking all the stored energy in the hydraulic system and throttling it, and that is converted to heat. So the next morning the shipyard commander came in, and he sent for me and he said, "You got that problem solved?"

I said, "Yes, sir."

He said, "What are you going to do?"

---

* On the night of 13-14 April 1945, Lieutenant Commander George L. Street III, USN, commanding officer of the USS Tirante (SS-420), took the submarine into a small harbor on Quelpart Island in the East China Sea, 100 miles south of Korea. The Tirante fired six torpedoes, which sank the 4,000-ton transport Juzan Maru and two 900-ton frigates. She then exited the harbor at high speed. For this exploit and others during the submarine's first war patrol, Street was awarded the Medal of Honor.

† There may have been a different input for this requirement. Lieutenant Commander Edward L. Beach, USN, was Street's executive officer during this mission and recalls that the Tirante was able to exit the harbor going forward; she did not have to back out.

I said, "I'm going to change the pressure in the stern diving."

"Oh, my God, you can't do that. We've got to tear all that stuff out and put in new stuff."

"No, no, Captain. We won't do that. I'm going to go down there, and I'm going to reduce the air pressure on the accumulator to get what I think it ought to be, and I'm going to take the ship out and try it."

He said, "You'd better explain to me what you're going to do." So I went through the whole thing that I'd spent all night worrying about, and he finally said, "Okay, you can try it." So we tried it alongside the pier, and it worked all right—as it should because there was no pressure—but it didn't heat. So we went out and ran ahead. Everything ran fine.

Then I said, "We'll back her down." We switched the system to emergency, and she backed all right. The thing that made it all possible was that in an emergency if you wanted to back at full power and go all the way, all you had to do was just shift to emergency, and then you'd go back up to 3,000 pounds. That worked all right, and it solved the problem. Before that we'd tried all kinds of weird things like putting in coolers and stuff like that, none of which worked. You had to go back to the first principles and say, "Hey, what's going on here?"

Paul Stillwell: Who was that shipyard commander?

Captain Jackson: Oh, E. C. Craig at that time.[*] He was not much force.

Paul Stillwell: Well, he found a way to solve that problem. Just confine you.

Captain Jackson: Yes, it did that for sure.

Paul Stillwell: Who was the first skipper of Tang?

---

[*] Captain Edward C. Craig, USN, served as Commander Portsmouth Naval Shipyard, 1950-52. He and Hyman G. Rickover were classmates at the Naval Academy, from which they graduated in 1922.

Captain Jackson: Enders Huey.*

Paul Stillwell: What do you remember about him?

Captain Jackson: Well, he was like a lot of submarine commanders. He was captain who felt he knew more about submarines than anybody else could possibly know, which really wasn't true. There were lots of people who knew about submarines. He tried to throw his weight around a little bit, but we coped with that. After we trained him, he turned to be a pretty good guy.

Paul Stillwell: How much dialogue did you have with Electric Boat, which was building the other three of these?

Captain Jackson: Oh, lots. Friendly competition. Yes. Another problem we had on the Wahoo—Wilkinson was there—we had inboard exhaust valves, and there were four of them, one for each engine.† Three of them worked all right, but one of them hung up and they couldn't close it. They put two guys on this big arm, and then we got heavier guys, and finally we got enough so I was afraid we were going to bend the handle, and it still wouldn't budge. But when it cooled down everything worked all right. And we ran a test on it during the nighttime.

We did all kinds of things, and each one of the things made certain changes. Didn't help things. We were pretty damn tired, and by this time it was about 2:00 o'clock in the morning, and I went home. I actually didn't change my clothes. I just lay on the bed I was so tired. I got to thinking, and then in my mind's eye I went through all the pieces of gear that went on that thing, and it was like turning a light on. What we were doing was heating up the lever, and the tolerances for the bearing were too low so that when it swelled up it bound up.

---

* Commander Enders P. Huey, USN, was the first commanding officer of the Tang (SS-563), commissioned 25 October 1951.
† Commander Eugene P. Wilkinson, USN, later first skipper of the Nautilus, was the first commanding officer when the USS Wahoo (SS-565) was commissioned 30 May 1952.

So I went down to the machine shop, and by this time I knew all the mechanics and the guys who worked on the night shift, and I said, "I've got one more task for you tonight. Go get that lever out, bring it out."

He said, "Jeez, you know, I've been in there three times tonight, and I don't think I can make it."

I said, "Well, hell, I'm no more tired than you are, so I'll go do it."

That was like waving a red flag. He said, "I'll go get it." We did and we took it up to the machine shop, and I got them to grind off ten thousandths, five thousandths on a side. Put it back in and got the motor mech up and we lit it off and ran it till it got nice and warm. And it had a little latch pin on it; you pinch it with your thumb. I said, "Just pinch it." He did, and it "swump," came right down, of course.

So next morning another big conference; the planning officer and production officer were around there, and the guy who was the design supe said, "The conference is called to find out what we're going to do about the exhaust valve."

I said, "Oh, didn't you hear?" I said, "We fixed that last night."

He said, "It sure didn't work when we left."

I said, "Well, you left too early." So, anyway, we went down, and we ran the engines up four hours to get them good and hot. I can remember just as clear as if it happened five minutes ago, the motor mach reaching up and pinching that thing, and it fell down and his eyes lit up. That's another example of when the chips are down you do something about it.

Paul Stillwell: Did you have any contact with Dick Laning?* He had the Harder then.

Captain Jackson: That's right. Since he was in a different shipyard the contact with him was minimal, but he did come up quite frequently to see what we were doing. And we'd go down to Electric Boat once in a while and see him down there.

---

* Commander Richard B. Laning, USN, was the first CO of the Harder (SS-568), commissioned 19 August 1952. Laning's oral history is in the Naval Institute collection.

Paul Stillwell: Well, we haven't talked much about the Guppies. How much of your attention did they take up?

Captain Jackson: A lot. When I moved up to design, that was a big problem, and I'd been ship superintendent on the Sea Robin when she was Guppyized.* That was very good experience. The design work on those ships was practically all done by the time I got there, but we took a lot of that design work and put it on the Salmon and the Sailfish. They were going to be radar picket ships, but they got overtaken by events. The kamikaze problem went away.† But much of the work that we developed on the Guppies was made in the initial design of those two ships, so I only had part time on that because I got shipped off to OpNav.

I got to go to OpNav because Admiral Mumma wanted to have a Ph.D. at the Model Basin, with which I agreed, but the only guy available was Frank Andrews, who was ordered to OpNav.‡ So to get Frank out to Model Basin Mumma offered me up as a sacrificial lamb saying that he'd send the best ED they had.

Paul Stillwell: Well, before that, let me ask what you remember about being ship supe on the Sea Robin project.

Captain Jackson: Oh, great. Had more darn problems than you can count, but they were all solved.

Paul Stillwell: What were some of them?

Captain Jackson: Well, the usual problems. Mostly the coordination of work going on. I had one run-in with the design division up there. We were going to put in some new electronic gear in the control room, and we needed a plan for a foundation. I kept hollering

---

* USS Sea Robin (SS-407) received the Guppy IA conversion in 1951.
† Kamikazes were Japanese suicide aircraft that began showing up in the Philippines campaign in the autumn of 1944. The pilots attempted to crash their bomb-armed aircraft directly into American warships. Hundreds of them successfully hit their targets and inflicted great damage.
‡ Rear Admiral Albert G. Mumma, USN, served as Chief of the Bureau of Ships from 1955 to 1959. Commander Frank A. Andrews, USN.

and saying, "We need it, we need it." It never did come, so in desperation I designed a foundation for it, put it in. About a week after we got it all in and the stuff all wired up and tested, down came the plan. So I just sort of filed it and left it there. Then one of the designers came down and looked and he said, "Hey, that's not the plan that I designed."

I said, "I know it."

He said, "Why did you do that?"

I said, "Had to get it done." That was another sea story. But <u>Sea Robin</u> turned out to be a good ship. They had a good crew on it, and I got to know them very well.

Paul Stillwell: In that role you're kind of the representative of both the shipyard and the ship and going both ways.

Captain Jackson: That's right, absolutely. <u>Nautilus</u> was in there and had another problem. When they raised the periscope they got a big thunk, and every time they'd raise it they'd get this thunk. The planning officer, Ben Strauss, got a number of us together, and we went down there to find out what the problem was and how to fix it.[*] The captain said they wouldn't take the ship to sea until it was fixed, and rightfully so. Scott Daubin was assistant design superintendent at that time, it was his ship, and he tried all kinds of things.[†] Weird. Didn't work. After everybody went away, Ben Strauss said, "Come on, Harry. You're not going to solve anything tonight."

I said, "Well, I want to think about it." So I sat down there and I had a guy raise the periscope, and I listened to where it was thumping. Then I thought about the pieces that went together and what makes them function. It appeared obvious that what was happening was there was a dash pot coming out there, and when you pulled it out it made almost a pure vacuum and as soon as that cleared the oil would go in there and cause this thump.

So I got the mechanics, and we tore the thing down and, sure enough, that appeared to be the source. Took it up to the machine shop, and we just bored a hole in the dash pot piston and put a little check valve in it. We went back and assembled it, closed it up, and

---

[*] Commander Ben A. Strauss, USN.
[†] Lieutenant Scott C. Daubin, USN.

tried it, and the thump went away. It had gone away. So once again in the morning I was able to report to the planning officer, "Hey, it's all fixed." And so he was amazed. Even after I explained to him what I did I don't think he understood it. Old Ben Strauss.

Paul Stillwell: Well, now, at lunchtime, when we weren't recording, you said that some people accused you of wanting problems to happen so you could solve them. Was that a fair accusation?

Captain Jackson: I don't know. That was Bob Carroll, who later was killed in an airplane accident.[*] He was one of the better submarine skippers by far. But it is a fair assessment. I enjoyed attacking a problem and finding a solution for it.

Paul Stillwell: The challenge stimulates you.

Captain Jackson: Yes, instead of frightening me, I do something.

Paul Stillwell: In a way that's the red flag for you.

Captain Jackson: Yes.

Paul Stillwell: What more do you have to say about that time in Portsmouth?

Captain Jackson: Probably the most enjoyable period in my career.

Paul Stillwell: Why would you say that?

Captain Jackson: Well, I was doing something creatively. I was solving problems daily. I enjoyed the people there, the counterparts that I was working with, so I have to say that I was at a level where I didn't have complete responsibility, but I had the opportunity to assume all the responsibility that I wanted to. So it was good.

---

[*] Commander Robert M. Carroll, USN.

Paul Stillwell: Well, I think also there would be a lot of satisfaction in just being able to see tangible results from ideas that have gone on in your head, and here they are in hardware and working.

Captain Jackson: Yes, that is exciting, yes. I have to agree.

Paul Stillwell: Who were some of the people that made it enjoyable?

Captain Jackson: Oh, Vandyke Johnson, Hal Hilmar.* Let's see, some of the younger guys. I have to close my eyes and think of them. But the civilians. I got along very well with the civilians because I treated them like equals. In other words, I didn't try to lord it over them because I was wearing a uniform and they weren't. I just said, "Hey, you guys are all humans. Some of you are better than others, but you're all humans. And you're entitled to the dignity that humans deserve." I think that made a big difference. When I left that time, they threw a party for me which was attended by practically everybody in the design division. Made me feel good.

Paul Stillwell: As well it should have.

Captain Jackson: Yes. But only because I treated them like equals.

Paul Stillwell: What was family life like in the far North?

Captain Jackson: Pretty good. We enjoyed skiing, so we would do a lot of skiing. We enjoyed sailing, so we did a lot of sailing. The kids did well in school. That was another thing I did. I felt that I ought to do some community service, so I was the treasurer of the Parent Teachers Association for four years, and I enjoyed that association very much. They made me a lifetime member of the Parent Teachers Association. Those people from Maine are good people.

---

* Lieutenant Commander Vandyke Johnson, USN; Lieutenant Commander Harold O. Hilmar, USN.

Paul Stillwell: Well, you mentioned the children. When did they come into the picture?

Captain Jackson: Let's see, when we were in Schenectady. They were both born in Schenectady.

Paul Stillwell: What are their names?

Captain Jackson: Harry Allen, Junior. That's my name. And Lisle Ann Jackson. Lisle is an old family name from my wife's side. Not a first name, but it's a family name. They've turned out to be both good kids.

Paul Stillwell: Where are they now?

Captain Jackson: Well, my daughter lives in New Jersey, and my son lives in Herndon, Virginia. He's working on the Y2K problem.*

Paul Stillwell: Well, I wish him luck.

Captain Jackson: Me too. I think he's got 27 programmers working for him on that problem. The only reason they don't have more is that they can't hire them. They're not available.

Paul Stillwell: It's a seller's market for those people that have that background.

Captain Jackson: Sure is.

Paul Stillwell: Anything else you remember about Portsmouth?

---

* In the years leading up to 2000 there was great concern that older computers would have problems in adjusting to a new century because they were programmed to recognize two-digit years and might indicate the year 1900. As it turned out, the Y2K problems were minimal compared to the fuss beforehand about a potential problem.

Captain Jackson: Well, I can talk about the first time I was there. I went from there down to OpNav, and then I went from OpNav to BuShips or really Special Projects to work on the design of the Polaris submarines.

Paul Stillwell: Well, why don't we cover OpNav then since about that's about the point where we are? What were your duties there after being the sacrificial lamb?

Captain Jackson: I was head of the Nuclear Power Section. Nominally that was the title of my job. But since I was interested in bigger things than nuclear power, that was the smallest part of my job. Then I spent my time with the Ship Characteristics Board and the submarine desk most of the time. As I told you, my brother-in-law, R. Y. McElroy was an admiral on duty there. He was in the upper echelons.

Paul Stillwell: I've heard the name. I've not met him.

Captain Jackson: He was an airdale.

Paul Stillwell: He was down at Key West in the early 1960s.

Captain Jackson: That's right. He was commanding officer of the base.

Paul Stillwell: Well, please tell me more about your work in OpNav.

Captain Jackson: Well, in working with the Ship Characteristics Board, that's how I got to know Admiral Knoll a little bit.[*] But I had a chance to make direct connections with the Ship Characteristics Board and BuShips Design Section, so I went through there, and at

---

[*] Rear Admiral Denys K. Knoll, USN.

that time we were talking about the Triton submarine, the big twin reactor, which was a political nightmare.[*]

Paul Stillwell: What made it so?

Captain Jackson: Well, once again, there was no logical reason for making a ship that big, except to prove that you could use two reactors in a submarine, and that's really what she was built for.

Paul Stillwell: And then to find a mission that would support that.

Captain Jackson: That's right. And that's where the politics came in. So, first of all, she started to be a radar picket ship. Then she was going to be a high-speed transport, but she didn't have any room in it. So lots of reasons why it was a misfit. The only thing she really did was demonstrate that she could go and run submerged around the world, which is nice, but any one of our ships now could do that. That's no problem to do it. The fact that it had two reactors, I guess we could say there was a measure of reliability, because if one of them failed you had another one that could take over.

Paul Stillwell: But that has not proved to be a problem.

Captain Jackson: No, that's right.

Paul Stillwell: I think she was the first nuclear submarine ever decommissioned.[†]

Captain Jackson: I think that's true, and when that went on I was a supervisor at Electric Boat Company and a lot of politics in that too.

---

[*] In the spring of 1960, the USS Triton (SSN-586), commanded by Captain Edward L. Beach, USN, made the first submerged circumnavigation of the world. Commissioned in November 1959, she was ostensibly a radar-picket submarine but actually a test ship for a two-reactor propulsion plant.

[†] The Triton was taken out of active service on 3 May 1969 and put into the reserve fleet. She was finally stricken from the Naval Vessel Register in 1986.

Paul Stillwell: What were the politics involved in decommissioning Triton?

Captain Jackson: Oh, the same thing. Radiation hazard. What are you going with the reactor? So she was really not decommissioned, but she was laid up and she had a crew on her for a good many years.

Paul Stillwell: I didn't realize that.

Captain Jackson: Yes.

Paul Stillwell: That was a step that had not been involved, I guess, too much in the planning, is get the ships out into the fleet and then what happens when they come to the end of their lives?

Captain Jackson: Yes, that's right. Or even what the end of their life was. It was undetermined.

Paul Stillwell: So was that the first time that question was confronted?

Captain Jackson: Yes, as far as I know.

Paul Stillwell: How was it eventually resolved?

Captain Jackson: They eventually took the reactors out, and they were disposed of. Let's put it that way.

Paul Stillwell: That's all you're willing to say?

Captain Jackson: Yes.

Paul Stillwell: About three or four weeks ago I was down near the mouth of Chesapeake Bay, and I saw a salvage ship towing the Sam Rayburn, what's left of her.

Captain Jackson: Oh?

Paul Stillwell: It looked like the missile section had been taken out and the ends welded back together and she was painted up very nicely. I don't know what was happening, whether she was going out to be sunk or just what.

Captain Jackson: No, they won't sink them. They have to cut them up in little pieces. I don't know what she was doing on the East Coast because they did cut up the missile compartments. On all those decommissioned Polaris boats they cut out the missiles. And they had to do that in accordance with the START Treaty.[*]

Paul Stillwell: Right. I saw a bunch of them out in Bremerton in the early stages.

Captain Jackson: Yes, there's a lot of them out there, right. But why would she be on the East Coast?

Paul Stillwell: The ones out there were just dingy looking. She had a bright coat of paint on including the hull number and the name of the ship painted on. I've got to track down somebody that would know what was happening there.[†] What else do you recall?

Captain Jackson: During that time, Lord Mountbatten, who was the First Sea Lord of the British Navy, came to visit Admiral Burke, who was CNO, and one of the things he wanted to do was see the Albacore.[‡] So Burke said, "Good, we'll take my plane and fly

---

[*] START—Strategic Arms Reduction Treaty.
[†] The former ballistic missile submarine Sam Rayburn (SSBN-635) was decommissioned and stricken from the Navy list in 1989. Her missile compartment was removed, and she was subsequently retained by the Navy as a moored training ship for nuclear propulsion plant operators.
[‡] Admiral of the Fleet The Earl Mountbatten of Burma served as Great Britain's First Sea Lord and Chief of Naval Staff from 1955 to 1959. Admiral Arleigh A. Burke, USN, served as Chief of Naval Operations from 17 August 1955 to 1 August 1961. His oral history is in the Naval Institute collection.

down and see it." Admiral Burke didn't know much about the Albacore, so he thought he'd like to have somebody on board who did. They asked around who knew about the Albacore, and I said, "Gee, I do."

So they said, "Well, we want you to go with Admiral Burke down to ride the Albacore, and he's going to take Mountbatten with him."

I said, "Gee, that's fine." You know, I'll jump at that chance.

So we get in the admiral's plane, and pretty soon the steward came and said, "The admiral would like you to come back in the cabin and talk to him." So I met Mountbatten and shook hands and so forth, and he started asking me questions about the Albacore, and I was able to answer most of them. We had a great time. So this was just the three of us all the way from Washington to Key West. I could see that Admiral Burke was getting kind of fidgety, because he wanted to talk about other things probably far more important than the Albacore. But Mountbatten wanted to talk about the Albacore.

Paul Stillwell: What were some of the things he wanted to know?

Captain Jackson: Oh, he wanted to know about why we adopted the shape we did. He wanted to know about the power plant. He wanted to know about the hydraulic systems. He wanted to know about the hydrodynamics of the control surfaces. He was very, very knowledgeable, and I was quite impressed with the questions he asked.

Paul Stillwell: Did he seem to have a technical grasp of it?

Captain Jackson: He did that. Boy, he sure did, and he wasn't really a submariner. He was a surface ship driver, but he asked all the right questions.

Paul Stillwell: What can you say about his personality?

Captain Jackson: I liked him. I said, "Hey, if all the Limeys were like that, it'd be a great country."

Paul Stillwell: Was that the first contact you'd had really with Admiral Burke?

Captain Jackson: No, I already knew Admiral Burke because my brother-in-law was an admiral on duty in Washington, too, in OpNav, and he was head of the Legislative Affairs Desk, and so he had lots of contact with Burke. And because of my relationships when we were there, I got invited to a lot of social events in which Burke was there, and so I got a chance to know him quite well. Enough so he called me by my first name.

Paul Stillwell: What are you observations on him?

Captain Jackson: Oh, once again, a great guy. I can't say that I think he was the best CNO we've ever had, because I didn't know many others, but he was pretty good.

Paul Stillwell: And he also had a great grasp of the technical details.

Captain Jackson: Not as much as Mountbatten.

Paul Stillwell: That's surprising.

Captain Jackson: Years earlier I had a chance to meet Nimitz too.[*] He was a very impressive character. I didn't know him very well, but I was walking down the passageway one night, and I'd stayed in BuShips for some reason, and here came Admiral Nimitz walking down there with two big briefcases full of paper and everything.

Paul Stillwell: When would that have been?

Captain Jackson: Well, I was just trying to think. It was when Nimitz was CNO.

---

[*] Fleet Admiral Chester Nimitz, USN, served as Chief of Naval Operations from 15 December 1945 to 15 December 1947.

Paul Stillwell: That would have been '45 to '47.

Captain Jackson: Yes, I was visiting down there. So I can remember how tired he looked. You know, he looked like he was completely exhausted, but he had these two big briefcases full of paper he was carrying home, and I know he was going to work on it at home at night. I said to myself, "Gee whiz, I wonder if it's really worthwhile being CNO."

Paul Stillwell: Well, what else did you do in OpNav? You mentioned the Triton. What other projects were coming through?

Captain Jackson: Oh, the 593s, or what are now call 594s.* The Tullibee, the Regulus boats, and there were lots of studies going on of various proposals and so forth, many of which were not accepted or sidetracked depending on the situation. It was in the heydays of new submarine development, and it was very interesting to see how that worked. But I was glad when my two years was up.

Paul Stillwell: Well, how was the role different in OpNav and with the Ship Characteristics Board compared with what you were doing in, say, BuShips or up at one of the yards?

Captain Jackson: Well, almost no relation.

Paul Stillwell: Just much more of a preliminary phase in OpNav?

Captain Jackson: Yes, and then the nuclear power. Since I was quote the expert in OpNav on nuclear power, I had to answer an awful lot of questions on that.

Paul Stillwell: Well, and an example is when Mountbatten and Burke were taking their trip.

---

* USS Thresher (SSN-593) was lead ship of her class of attack submarines. After she was lost on 10 April 1963 the remaining ships came to be called the Permit (SSN-594) class.

Captain Jackson: Yes, that was very enjoyable and that was really one of the highlights of my tour of duty there.

Paul Stillwell: What other examples do you have?

Captain Jackson: Well, there was a letter went through actually on the Trident, whether it should be built.* I knew what the policy was of our admiral, but I didn't agree with it. But I prepared an endorsement on the letter that I thought he would like. But then I appended to it an additional interoffice memo saying, "Hey, if we do this we're condoning the fact that you will build a power plant and then develop a submarine around it. And if you don't stop it now, you never will."

I still have a copy of that and it's come to pass. That's the way we build submarines now. We build a power plant and then we wrap what we want around the outside. But that's not new. I was reading a discussion on submarine design and the Transactions of SNAME for 1909, I think it's 1909, and one of the commenters said, "You guys in the submarines have got it easy. All you do is select a power plant and then wrap a submarine around it."† So it's been going on for a long time. Even before nuclear power.

Paul Stillwell: How much contact did you have with Admiral Rickover during that period?

Captain Jackson: Oh, I would go over and see him, I guess, once every two weeks. I avoided it as long as I could.

Paul Stillwell: How would you characterize the relationship at that point?

Captain Jackson: Oh, mutual standoff.

---

* The Trident submarine-launched ballistic missile entered the fleet in the late 1970s. The first submarine designed specifically for the Trident missile was the USS Ohio (SSBN-726).
† SNAME—Society of Naval Architects and Marine Engineers. Transactions is the name of the society's periodical publication.

Paul Stillwell: Did he try to intimidate?

Captain Jackson: He never tried to intimidate me. Maybe he didn't think he had to.

Paul Stillwell: Or maybe he didn't think he could.

Captain Jackson: Well, I don't know about that. He prodded me a couple of times. He called me back. As a matter of fact when I found out I was going to leave to do the Polaris design, he said he had heard I wanted to come back and work in his shop.* I said, "No, Admiral, I have nothing against nuclear power. As a matter of fact, I've been a big champion of it. But I want to go on to something bigger and better. And what I'm interested in is the whole thing, the whole ship."

He said, "I can understand that. Good luck to you."

Paul Stillwell: It sounds like an unusual response.

Captain Jackson: Yes, but it was true. Here I was given an opportunity to design one of the real advancements in submarines.

Paul Stillwell: Revolutionary advance.

Captain Jackson: I had desires to do just that for a long time, and so Admiral Mumma was also the guy that gave me that chance. It boiled down to a selection between me and Roseborough, and once again Niedermair and Oakley swung the tide to me.†

Paul Stillwell: Do you know what the basis was for choosing you?

---

* The Polaris ballistic missile program began in the mid-1950s. Initially intended for launch by both submarines and surface ships, it entered fleet service in 1960 in the ballistic missile submarine George Washington (SSBN-598).
† Commander William D. Roseborough, Jr., USN. Owen Oakley was a civilian in the Bureau of Ships.

Captain Jackson: No. As a matter of fact, on paper Rosey was a lot better qualified than I was, but I think that Niedermair and Oakley liked me better than they liked Rosey.

Paul Stillwell: Did they know you better?

Captain Jackson: I don't think so. I don't think they knew me as well. Maybe that's what turned the favor.

Paul Stillwell: Well, we haven't talked much about the Regulus boats.* What do you remember about that program?

Captain Jackson: They were tremendous boats. They really held the line in the Cold War until we could develop Polaris. And there were three of them, one nuclear powered and two conventionally powered.

Paul Stillwell: Halibut.

Captain Jackson: Halibut was the nuclear powered one.

Paul Stillwell: Cusk was used for a test ship earlier.

Captain Jackson: Yes, that's right, they did, but that was just a development ship. But, no, these were Grayback and the Growler.

Paul Stillwell: I thought there were five altogether.

---

* Two Regulus missiles were designed to be fired from surface ships or surfaced submarines. Regulus I, which entered the fleet in 1952, was 34 feet long, weighed 12,000 pounds, and had a speed of Mach 0.9 and range of 500 miles; Regulus II, which had its first flight test in 1958, was 57 feet long, weighed 22,000 pounds, and had a speed of Mach 2.0 and range of 1,000 miles. The Regulus-armed submarines were the Grayback (SSG-574), Tunny (SSG-282), Barbero (SSG-317), Growler (SSG-577), and Halibut (SSGN-687).

Captain Jackson: Well, there were, but there were only three boats built. Polaris overtook them.

Paul Stillwell: I see.

Captain Jackson: Grayback and Growler were the two that I was involved with during the design. They were good submarines, and they stayed out there on patrol with their Regulus missile ready to fire them at any time. So they only had three of them, and they kept one on station all the time until we developed Polaris. Once we developed Polaris, then Regulus was really not competitive.

Paul Stillwell: Well, it was competitive in that it was eating up funds, and so it went by the wayside.

Captain Jackson: Well, the Halibut changed her mission.[*]

Paul Stillwell: But Admiral Burke had evidently to make a choice between Polaris and Regulus because he couldn't fund them both.

Captain Jackson: Oh, sure. And the promise of Polaris was so much greater than Regulus that there was really no question. He actually took money out of the operating funds for the Navy to fund Polaris. When I talk to my students about the history, I say that Admiral Burke deserves a tremendous amount of credit for his courage in doing that.

Paul Stillwell: Sure.

Captain Jackson: It's really the thing that made it go. You know Raborn gets lots of credit, as he should. There's no question about that. And Burke doesn't get much credit for his leadership in distributing the funds.

---

[*] USS Halibut (SSGN-587), commissioned on 4 January 1960, was the first submarine in the world designed from the keel up to launch guided missiles, the Regulus I. After Regulus was phased out in favor of Polaris, the Halibut in 1965 was converted to an attack submarine and on 6 September 1965 redesignated SSN-587.

Paul Stillwell: Well, the downside was that there was not then a surface-to-surface missile for surface ships, and that waited a long time till Tomahawk came along.*

Captain Jackson: That's right.

Paul Stillwell: One of the proponents I talked to of Regulus boats was Grayson Merrill, who worked initially in Polaris.†

Captain Jackson: Oh, yes. He was there when I went there.

Paul Stillwell: What memories do you have of him?

Captain Jackson: A good guy. He was an AEDO and well qualified. He had lots of missile experience. He wasn't there too long. We didn't overlap too long, but I got to know him pretty well.

Paul Stillwell: He was one of the few who did not respond well to Raborn's leadership, and he retired because he just couldn't take it.

Captain Jackson: Well, and it's unfortunate, too, because he had a lot to offer, but in his place came Levering Smith, who probably did a much better job than Grayson would have done.‡ You never know whether it was the right move or not.

Paul Stillwell: Well, Levering Smith is just universally admired for the role he played.

---

* Tomahawk is a long-range cruise missile that entered the fleet in the early 1980s, capable of delivering either conventional or nuclear warheads. Originally conceived to have both antiship and land-attack versions, the antiship type is no longer in service. For details see Miles A. Libbey III, "Tomahawk," U.S. Naval Institute Proceedings, May 1984, pages 150-163.
† Captain Grayson Merrill, USN, was the first technical director for the Polaris program. See his Naval Institute oral history for details.
‡ Captain Levering Smith, USN, succeeded Merrill as technical director. Eventually he became head of the entire Special Projects Office as a flag officer.

Captain Jackson: Yes, he is that.

Paul Stillwell: Anything more on the specifics of the program development for the Regulus boats?

Captain Jackson: No. My real association with it was with the Growler.* We built the Growler but from Mare Island plans. So the design activity up there was really minimal. It wasn't until they started wanting to go on sea trials that we were called upon to help them.

Paul Stillwell: What do you remember in that regard?

Captain Jackson: Oh, there were lots of minor problems and they had to be resolved. The production department at that time was led by a guy that said, "Hey, we can't think. We have to be told every single thing what to do." He was sincere about that because he'd gone to Harvard Business School. I don't know if he was repeating that from bitterness or whether he really believed it. It's hard for me to believe that you tell people that your employees can't think, they have to be told.

Paul Stillwell: Well, one of the issues you'd have to deal with, I think, would be how and where do you store the missiles.

Captain Jackson: Oh, yes. Well, that was already decided because the design had been developed. That was the big thing that was against Regulus. A ballistic missile was much more attractive. I think everybody recognized that by the time we initially started on Polaris.

Paul Stillwell: Well, that would affect the hydrodynamics, wouldn't it? And the storage cell?

---

* The missile-armed submarine Growler (SSG-577), commissioned 30 August 1958, was built by the Portsmouth Naval Shipyard.

Captain Jackson: Oh, sure. When we talk about Polaris I'll tell you a lot about the philosophy of how that was designed. And to do the concept design there were only eight of us. In less than 18 months not only did we design the 608, which was pretty much designed—we designed the George Washington as well. That was another heady day, a heady time.

Paul Stillwell: Wonder if you want to tackle that one tomorrow. We've been going for a long time today.

Captain Jackson: I think that probably would be a good idea, because I don't think we have time to finish it even if we stay late tonight.

Paul Stillwell: Well, this has been an interesting start today. I look forward to the next chapter. Thank you.

Interview Number 2 with Captain Harry A. Jackson, U.S. Navy (Retired)

Place: Captain Jackson's home, Groton, Connecticut

Date: Wednesday, 2 September 1998

Interviewer: Paul Stillwell

Paul Stillwell: Well, we've got another wonderful New England morning here for the interview and big picture windows in your office to look out of. In this environment I wonder if there are any catch-ups you want to do from the things we talked about yesterday.

Captain Jackson: Yes, there's one person that had a big influence on my life, and he was a neighbor, Fred Klein.[*] He was four years older than I was, and so he had developed an interest in boats before I did, and he was very industrious. He belonged to Charles Christy's Model Boat Club previous to the time that I belonged to it. His interest caused him to want to build big sailboats, and Christy helped him build a 15-foot sloop named the Flying Dutchman, which he did, and it turned out to be quite successful.

    While he was still in high school and I was in junior high school he built a 22-foot yawl, which also turned out to be quite successful. Both those boats were designed by Christy, and Christy really shepherded us all during the construction of both of them. Fred wanted to be a naval officer. He couldn't get an appointment to the Naval Academy, so he enlisted in the Navy and went to the Naval Academy Preparatory Course in Norfolk, and he failed the physical exam. He came back to Saginaw and joined the Naval Reserve unit, and he got a commission there. The Meteor and the Flying Dutchman were sailed very, very extensively by Fred, and I made many cruises with him.

    When the war started, Fred went to active duty. His first assignment was on the New Mexico. He spent two years on it, and then he applied for naval air training in lighter-than-air craft, and he was blimp flyer. Near the end of the war he was a squadron

---

[*] Frederick M. Klein, Jr., who was born in 1913, became a naval aviator, and eventually retired as a captain in June 1962.

commander for blimps out in California at Moffett Field.* As a matter of fact, during Christmas period in 1943 I was up in San Francisco, and he invited me to come down and spend Christmas with his family.

Transportation was pretty difficult in those days. There were lots of people riding trains, which was about the only way to get there. But he had a blimp that was up near San Francisco at Moffett Field. It was going to go back to San Diego, and he said if I could get down to Moffett Field I could ride the blimp. So that was a pretty good way to go down, and fortunately he had another blimp coming back after Christmas, and so I made a round trip in the blimp.

Paul Stillwell: What do you remember about the blimp rides?

Captain Jackson: Oh, fine. At that time I didn't know I was going to be involved with submarines, but they let me fly it. It was great, because you could manipulate the control surfaces and look over the side and see what happens. You can't do that in a submarine. You have to do it all by feel. But in the blimp you could fly it and not only feel what you were doing but look over the side and see what you were doing.

Paul Stillwell: And the shape of a blimp is roughly similar to that of a submarine.

Captain Jackson: Yes, I have a picture of a submarine on the surface and a blimp flying over it, and I can remember when I first got that, that's what a submarine ought to look like. A lot of the work that was done on the Albacore was the result of the wind-tunnel tests that they had made on the big dirigibles.

Paul Stillwell: That's interesting.

Captain Jackson: As a matter of fact, the hull of the Albacore is quite similar to the British R-101, which was a famous blimp. So the association with blimps in the Navy is long

---

* Moffett Field Naval Air Station, Sunnyvale, California, was located ten miles north of San Jose, at the southern tip of San Francisco Bay. It was named in honor of Rear Admiral William A. Moffett, USN, first Chief of the Bureau of Aeronautics.

standing. At the end of his naval career Fred was at the naval air station down in Lakehurst, New Jersey. He stayed down there and he retired there. Because he'd had enlisted time, he put in 33 years of active duty.

Paul Stillwell: That's a full career.

Captain Jackson: Yes. So, anyway, I thought that might be interesting. And the whole purpose of that is that he really got me interested in the Navy and becoming a—well, not so much a naval constructor, because that was my nature and the way I ended up.

Paul Stillwell: Well, I think you had some interest already from having built the model of the S-4 and rescuing it.

Captain Jackson: Yes. I had some pictures, you know, photographs of that S-4 fleet that I made, and during the war they disappeared somehow. My mother cleaned house, you know.

Paul Stillwell: Mothers have a way of doing that.

Captain Jackson: Yes.

Paul Stillwell: Well, are we ready to move back to the 1950s?

Captain Jackson: Yes.

Paul Stillwell: All right. You want to talk about the Barbel then this morning.

Captain Jackson: Yes. When we were designing the Albacore and building it, we got very much interested in what we thought of as a future for submarines. We knew it was an experimental ship, and we knew that there were many features of that ship that would be advantageous to put into a military submarine. But, strangely, there was a very strong opposition to the Albacore by many high-ranking people and also a lot of people who depended on hearsay of the senior people that it was unsatisfactory. The main objection was it only had one propeller.

The first proposal for the Albacore was to make it a complete military ship, and then it was a compromise to make it a research submarine, which in hindsight was good, because we were able to do a lot of things on it that we wouldn't have been able to do if it had military characteristics.

Paul Stillwell: Such as?

Captain Jackson: Oh, changing the stern every three or four months. Changing the way the roll—let's see. In order to reduce the snap roll, which occurs when making a sharp turn at high speeds—submarines will roll inward, and Albacore did that in spades. She would roll over to 30 or 35 degrees. In order to destroy that feature, we put a big dorsal rudder on the sail, not to help in turning but to destroy the lift on the sail so that it wouldn't roll so much. Good idea, but it really didn't work.

We were also concerned about if they had a casualty while the ship was going at high speeds with a down angle—how do you cope with it? We put some big dive brakes set in the hull, so in an emergency you could open them up and slow the ship down, which is the proper procedure for any submarine that gets in extremis, slow down. That was a good idea that didn't work. Then another thing we did, we went over to the Pease Air Force Base and got a drag chute off of a B-47 bomber.[*] We put that at the trailing edge of the sail, up at the top of it. We tried that at low speeds. It didn't have much effect. We tried it at higher speeds. Had a little more effect. But, once again, it really didn't do all the things we wanted to do.

Paul Stillwell: Plus a parachute might not be too practical under water.

---

[*] Pease Air Force Base, which closed in 1991, occupied approximately 4,365 acres of land in southeastern New Hampshire, adjacent to the city of Portsmouth.

Captain Jackson: Well, the whole project ended when we wrapped the parachute wire up in the wheel.

Paul Stillwell: By the wheel you mean the propeller?

Captain Jackson: Right. That ended that experiment. So that's the kind of things that we did, and you couldn't have done that on an operating submarine.

Paul Stillwell: Well, it's interesting. You say it was good not to have military characteristics in Albacore, but it was good to have them in Nautilus. How do you draw the distinction?

Captain Jackson: Changing times and for different purposes. Different purposes. The Nautilus really was not a research project itself because all the research had been done on the plant out at Arco. And everything else on the ship was just like the Trigger.

Paul Stillwell: I see.

Captain Jackson: But, anyway, we got talking about what we were going to do after the Albacore. All the assistant design superintendents up at Portsmouth had a little conference among ourselves. At that time the shipyard commander asked all of us to take a more active participation in the technical societies and prepare papers for them. I took the initiative and wrote a paper on redesigning the Albacore into an attack-type submarine, which outlined all the features which eventually showed up in the Barbel. The Barbel was a major advancement in submarine philosophy and design construction and eventually operations.

Paul Stillwell: In what ways?

Captain Jackson: Well, first of all it was designed to primarily operate submerged, and the surface characteristics were all sacrificed to improve the underwater characteristics. The maneuverability of the Albacore was really fantastic, particularly with the X-sterns. As a matter of fact, it was so great that ComSubLant got concerned about the fact that these crews were doing too much aerobatics.* Instead of saying, "Gee, isn't it wonderful that they can do all those things?" he said, "Hey, you guys are going to kill yourselves." And that philosophy also held back the development of the Albacore. They thought it was too risky to operate.

Paul Stillwell: Well, we're all creatures of our upbringing and experiences.

Captain Jackson: Yes, but it was a change in technology, a leap forward.

Paul Stillwell: Did the younger operators eventually sell the new concepts to the seniors?

Captain Jackson: Oh, sure. Johnny Boyes was the leader.† And as they rose up in rank they carried with them their philosophy and they figured, "We'll change it." But the Barbel was really the trial horse for many of the concepts that were put on the Skipjack. The interior equipment that was developed for Barbel was just lifted and put in the Skipjacks. The major difference, of course, was the nuclear power plant, which increased the range of the Skipjack dramatically and also the speed at which it could go. But the basic philosophy came out of Albacore and Barbel. Most people today don't ever remember the Barbel. Of course, she wasn't nuclear powered. They say that's unimportant. There's more to a submarine than just the power plant.

Paul Stillwell: Good that some people recognize that.

Captain Jackson: Yes.

Paul Stillwell: Well, was the philosophy then that there would still be a mix of diesels and nuclear-powered submarines in the fleet?

---

* ComSubLant—Commander Submarine Force Atlantic Fleet, the type commander.
† Lieutenant Commander John L. Boyes, USN, commanded the Albacore (AGSS-569) from 1955 to 1957.

Captain Jackson: Yes, it was inevitable that they thought that, because there wasn't enough money to build a whole fleet of nuclear submarines. But as they began to expand in the numbers and so forth, particularly the Congress said, "That's what we need. We need lots of those."

Paul Stillwell: Because Rickover was a very effective salesman in that arena.

Captain Jackson: Yes, that's right. They built three Barbels, and there were four big shipyards that wanted to get into submarine building: New York Ship, Ingalls, Quincy, and Newport News.

Paul Stillwell: So four more in addition to EB.

Captain Jackson: It was pretty much a disaster, because New York Ship went bankrupt because of it.* Quincy had other problems, but they went bankrupt, closed down. Ingalls had a very difficult time, but they did survive and built a number of nuclear submarines. When the number of contracts for those ships went down, Ingalls couldn't support the big shipyard, so they started making other things like railroad boxcars and anything they could get.

Paul Stillwell: Well, plus you had Portsmouth and Mare Island in the picture also.

Captain Jackson: Yes, but they'd been in the business for a long time

Paul Stillwell: I see.

---

* The attack submarine Pogy (SSN-647) was under construction as business dwindled at New York Shipbuilding Corporation in Camden, New Jersey. Soon after she was launched on 3 June 1967, her contract was cancelled and the unfinished ship was towed to Philadelphia for temporary berthing. She was subsequently assigned to Ingalls Shipbuilding, Pascagoula, Mississippi, for completion.

Captain Jackson: A lot of people don't realize it, but between World War I and World War II all the submarines for the Navy were built by either Portsmouth or Mare Island, and that was a period of really trial and error. They tried many different schemes of submarines and eventually decided on the fleet type, which was good. Those submarines provided a real service during World War II, and we probably wouldn't have won the war without them.

Paul Stillwell: Well, it's good that they didn't use the Marlin and Mackerel as models for the fleet boat.*

Captain Jackson: Well, that was one of the errors in the trial and error. Also the big V boats. They had 6-inch guns on them.† But it's great that we did that, because we learned what we didn't want as well as what we did want. I can talk about that mostly because of my association with Admiral Andy McKee who played a big part in that development.

Paul Stillwell: Anything more to say on the Barbel class?

Captain Jackson: Well, everybody that sailed on them liked them. They did things that they're just now bragging about as being revolutionary. We made all the submarines capable of single-stick control, like flying an airplane, but they never used it. The fleet never used it. The only guys that really did that were the fellows that served on the Albacore on their way up through the ranks, and most of them went to the Barbel-class submarines. Actually the Albacore developed a single-stick control. If you go look at it now up at Portsmouth, you will look at the control room and see the control stick. They say, "That looks just like an airplane control stick."

---

* The Marlin (SS-205) was commissioned 1 August 1941 and the Mackerel (SS-204) on 31 March 1941. Their range was too short to serve the role that the fleet boats did in World War II, so these two were used primarily as training submarines. The Naval Institute oral history collection contains the oral history of Rear Admiral John F. Davidson, USN (Ret.), who had been the first commanding officer of the Mackerel.
† In the 1920s and 1930s Mare Island and Portsmouth navy yards built six submarines originally classified V-1 through V-6. The latter three—Argonaut (SS-166), Narwhal (SS-167), and Nautilus (SS-168)—were armed with two 6-inch guns apiece.

When I talk to them I say, "No, that came out of a blimp." And I'll leave it to you to see why it came out of a blimp.

Paul Stillwell: Well, you made that pretty clear a few minutes ago.

Captain Jackson: So, anyway, the <u>Barbels</u> don't get the recognition that they really should, because they were a big step in the development of submarines, in the ones that we have today.

Paul Stillwell: When you were in Washington in the mid-1950s you really got in on the ground floor on the Polaris program. Had there been any preliminary meetings and so forth at the time you reported to that?

Captain Jackson: Oh, yes. As a matter of fact, there was also a concept design of a submarine that would carry just one missile and had a huge tube in it which extended well above the pressure hull. The missile tube was almost as big as the submarine. Just looking at it, you could tell that it was impractical.

Paul Stillwell: Was this still at the time of trying to accommodate the Jupiter missile?

Captain Jackson: I think it was called the Redstone missile. It was liquid fueled with liquid oxygen and JP-5. I reported in to BuShips from OpNav, and so it was just a short bus ride to change duty. There was a lot of debate on how the Polaris program would be organized and operated. It was not called Polaris program at that time; it was missile development.

Admiral Raborn had been designated as the leader, and he had strong feelings that his organization should be separate from the bureaus, and that they would do all of the development from that office. As the debate ended I was assigned to SP, the Special Projects Office, for what was thought to be temporary duty over there. Eventually I had eight engineers—seven engineers, and I made the eighth person—to work up the design studies for submarines that would carry missiles. We worked very closely with the SP people and particularly those that were developing the missile itself.

We were pretty much locked in to liquid-fueled missiles because that's all there were at that time. They were huge big missiles, and they weighed about 106,000 pounds, which is a little over 50 tons. The only way they could fire them was to have them erected vertically, fueled when the submarine was surfaced, and the guidance capsules energized so they would guide them on the proper course, and then fire the engines to make them go.

Our problem was to do that on a submarine, and we had many schemes, most of them which were really Rube Goldberg.* One of the problems was how to elevate the missile to the top of the sail so that it could be fired. We never really did get an elevator that would do that. Later on, we found out that the Russians had developed an elevator. Don't know much about the details. We've seen missiles standing up there. The first sketch that our team made was one in which the missiles were in line in an amidships compartment. It had four big tubes and they extended—about 50% of the tube was outboard of the pressure hull. There was room for an elevator underneath, although we didn't know what that was going to look like. We just left the room there.

Paul Stillwell: So the tube penetrated the pressure hull?

Captain Jackson: Oh, yes, and it was 10 feet in diameter, a huge thing. We also put in a tank that would carry 400,000 gallons of liquid oxygen, and that had to be cryogenic, and so there was a lot of insulation all around it and equipment to keep it cold. It probably would have worked. We had to do some manipulation with the main ballast tanks and locate them high up on the hull so you could get enough stability to hold the missiles up on the sail. We struggled with how to get them out.

When we were working on the Thresher, we developed a retractable whip antenna, a radio antenna. It was an all-purpose thing, and it was pretty big. We had a scheme in which we raised it with compressed air. In order to hold it back and not let it go up and bump against the stops at the top, we had a nylon line on it. We were testing it out

---

* Reuben L. "Rube" Goldberg (1883-1970) was a popular syndicated newspaper cartoonist best known for drawings of mechanical devices that used absurdly unnecessary complexity to achieve simple actions.

alongside the machine shop, and after a couple of trials the line broke and the antenna went up and landed on the roof of the machine shop. That made an impression on me, and we decided that that was not the way to go.

Paul Stillwell: This whole description of a liquid-fueled missile just makes me shudder.

Captain Jackson: Yes. Well, it did us, too, but that's all there was. To get back to the launching thing, as we were working on it, I remembered this whip shooting out like a skyrocket. So I said, "Why can't we do that with a missile? Why can't we just put a bunch of compressed air in there and let it go?" We made some computations about the size of air bottles and so forth that were required, and it all looked very practical. But also I remember the restraining line breaking and what happened. So instead of trying to stop it up there and to put in all the alignment of guidance capsules and so forth, why don't we just let it go?

    I worked up a little sketch of it, and I took it down to the people in charge of launching the missile, and I described how I was going to do this. I can remember Deke Ela saying, "You mean you're going to take that missile and you're going to throw it up in the air like that and have it light the engines and go 2,500 miles and hit the target?"*

    I said, "Yes."

    He said, "You're nuts."

    But I wasn't too nuts because that's what we did.

Paul Stillwell: What had been the purpose of the restraining line before that?

Captain Jackson: Oh, so that the antenna wouldn't become a skyrocket.

Paul Stillwell: Turned out you did make a skyrocket out of it.

Captain Jackson: The restraining line was put on the whip, which had to be connected to the submarine so it could transmit messages on the surface.

---

* Captain Dennett Keith Ela, USN, an engineering duty officer.

Paul Stillwell: I see.

Captain Jackson: Yes, that's how that happened. On the missile we never had it restrained. We said that the only way it's going to work is to blow them out. But to give the missile guys credit, they did it, and Willie Fiedler really was the guy that did it.* He looked at what we were proposing, and he said, "Yes, we can make a missile do that. And even more we can make it go through the water so we can launch it submerged."

Paul Stillwell: That was another significant step.

Captain Jackson: It was a big step. Sure was. Then we had troubles with alignment of the guidance capsules, and we had a big SINS in there.† And we developed the optical alignment system. We didn't know how much a submarine really bent and moved, because now we were talking about fractions or thousandths of an inch linear movement being effective—or undesirable, let's put it that way. We had some long-hulled submarines, and we took them out to sea and instrumented them. We were looking for heavy weathers and, gee, for about three months it was a dead flat calm every time they went out. The crew liked it, but we sure didn't get much data.

Eventually one day we did get some. So we worked on that, and we finally made some computations mathematically how much it would move, and it looked like it would be all right. Another thing, when we had the fueling process at the top of the sail, the only way you could do that, to get enough stability, was to run with the waterline about halfway up on the sail.

Another big question was could depth be maintained on a submarine with that. So we went out on the Trout.‡ I made a run down from New London to Norfolk and back. We were looking for heavy weather, and we found it. We had one of the usual hurricanes along the East Coast at that time, and we figured that we could do it for a short period of

---
* Fiedler was a German missile engineer who went to work for Lockheed.
† SINS—Ship's inertial navigation system.
‡ USS Trout (SS-566), commissioned 27 June 1952, was a Tang-class fast-attack submarine.

time, but if we had to be there four or five hours we would probably get in difficulty. But that problem went away as soon as we said we could have a submerged launch.

We tried all kinds of arrangements. One of the big questions was, "How many missiles do you want to carry?"

The answer always came back, "Well, how many can you carry?" We made studies all the way from one, which was the first one—we had discarded that—up to 128. If we put 128 missiles in it, then we needed a much bigger power plant, and so we looked at the Triton's power plant with twin reactors. The best way to describe that arrangement: "It was humongous."

Paul Stillwell: Well, you'd have to have an awfully long submarine for that many missile tubes.

Captain Jackson: Yes, you would. So there was no consensus of how many you should have. By this time we had a design study that just looked pretty good. It had 16 missiles. The steering group, of which I was a member, had a meeting to decide how many there should be. All the department heads and all the contractors were there. There was a lot of chatter. Each guy would get a chance to make his say.

I was the last guy to be able to say what's what. I said, "I don't know how to figure this out, but there is some way that we can do it." I went to the blackboard and put the graph coordinates on here and I said, "This is the number of missiles." And I was very careful to make 16 in the middle, you know, like this with 4, 8, 12, 16, and 24, like that.

I said, "Now, from a submarine point of view we've never put a 6-foot hatch in a submarine, and here we're talking about putting in 128. All I can say is that the more missiles you have, the less good it is. So I'll make this ordinate. I'll call it 'goodness'. Undefined but higher better than lower." And in my mind's eye I put a point here, and I said, "This goes something like this." Then I said that, "There's no doubt about it, that the more missiles you carry, the better the system is. So once again goodness is a number of missiles." So I said that, "If you don't have any, it's not very good. So you come down here. The more you get, you get a curve like that." Then I said, "You've got an intersection there so that ought to be an optimum point, but what is it?" So I said, "We'll take the inverse value and we make a curve that looks like this, and that's a maximum."

Paul Stillwell: You very cleverly had all your curves come out at 16.

Captain Jackson: Very carefully. Very carefully. Then they took a secret ballot, and there were, I think there were 18 guys voted. Seventeen of them voted for 16. And I was one of the 17.

Paul Stillwell: You were very convincing.

Captain Jackson: No, not necessarily, but I was the only one that had a basis for making a selection because everything else, you know, they'd wave their arms and say, "Well, I think you ought to have all those."

Paul Stillwell: At what point in this whole process did it become apparent that you could go with a solid-fuel missile?

Captain Jackson: Oh, before this happened.

Paul Stillwell: Before the settling on 16?

Captain Jackson: Yes. They had the Nobska Conference up at Woods Hole.[*] The Nobska Conference was held in those days annually at various places but in, I think the year was 1956, they had it at Nobska, which is near Woods Hole. Admiral Raborn was a participant in that, and he said if we could make a smaller warhead we could make a smaller missile. And he said that the missile people told him that if we could get a 600-pound warhead we could make a nice missile. He encouraged all the people there who were involved in missile development to work with the warhead people and see if they could do that.

---

[*] Project Nobska was named for a point of land near Woods Hole, Massachusetts. For details on the beginning of the program, see William F. Whitmore, "The Origin of Polaris," U.S. Naval Institute Proceedings, March 1980, pages 55-59.

Paul Stillwell: I heard that Doctor Teller had a role in suggesting that.*

Captain Jackson: He sure did, but Raborn was the spokesman. He and Teller had talked about it, and Teller carried the day up there when he said, "I think we can do that." So when we got the word out that the missile would be much smaller and they gave the dimensions of the Polaris missile, we made one study of a submarine that was not much larger than the Skipjack, about 20 feet longer.† We had missiles that were stored all inside the ship and a device that could rotate the storage rack underneath the missile tube, and that could eject it like a torpedo going out of the torpedo tube.

That looked pretty good, and the only problem was it was limited in number. We had several studies, and the most we could carry was nine in it. Unfortunately, the dimensions of that missile grew during the development. Then we started looking at other arrangements, and we finally settled on the one with 16, which was what the Polaris submarines came out with

We went to preliminary design on that, and it was quite well along when the Russians put up the Sputnik.‡ Lots of consternation in Washington about the situation. They said, "The Russians are one up on us. They got a satellite up there before we did, and therefore they must be better than us." Big question was what are we going to do. Well, one of the things, we'll upstage them by going to the moon, and that's what led Kennedy to say in an address that we would go to the moon within a decade.§ The other thing was that if we could develop a submarine that would carry a missile with the nuclear warhead in it and fire it for 2,500 miles and have it hit the target, that would demonstrate to the world that we were better than the Russians.

---

* Dr. Edward Teller, a highly respected Hungarian-born physicist, was the prime mover in the creation of the U.S. hydrogen bomb, which was first detonated in 1952.
† The first version of the submarine-launched Polaris ballistic missile, the A-1, was 28 feet long, 4 feet in diameter, and weighed about 30,000 pounds. It had a range of 1,200 nautical miles. The missile entered fleet service in 1960 in the nuclear-powered submarine George Washington (SSBN-598).
‡ On 4 October 1957, the Soviet Union launched Sputnik I, the first artificial earth satellite. It caused great uproar in the United States, which had expected to be first in space.
§ In a speech to a joint session of Congress on 25 May 1961, President John F. Kennedy addressed urgent national needs. Among the points he made that day: "I believe that this nation should commit itself to achieving the goal, before this decade is out, of landing a man on the moon and returning him safely to the earth."

Paul Stillwell: Sputnik was a great embarrassment for the United States.

Captain Jackson: Oh, it sure was. But maybe it was even fortunate, because what it really did is it brought all the technology together to do what we wanted to do. I mean, the going to the moon was a direct result of the Polaris system.

Paul Stillwell: Well, Polaris was already under way by then, wasn't it?

Captain Jackson: Oh, yes. I say we had almost a complete preliminary design for what turned out to be the 608 class.* But we wanted to make it and build it fast, and one Saturday morning—I've forgotten the day in which the Sputnik went up—we had a conference in the BuShips front office about what were we going to do.† A number of people had suggestions, and when it came my turn they asked me, and I said, "Well, the biggest bottleneck in building a submarine these days is the long lead time material that you have to get, like reactors, turbines and gears, steel, etc. So if we can rob from the pipeline stuff that's already available, destined for other ships, and then delay those ships and use their material, we could expedite the construction."

Both Admiral Raborn and Shugg give me credit for suggesting that.‡ So it's a matter of record it was decided to do it. So some parts of the Scorpion were already on the ways.§ We used those parts, and that led people to say, "Well, it was a simple matter. All we did was take a 585-class submarine and cut in two and put in a missile compartment." One of the encyclopedias says that once they had nuclear power it was a simple matter to put in missiles. It was far from it. When you're using all the material that was assembled for some other ship and you try to use it, you find that most of it doesn't fit, and you've got to make it fit.

---

* USS Ethan Allen (SSBN-608) was commissioned 8 August 1961 as the first of her class.
† The launch was on 4 October, which was a Friday.
‡ Carleton Shugg was president of the Electric Boat Division of the General Dynamics Corporation. His recollections are in the Naval Institute oral history volume on the Polaris program.
§ The original hull for the attack submarine Scorpion (SSN-589) was laid down on 1 November 1957 by Electric Boat. In December of that year the portion of the hull already built was split, extended, and renamed George Washington (SSBN-598), effective 6 November 1958. A new Scorpion with the original hull number of SSN-589 was laid down at Electric Boat on 20 August 1958.

Paul Stillwell: So you then redesigned the 608 class?

Captain Jackson: No, we didn't. We started out a new design, but we used all the material that was already available, and that made the design problem far more difficult. And we made some mistakes. One of my contributions to the mistake area was when we said we were going to retain the missile compartment that we were developing for what turned out to be a 608 class. It was a bigger diameter than the Skipjacks, but yet we were going to use the material already bought for the ends, which was lighter. You couldn't make it bigger and use that material. All the control surfaces were much larger; therefore you needed bigger, stronger hydraulics. You needed vast more quantities of compressed air. All those things were problems which had to be solved. It annoys me no end to have them say that it was a simple matter of just cutting it in two.

Paul Stillwell: How much would you say that the timetable was speeded up by reacting to Sputnik?

Captain Jackson: Oh, about three years.

Paul Stillwell: That's substantial.

Captain Jackson: Oh, sure. From that day of that conference when we decided that that's how we were going to go, it was 27 months until the ship went on sea trials, and six months later she fired the first missile.* That is remarkable, really. But the only way that happened is because there was a national will to do it. It's the same as in wartime. The miracles of production in World War I and World War II also came about only because there was a national will to do it. The people, the leaders of industry, the leaders of the government all wanted it to happen, so it happened.

---

* The George Washington (SSBN-598) was launched on 9 June 1959 and commissioned on 30 December 1959. On 20 July 1960 she became the first submarine to launch ballistic missiles from underwater. Her first deterrent patrol began in November 1960. She served until being decommissioned on 24 January 1985.

Harry A. Jackson, Interview #2 (9/2/98) – Page 151

Paul Stillwell: Well, and Admiral Burke really personified that national will.

Captain Jackson: He did that. There's no question about it. And the most impressive thing to me was that when he announced that he had taken money out of the operating funds, which meant tying up a number of ships to finance the Polaris system, it was a real signal that this was serious business.

Paul Stillwell: Well, another ingredient beyond national will was almost giving Raborn a blank check to get the best people he wanted to do the job.*

Captain Jackson: Yes. Sometimes I think he misjudged some of the people, but he had that capability and he did have some tremendous guys. Most were ED officers. When Admiral Smith came, there was a big change in philosophy and energy, working conditions—all the other things that make projects go.

Paul Stillwell: Do you think that the PERT chart program was a useful ingredient?†

Captain Jackson: Strange that you should bring that up.

Paul Stillwell: Well, it's not strange. I think that's a logical question.

Captain Jackson: Well, later on, long after I had retired and Admiral Raborn had retired we were on a trip together, just the two of us. We were having dinner, and so I said, "Admiral, how come it was that we never used the PERT system? That we just fell back and used the same old methods that we'd been using to build ships for a long time?"

He said, "Well, I'll tell you. I thought about the situation, and I thought that I could do much better if I didn't get help. So I had to demonstrate that I had the management of this program under control. And how did I do it?" He said, "I created a system." So he got this room with all these great big charts and stuff in it, and he got young naval officers

---
* Rear Admiral Raborn became head of the Special Projects Office on 5 December 1955.
† PERT—Program Evaluation Review Technique, a system of milestones for tracking the progress of a program against its schedule.

who were assigned that as their duty station. They were supposed to be there every day, and then if something either happened or didn't happen they were supposed to take action on it. It was very, very impressive, but it was a show.

Paul Stillwell: Are you saying it was completely show?

Captain Jackson: That's what Raborn told me.

Paul Stillwell: So how were things actually tracked?

Captain Jackson: Oh, just like shipyards did. They had systems to track progress, and that system was tied into their getting paid on it, so they had a good system.

Paul Stillwell: Well, Grayson Merrill agrees with you.[*] He thought that PERT was a lot of busywork but that it detracted from getting the real job done.

Captain Jackson: Well, that's why we didn't use it. But Raborn invited McNamara over to see what a wonderful job he was doing, and McNamara bought it hook, line and sinker.[†] He said, "Hey, this is for the whole Defense Department. This is what they've got to use."

Paul Stillwell: So he was clever enough to talk to McNamara in McNamara's language.

Captain Jackson: Oh, sure, and therefore McNamara didn't bug him. He said, "Hey, I've finally found a guy that knows how to do it."

Paul Stillwell: Well, of course McNamara didn't come along till the first ship had already gotten operational.

---

[*] See the Naval Institute oral history of Captain Grayson Merrill, USN (Ret.).
[†] Robert S. McNamara served as Secretary of Defense from 21 January 1961 to 29 February 1968.

Captain Jackson: Well, no, he was there before then. I don't know what he was doing, but I can remember him as being there when we were talking about the PERT system.

Paul Stillwell: Well, I'm sure it was still in existence after George Washington got to sea. He was still at Ford back in the late '50s. He started with Kennedy at DoD in 1961.

Captain Jackson: Right.

Paul Stillwell: Seems to me the George Washington got commissioned right at the end of 1959.

Captain Jackson: That's affirmative. I was in Portsmouth when she was commissioned. Well, I'll have to go back and check my records on that. I used to keep a notebook on things like that and I have it there. Let's see, when was the Cuban Crisis?

Paul Stillwell: That was in October '62.

Captain Jackson: Okay, well, Kennedy then when he was talking to Khrushchev about, "Take your damn missiles out of there," he was talking from what appeared to be strength of the Polaris system.*

Paul Stillwell: Oh, absolutely.

Captain Jackson: But we'd had some submarines—they had George Washington at sea then, I think, but I'll go check.

---

* The Cuban Missile Crisis was triggered in mid-October 1962, when a U.S. reconnaissance plane photographed a Soviet nuclear missile site in Cuba and the presence of Soviet bombers. On 22 October President John F. Kennedy went on national television to announce a naval quarantine of Cuba, to be implemented on 24 October. On 28 October Premier Nikita Khrushchev of the Soviet Union notified President Kennedy that he was ordering the withdrawal of Soviet bombers and missiles from Cuba.

Paul Stillwell: I think there were more than that, because Admiral Shear said they had some in Holy Loch that they cleared out just as a signal to the Russians that the United States was ready.

Captain Jackson: Yes, well, so the Sputnik went up in, must have been—

Paul Stillwell: It was October 1957.

Captain Jackson: Fifty-seven, yes. That's right because I was—and so the first sea trials were 27 months later, two years, three months, so that would be October '59. It'd be early '60. And when was Kennedy elected?

Paul Stillwell: He was elected in November 1960 and he took office in January '61.

Captain Jackson: Yes, so that's when McNamara came.

Paul Stillwell: Right. But the PERT system was I presume still in existence by then to show to McNamara.

Captain Jackson: Oh, it was still being developed at the time because—but it did just exactly what Raborn wanted. It kept the upper echelon of the government out of his hair, kept people from bugging him with all their design reviews and stuff like that. It said, "Hey, we've got it under control." There's a book about it by Sapolsky.[*]

Paul Stillwell: I've seen that, yes.

Captain Jackson: He talks about that situation with great detail. He doesn't say that it was a sort of a sham, but he talks about how good it was.

---

[*] Harvey M. Sapolsky, The Polaris System Development: Bureaucratic and Programmatic Success in Government (Cambridge, Massachusetts: Harvard University Press, 1972).

Paul Stillwell: Well, what other milestones do you remember from that time that you were with Special Projects from '56 to '58?

Captain Jackson: Well, the other one was the development of the guidance system for the ship, as well as the guidance systems for the missiles. In the big picture it was one of the few things that I've been associated with where we developed the weapon system at the same time we developed the submarine. It made it much better to do it that way than what we had done most of the time. That is, develop a weapon system over here and then a submarine over there and then say, "Hey, how do we put it together?" I was quite impressed with that.

BuShips fought against my team being assigned to work inside of SP, because they felt they were losing control of the submarine design. So to solve that problem I had two bosses. I had to report to the design section in BuShips as well as SP. I had to walk a tightrope all the time on that to keep the BuShips guys informed well enough and seek their advice enough times so they didn't feel left out. At the same time, I had to satisfy Admiral Raborn and his group to get on with the job quickly. So there were pros and cons.

Paul Stillwell: Now, by using the existing materials for an attack submarine, did that enable you to keep Admiral Rickover from having too much interference, rather than it being a totally new design?

Captain Jackson: Well, yes. Admiral Rickover fought it bitterly, because he didn't want his submarines to be associated with a failure, and he said that in his opinion it would be nothing but a failure. But we said, "Hey, we're not changing your power plant," and that was one of the good reasons for taking the stuff that was already in existence. We said, "We're not changing it, and therefore we're not going to interfere in your area of responsibility at all. You're going to operate just like you always did. And just because it's a different kind of ship isn't going to affect the power plant."

Shugg deserves credit for bringing him around. Rickover was up here visiting EB, and Shugg invited him to stay at his house that night, and they stayed up talking practically the whole night, I guess. I got this from Shugg, so it's Shugg's point of view that he said,

"Look, if we build this submarine and the missile works like it's supposed to work, it's a tremendous development. But suppose it doesn't work. Then we just put the publicity out, and the Russians don't know whether we have something or whether we don't have. You know, we can put some dummies in there and practice blowing them out and things like that. And saying that well, we don't want to make them long range because they will cost too much, and we don't want to excite the world by shooting these things all over. So the Russians will never know whether they're dummies or not, and they have no choice but to say, 'Well, maybe they are.'"

So Rickover said, "Okay, that sounds reasonable. You guys go ahead, but I'm running the power plant."

Paul Stillwell: Well, another area he was running was the personnel, and he was slow in getting enough people qualified for the Polaris submarines.

Captain Jackson: Could have been because that was a rapid expansion, and he had quite a pipeline going by that time. But there were a lot of guys that went on the Polaris boats that probably were not fully trained.

Paul Stillwell: I talked to Admiral Train, who was in BuPers in submarine detail in the early '60s, and he said there was practically a one-for-one match of billets and qualified personnel.[*] He said there was no excess at all.

Captain Jackson: Yes, that can happen when you get an accelerated program.

Paul Stillwell: Right.

Captain Jackson: Another thing I remember very much is the first time we fired a missile, or a dummy. It was out at San Francisco Naval Shipyard, and we had a dummy missile tube, but it had all the compressed air and the valves and everything. It was put on a pier and pointed away from the pier. We had big questions of whether it would work or not.

---

[*] See the Naval Institute oral history of Admiral Harry D. Train II, USN (Ret.).

We were all standing there, and they fired it. There was a big whoosh, and then you see this dummy missile sailing out through the air—beautiful arc. Came down and hit the water and broke all up. But that was rewarding to see it happen.

Later on they rigged up underneath the big crane a device to fire the missiles and then catch it in an arresting gear, a carrier arresting gear for the airplanes. That worked real well. Then later on did the same thing submerged down at Catalina Island, and that was pretty exciting, too, to see when that big missile went out. I wrote a paper on the development of the Polaris system, and I got lots of pictures of those things going off.

Paul Stillwell: Well, and Observation Island fired some missiles, too, I think.[*]

Captain Jackson: Yes, they did. That was a fallback position, they said, if you can't develop one that will fire out of a submarine. There were a lot of people who said that you couldn't do it. Fortunately, enough of us were too stupid to know we couldn't do it. But the fallback was that they would put a missile tube or several missile tubes in all the Navy ships that were big enough to carry it. And if need be, all the U.S. merchant ships, and could fire them there, so we did outfit a missile tube in the Observation Island and proved that you can fire the missiles out of there. To my knowledge we never fired a live one. They were all dummies.

Paul Stillwell: Well, there was a plan to put Polaris in the cruiser Long Beach, for example.[†]

Captain Jackson: Yes, that's right.

Paul Stillwell: And the Italians had a cruiser, Garibaldi, that was supposed to take them,

---

[*] The first test firing of the Polaris AX-1 test vehicle, on 24 September 1958, was unsuccessful. The first successful firing was the AX-6; on 20 April 1959 it was flown 400 nautical miles down the Atlantic Missile Range. A shipboard test of the AX-22 followed on 27 August 1959 from the test ship Observation Island (EAG-154).

[†] USS Long Beach (CGN-9), the Navy's first nuclear-powered cruiser, was the only ship of her class. She was commissioned 9 September 1961.

but I don't think she got them either.*

Captain Jackson: Certainly didn't get any of ours. They could have gotten them from the Germans or the Russians.

Paul Stillwell: Well, I thought this was from us, that that was the plan, but it was not implemented.

Captain Jackson: I'd never heard that.

Paul Stillwell: When did all these paper studies start to take place in steel?

Captain Jackson: In steel? Let's see, the conference was on November 7. They started on November 8. I'm serious. They really did.

Paul Stillwell: Where, up at Electric Boat?

Captain Jackson: Yes, that was the place they were going to build the ship.

Paul Stillwell: What did you have in the way of plans at that point?

Captain Jackson: Sketches. And we turned them out. EB sent a bunch of guys down to BuShips, and they took our sketches and sent them up to EB and said, "Hey, this is it. Start with the plans." Things were moving, and there wasn't a question about negotiating great contracts and design reviews and management reviews and all that stuff. People said, "Go do it."

Paul Stillwell: How of much of a role did Admiral Andy McKee have in this?

---

* The Italian light cruiser Giuseppe Garibaldi was built in the 1930s and then extensively modernized between 1957 and 1962. Her after 6-inch turrets were replaced, one by a twin Terrier missile launcher and the other by four Polaris missile tubes. She test-fired Polaris but did not carry it on an operational patrol.

Captain Jackson: Not too much. He had retired from Electric Boat Company as vice president, and they called him back as a consultant, and he still kept his office there, I think. But he wasn't in the direct line of things at that time.

Paul Stillwell: So did Electric Boat do the detail design on it?

Captain Jackson: Yes, they did.

Paul Stillwell: How long a period did that take?

Captain Jackson: Well, see, they had two classes of ships now that they were working on at the same time. That was the great thing. And there were a lot of similarities in the two ships. Some of the plans could be used for both ships. But in 27 months the George Washington went to sea. And the 608, I have to go check the records, but she came out about two years later.* It was a wartime production. That's really what it was.

Paul Stillwell: That kind of urgency, yes. It was the Cold War.

Captain Jackson: Yes, it was.

Paul Stillwell: And that period was about the height of it, when Khrushchev was in power.

Captain Jackson: Yes. When Kennedy made him back down, that probably really changed the history of the world, because if he had not backed down it's pretty hard to predict what would have happened, but I'm sure there would have been a confrontation of some sort.

Paul Stillwell: Yes.

---

* USS Ethan Allen (SSBN-608) was commissioned 8 August 1961 as the first of her class.

Captain Jackson: And in my opinion it was the Polaris system threat that made him back down.

Paul Stillwell: Well, that was certainly part of it, if not completely.

Captain Jackson: Yes.

Paul Stillwell: I mean, we had the SAC bombers at that point and the land-based missiles.*

Captain Jackson: Right.

Paul Stillwell: What more do you have to put on the record from that time in Washington before you went up to Portsmouth?

Captain Jackson: Well, those were busy times. When I was doing my BuShips connection, I had an opportunity to look at the development of all the preliminary designs that were going on down there, and one of them was for the Thresher class.† So I knew quite a bit about it, what was being proposed, what would be the features of it, and so forth. I wasn't directly involved, but I had an opportunity to observe.

Paul Stillwell: How was that an advance over its predecessor?

Captain Jackson: Oh, that was a major step forward, and we can get into that now. The six Skipjack-class submarines were authorized for construction, but the sixth one was picked off and said, "Make a significant improvement."

Well, the Skipjacks were already pretty darn good submarines, and here they say you've got to make significant improvements. Well, you say, "What is a significant

---

* SAC—Strategic Air Command.
† The nuclear attack submarine Thresher (SSN-593) was commissioned 3 August 1961 as the first ship in her class. She was 278 feet long, 32 feet in the beam, and displaced 3,700 tons surfaced and 4,300 submerged. She had a top speed on the surface in excess of 20 knots submerged. She was armed with four 21-inch torpedo tubes. She was later lost during trials on 10 April 1963.

improvement?" Depth at that time was a big selling point, so if you could go twice as deep or thereabouts that's a significant improvement.

Paul Stillwell: Certainly is.

Captain Jackson: Yes. Also noise was a big thing, so if you could reduce the noise level by a half that's a significant improvement. If you could fire the SubRoc missile, which was being talked about then, that was a significant improvement.* If you could extend your listening range on the sonar by a factor of two, that was also a significant thing. So the factor of two kept coming up all the time, that you had to be twice as good as the Skipjacks. But speed was also a real attribute, and the Skipjacks prided themselves that they were the fastest nuclear submarines around.

Paul Stillwell: You couldn't increase that by doubling the horsepower.

Captain Jackson: No, but we could maintain it. With all this other advance that we did on the ship, the Thresher turned out to be 600 tons heavier than the Skipjacks, so it meant it was a bigger ship. You had to float 600 tons. We were determined that there would be no reduction in speed with the same power plant. And on the initial sea trials we had a speed/power curve of the Skipjack, and we were plotting the speed and power of the Thresher on the same chart because this was our objective.

Well, we were under the Skipjack's speed and power curve all the way out to the end. I got a little bit of across the breakers about that, because we'd get a point, you know, "Oh, gee."

Rickover came down and said, "What's all this noise about?"

I said, "Well, we're getting pretty good results, Admiral."

He says, "Well, you get the results, but keep your mouth shut." That was quite a trial because the only two people on the ship that both Rickover and Moore, who was the

---

* SubRoc was a submarine-launched ballistic rocket, fired from underwater and guided to its target by an inertial system. Development began in June 1958, and it was approved for service in 1966. It had a range of about 35-40 nautical miles.

deputy in BuShips, would talk to were Dean Axene, who was captain, and me.* Well, Dean was busy running the ship, so I was the messenger boy. Rickover and Moore disliked each other immensely. Rickover saw Moore as a threat to relieve him, and he didn't like that. And Moore didn't like Rickover, because he felt that Rickover was holding him back from better jobs.†

Paul Stillwell: Which he was.

Captain Jackson: Yes. So anyway those are a couple of things I remember.

Paul Stillwell: Well, after that very busy tour in Washington, then you headed back up to Portsmouth. I'm just curious. In terms of the pace, what was your workday, what was your workweek like in Washington? How many hours?

Captain Jackson: Well, most of the days I'd get to work about 6:00 o'clock, and the rest of the guys would get there at 8:00 o'clock, and we'd work till about 5:00, 6:00 o'clock at night. Worked every Saturday, most Sundays.

Paul Stillwell: So that's a 12-hour day for you times six full days, so you're talking about maybe an 80-hour workweek?

Captain Jackson: Yes, something like that.

Paul Stillwell: That's a demanding pace.

Captain Jackson: Yes.

---

* Commander Dean L. Axene, USN, was the first commanding officer when the nuclear attack submarine Thresher (SSN-593) was commissioned 3 August 1961. Rear Admiral Robert L. Moore, Jr., USN, served as Commander Portsmouth Naval Shipyard, 1956-59. From 1959 to 1963, including the period of the Thresher trials, he was Deputy Chief and Assistant Chief, Bureau of Ships.
† For further details on the relationship between Moore and Rickover, see Norman Polmar and Thomas B. Allen, Rickover: Controversy and Genius (New York: Simon and Schuster, 1982).

Paul Stillwell: How much did that allow you to spend with your family and relaxing?

Captain Jackson: Well, not much with the family and none for relaxing.

Paul Stillwell: This is what Grayson Merrill said was the problem that he had. It was so demanding that it was affecting his physical health.

Captain Jackson: Yes.

Paul Stillwell: You survived evidently.

Captain Jackson: Yes, I did. I not only survived but thrived on it. The family bore up. We had a nice place to live. We lived at Lake Barcroft, down there. That was a good point when we had a good place to live.

Paul Stillwell: What sort of duties did you then move into at Portsmouth?

Captain Jackson: I went back as the design superintendent, and I had that job temporarily for four months before I left. I didn't know that I was even under consideration for being transferred until I got a call from the BuShips personnel office that I was going to be transferred to Portsmouth. I thought this was rather odd that I would go right back to the same place.

Captain Jackson: Was it a disappointment to be leaving SP?

Captain Jackson: Well, mixed disappointment and anticipation of going back doing something that I liked. But one of the guys, my seniors, Eddie Arentzen, was in on the action.* He later told me that there were a number of candidates, and we were all equally well qualified, I think, to do the job. But he said that I was the only guy that both Admiral

---

* Captain Edward S. Arentzen, USN.

Morgan and Admiral Moore, who was going to be shipyard commander, could agree on, and so I got nominated to go.

When I reported in there, I had an unusual situation. They had a welcome and farewell party at the same time, and so I was introducing many of the employees to the guy I was relieving, because I had known them when I was there before. I had made a point not only of knowing them but knowing their families and so forth and they were in the receiving line, and Lewie Rupp was the next guy in line and I'd say, "Oh, yes, this is So-and-So and this is his wife."* Unusual situation.

Paul Stillwell: Rupp was leaving, and you were coming in.

Captain Jackson: Right.

Paul Stillwell: But you knew some of the families better than he did.

Captain Jackson: Much. Many families.

Paul Stillwell: What projects were you involved in once you got up to Portsmouth?

Captain Jackson: Well, the big problem was that Portsmouth had been assigned to make the detail design and build the Thresher, and that was the big project. We were still designing the Barbel, the detail designs, and she was under construction. And we had the Abraham Lincoln. It was a Polaris boat we were building. Then we were still making some Guppy conversions—not many. And then they had a big repair load.

Paul Stillwell: Well, now, on the Abraham Lincoln, how much could you just take EB's plans and work from those?

Captain Jackson: Oh, we did. Entirely. The only time we'd change them was to suit equipment that we had. We had bigger rolls than EB so that we could roll bigger plates,

---
* Captain Lewis A. Rupp, USN.

and by that time we were buying some new plates. And we could save quite a bit of welding by using the big rollers so we had to change many of the structural plans just to accommodate the equipment we had. But fundamentally it was all the same.

Paul Stillwell: Was there any problem with getting equipment from the defense contractors on time to fit into this hectic building schedule?

Captain Jackson: Always. Yes, and we had a full team of expeditors to ensure that that didn't happen. Sometimes they, I won't say, got out of control, but there were things that occurred that were beyond their control to have them there on time, so you have to work around it and say, "Well, we'll put it in later."

Paul Stillwell: And sometimes the quality control suffers because something is so new they really haven't set up all the procedures yet.

Captain Jackson: Yes, but we had pretty good assurance that everything was going to work.

Paul Stillwell: Were there any special requirements for cleanliness on these submarines?

Captain Jackson: Oh, man. Oh, I'll say. That goes back really to the things I said when we were talking about the <u>Tang</u> class. We'd gone to 3,000 pounds per square inch hydraulic pressure, and they had problems with dirt getting in them, so we had to put strainers in. We had to clean them out, put water in them, and then we put oil in them to get rid of the water. And then you put hot air through them to dry them out so there is no water in them. Big problem. That's another paper I wrote, on all the things we had to do to keep the systems clean.

Paul Stillwell: Well, that would especially apply, I would think, to the guidance systems on the missiles and the fire control system in the submarine.

Captain Jackson: Yes. A note about my first time there. The yard was just gearing up to handle nuclear power, and so we built a building down near Pier 7. And that was to be the nuclear power building. And to practice and to show the people how you rope off spots that contain radioactivity and so forth, we had a bunch of signs and some rope around the building. At the same time we were developing a closed-cycle diesel for the X-1, and that was to use hydrogen peroxide, high concentration, carried in plastic bags in the main ballast tanks.* If the water gets in hydrogen peroxide, it will cause the peroxide to disassociate and you get a release of oxygen and you could get through contacts with something that's combustible it'll start a fire and burn up.

So we were trying to experiment and see what would happen if one of these bags leaked. We made a bunch of wooden staging on the pier so that we could hang this device down into the water. That device was a tank which we could flood with seawater, but in it was a bag, and inside the bag was the high-concentration hydrogen peroxide. Then we had a little spring-loaded knife that on demand would puncture the bag, and so the hydrogen peroxide was supposed to run out and mix with the water.

We didn't know what was going to happen, but that's what we were trying to find out. In order to flood the tank with seawater we had pipe, about a 2-inch pipe, on the side, which eventually acted like a nozzle. The first time we did it, everything was going and we excited the plunger. It penetrated and nothing happened. So we said, "Gee, we must have done something wrong." Took it all apart. The puncture was there. So we got a new bag and filled it and tried it again and the same thing happened. So this could be good or bad. If that's the only thing that was going to happen, it was good.

Paul Stillwell: You've got no problem.

Captain Jackson: Got no problem. But how do we know that it was working like it was supposed to work? Well, one thing you can do, if you get a little of silver in the hydrogen

---

* The X-1 was the U.S. Navy's only midget submarine. Construction began on 8 June 1954 at Deer Park, Long Island; the vessel was launched 7 September 1955 at Oyster Bay, Long Island and delivered to the Navy at New London, Connecticut. It was placed in service at New London on 7 October 1955 under the command of Lieutenant Kevin Hanlon, USN. It was used in a research and test capacity. An explosion of the vessel's hydrogen peroxide supply on 20 May 1957 resulted in conversion to diesel-electric drive.

peroxide it will accelerate the disassociation, so we said, "Put a little piece of a silver dime on the knife," which we did, and I provided the dime to cut out the little piece.

Paul Stillwell: That's when we still had silver dimes.

Captain Jackson: Yes. And so I told the planning officer and the design superintendent and everybody that we were going to do it and about the time and everything. Captain Mandelkorn was planning officer, and he had just gone over to the PX to pick up his brand-new uniform.* He had it on, and he came down there to see the show. Well, we went through the same process of lowering it away to get it started, and everything was right. Excited the plunger, and the knife went in the bag. And for a few seconds nothing happened, and we said, "Well, it's the same thing."

Then, all of a sudden, it started to go. It was hanging on a chain fall, and unfortunately the nozzle we were talking about was pointing right toward the seawall. So this thing actually swung around in an arc like this, and it took all the wooden staging area and threw it up in the air, and there was enough hydrogen peroxide so that it all caught on fire. It was flaming up there.

Paul Stillwell: That dime had quite an impact.

Captain Jackson: Oh, man, did it have an impact. The Marine colonel's quarters were just up the hill there. His wife heard the explosion, and she came running out to see it just at the time the cloud of hydrogen peroxide vapor drifted up over her. Nothing really happened at that time, but we were busy putting the fire out. But the woman was looking down there, and she saw all these radiation signs around the building. There was no radioactivity. It was just a practice thing we were doing. So we put the fire out and were cleaning up.

I eventually went home and had my supper, and it was about 10:30 that the telephone rang and said, "This is the duty doctor at the hospital, and we have a hysterical woman here who says she's been radiated. Can you help me?"

---
* Captain Richard S. Mandelkorn, USN. PX—post exchange.

I said, "Well, where did she come from?" So he said that she was in her quarters, and I knew which ones they were.

"And she said there was a big explosion down at the radioactive building and that she's been radiated. She's completely hysterical."

Captain Jackson: Was there any physical damage to her?

Captain Jackson: Not yet.

Paul Stillwell: Okay.

Captain Jackson: But I said, "Well, how do you know that she's been radiated."

He said, "She's got white specks all over her."

I said, "Are they little round ones?"

He said, "Yeah."

I said, "That's just where she's bleached." I said, "Tell her to take a hot shower with good soap and water and wash off and go to bed."

So he said, "Well, what was it?"

I said, "Hydrogen peroxide."

He said, "I've never seen any hydrogen peroxide like that."

I said, "Well, maybe you've never had any 95% oxygen." So he gave her some pills to calm her down and told her to go take a shower and go to bed. But the next day the colonel came to see me, and he said, "What in the hell did you do to my wife?"

Paul Stillwell: So I take it the problem was completely superficial.

Captain Jackson: Yes, oh sure.

Paul Stillwell: Well, you mentioned Captain Mandelkorn in his uniform. Did something happen to his uniform?

Captain Jackson: Yes. He started running to get out of the way, and he tripped and he fell on his hands and knees and took the knees out of both legs of his trousers.

Paul Stillwell: Well, so what then could you do now that you'd had this experiment? What did that tell you about running a submarine?

Captain Jackson: Don't have any leaks. That just reinforced what the Germans had told us. It's bad. But they eventually gave the contract to develop the X-1 to Grumman over on Long Island, and they built a submarine and they ran it for a number of years. As a matter of fact, Kinnaird McKee was the commanding officer of it.[*] She ended her days when it blew up alongside the pier. It got a leak and it actually blew the whole bow off. Nobody was hurt thank goodness.

Paul Stillwell: So it really was dangerous.

Captain Jackson: You bet your bottom dollar it was dangerous. Yes, it blew up. It was just sitting alongside the pier, and they got a leak, and it did like we did at Pier 7.

Paul Stillwell: Well, that was the end of that program.

Captain Jackson: Pretty much. I think they did put a new bow on and put some batteries in it, and then she was used as a research submarine down at the Naval Research Laboratory. They put a bunch of detecting material on one of the bridges and rode the X-1 back and forth under the water to see if they could find it.

Paul Stillwell: I think it sits down in Annapolis now near the swimming pool building.

Captain Jackson: Well, I wouldn't argue that a bit. As a matter of fact, that sounds like a pretty good thing.

---

[*] Lieutenant Kinnaird R. McKee, USN, took command of the X-1 in 1956. Eventually, in 1982, he became a four-star admiral when he relieved Admiral Hyman G. Rickover, USN (Ret.), as head of the Navy's nuclear power program.

Paul Stillwell: What was the purpose of that submarine?

Captain Jackson: Well, really the forerunners of the SEALs and the special forces of Great Britain wanted a submarine that had quite long legs, a little one where they could land SEALs and saboteurs and so forth on a beach.* That was the purpose of it. They were all called the X-boats. In World War II they were run on batteries, and they all did a good job, but they wanted longer legs.

Paul Stillwell: Well, one of them went against the Tirpitz up in Norway.†

Captain Jackson: Yes. But she was towed by a big submarine in close, so she didn't have to make the whole long passage.

Paul Stillwell: Well, now that I think about it, somebody told me that the purpose or intent was to assign these to the amphibious force. But then once it got developed it was seen, "Well, this is a submarine so it belongs to the submarine force," so it didn't really get to do its job.

Captain Jackson: I wasn't in that part of it. We started out, and we made the preliminary studies for it, and that was given to Grumman to finish up. Portsmouth had enough to do with the big submarines.

Paul Stillwell: Well, you've talked about a number of the various personalities. What do you remember about Moore as a leader, as a technical man, and so forth?

---

* SEALs—individuals trained for sea, air, and land operations. In previous years similar individuals were designated as part of underwater demolition teams (UDTs). In addition to that specialty, the SEALs have a broader mission that includes commando-type operations ashore.
† The German battleship Tirpitz was a sister ship of the Bismarck, which was sunk by the British in May 1941. To avoid a similar fate, the Tirpitz holed up in Norway for protection. After being damaged by a midget submarine attack in September 1943, she was sunk by aerial bombing on 12 November 1944.

Captain Jackson: Well, as a technical man he was very good, super. Not only did he know the engineering principles, he knew how to apply them. We all had a high respect for him. He was very, very energetic. He worked hard and he worked long hours and in general did a very good job.

Paul Stillwell: Much different personality from Rickover.

Captain Jackson: Yes—much.

Paul Stillwell: What do you remember of Admiral Moore in terms of personality?

Captain Jackson: Well, I was always impressed with his integrity. He had good moral standards and he, I wouldn't say insisted, but he tried to lead his people to measure up to the same moral standards.

Paul Stillwell: Do you remember any examples of that?

Captain Jackson: Oh, gee, pretty hard to pick out some specifics because, you know, it was just continuous. He had a few personnel problems that he handled, and I don't know the details on them, but things were corrected, not on his part but on the guys he was leading, and I thought the results of what he did, whatever it was because I don't know, were good.

Paul Stillwell: Well, was he the kind of man who could inspire you?

Captain Jackson: Did me, very much. Yes. And I think the reason that I went up there is that he probably had more force than Admiral Morgan, who had his candidates, and I was one of Moore's candidates. The biggest competition was Roseborough, who relieved me as—I was temporary planning officer at Portsmouth, and Rosey came to be planning officer. Unfortunately, he was there when the Thresher was lost, and he took a lot of flak probably.

But to get back to the Thresher, she was a significant advancement, and we had to do a lot of things on it. When we were going deeper, we needed more air to blow the main ballast tanks. We had our choice of putting more air in at 3,000 pounds or increasing the pressure up to 4,500 pounds, and we'd carry 50% more air in the same tanks. We did a little bit of both. We went to 4,500 pounds of air pressure and put in more bottles, and that's when the ship got bigger.

Then we put the big ball; that was the first sonar that used a spherical array. That caused some problems because the shell plates were all thicker than we previously used, although they were the same material, HY-80.[*] We ran into a number of welding problems that were corrected, but the metallurgy of welding thick plates is different than thin plates. So we had to do an awful lot of development work there. We also had to use stronger piping for the seawater systems that we brought inside the ship, and we had lots of problems with those.

The biggest thing is that we wanted to make the ship substantially quieter, and that was a big development program. It involved more than just what we did with the Thresher. It was developing a whole new technology for all submarines. The guy that led that worked for me, Bob Baylis, and was superb.[†] Did an excellent job. And there were a lot of problems on it. We had some problems in launching the ship. It's traditional to launch ships stern first into the water, and that's been going on since I guess Noah launched the ark that way. Or maybe he didn't launch it. He just waited for the water to come up. But, anyway, we decided that we would launch her bow first, and that caused some problems because of the shape of the ship. They get lots of buoyancy at the forward end, and it wants to lift the ship and rotate it.

Paul Stillwell: Well, what factors made it more desirable to launch her bow first?

Captain Jackson: Well, we had to. It was a heavy ship, and it was short because we wanted to make it short. We made lots of studies of which was the best way and actually made some models and launched them. We decided that we would launch it bow first.

---

[*] HY-80 is a grade of steel used in building submarines.
[†] Lieutenant Commander John Robert Baylis, USN.

There were no control surfaces on her. But in order to do that, we had to drop it 22 feet off the end of the ways, and that caused an awful lot of heartburn to decide to do that. One group of guys would make the computations and say, "Okay, you've got an answer," and then you'd go to another group and say, "You guys do it independently of these guys and see what you get." Then it was checked and rechecked. The great day came, and so we had all the ceremonies and got ready to launch her. The sponsor was up there with a bottle of champagne, and everybody was waiting.*

Paul Stillwell: With fingers crossed.

Captain Jackson: Yes. They tripped the triggers, and so she started and went down and did just what it was supposed to. It dropped 22 feet. You took a big thing down there and bounced out. The river up there where we launched it was pretty narrow, so we had a big old steam tug there with a big line that had already been tied on. So as soon as she got in the water, the big tug tried to pull her up the river and rotate it around so it would stop the forward motion. That worked too.

Paul Stillwell: Well, I'm still not clear. What were the benefits or advantages of bow-first launching?

Captain Jackson: Well, I have to draw a picture. If you have a submarine that looks like this, the center of buoyancy and therefore the center of weight's way up here. Right now it enters the water something like this. So now you're picking up buoyancy back here, and the after end is still supported by a cradle up here. As you're going down, you pick up buoyancy, now the ship wants to rotate about this point here.

Paul Stillwell: And kind of move upward at the stern.

---

* The submarine <u>Thresher</u> (SSN-593) was launched at the Portsmouth Naval Shipyard on 9 July 1960. The sponsor was the wife of Rear Admiral Frederick B. Warder, USN, who had served as Commander Submarine Force Atlantic Fleet from 24 September 1957 to 13 January 1960.

Captain Jackson: This way, sure. Okay. Now, if you turn it around the other way, and let's put it—this is bow first, like this. If you're going stern first, going this way, now this is much fuller back here, and your center of buoyancy is here, so you get a bigger lever to rotate. When you're like this, you get a smaller one to rotate. If you have it so that you're going in tail first, the possibility is you'll come out here and stick the tail in the bottom. So the advantages of doing it bow first is that you get a buoyancy and so you don't hit the bottom.

Paul Stillwell: I see. Well, that then would determine how you build it on the ways, wouldn't it?

Captain Jackson: Oh, it sure does.

Paul Stillwell: You're going to decide that before you start.

Captain Jackson: That's why everybody had their fingers crossed. It was the first time it had been done at Portsmouth, and the decision was made almost 24 months before that.

Paul Stillwell: But that did not become a standard practice, did it?

Captain Jackson: For that type of boat in Portsmouth it did. We got pretty good. On the next one we put some temporary tanks up forward to provide buoyancy up there.

Paul Stillwell: But that was not widely adopted for submarine launching, was it?

Captain Jackson: No, and it depends on the bottom conditions at the end of the launching ways.

Paul Stillwell: I see. So that was really to adapt it to the locale.

Captain Jackson: Yes, absolutely.

Paul Stillwell: Did you go out on the initial trials with Thresher?

Captain Jackson: I made all the trials on the Thresher.

Paul Stillwell: Well, please tell me about those.

Captain Jackson: The first one was exciting. Then we had a number of problems. As I told you, on that trial Dean Axene and I were the only two guys that both admirals would speak to. And Rickover would almost only talk to Axene. In other words, if he wanted to tell Moore something, he would tell Axene to tell him. But Axene was busy driving the ship, so that left me. Moore would talk to me all right. There was no question about that.

Paul Stillwell: Well, you worked for him.

Captain Jackson: Yes. But I had Moore tell me to go tell Rickover something, and I'd tell him. And he says, "You go tell Moore . . ." It was sort of childish.

Paul Stillwell: No kidding.

Captain Jackson: But we had some major problems on the first sea run. The power plant worked fine. The ship was designed to be quiet, and therefore we put sound mounts under everything, including the main propulsion. But Rickover didn't think that would work, so he wouldn't let us go to sea on sound mounts. We had to take them all out and put in steel blocks in their place and bolt it down. It turned out that there was no need to do that. When we did finally put it on the rubber, they worked fine.

We had some trouble with measuring the stress in the pressure hull, and we weren't quite sure whether it was an instrumentation failure or that the stresses in the steel were getting as high as the instrumentation showed, which was approaching danger. So we decided it was prudent to abandon the trial and come in and get inside the tanks and see what was happening and also to check the instrumentation. Finally we came to the conclusion it was the instrumentation. That was repaired, and we went back out and finished the trials. But we found some other problems that we had to correct. But, all in all, it was very successful, and the fact that we didn't lose any speed compared to the Skipjack was quite rewarding, since the Thresher was 600 tons heavier.

Paul Stillwell: Did she live up to your expectations in terms of all these gains you were trying to achieve?

Captain Jackson: Yes, sure did. And the whole class of ships really turned into the 637 class, the 637 class, which is a Thresher class extended to put more room in it. We had so much gear, and we really did too good a job of packing stuff in. So when the 637s were authorized, they put in a middle body, I think, of about 20 feet.*

Paul Stillwell: It was just too crowded?

Captain Jackson: Yes. Well, we had put sound mounts all over, and that takes a lot of room. And they had the captain's and exec's staterooms down on the second level and ops compartment on the upper level, and all the operators wanted the captain up on the upper level where the operations went on. There were good reasons for it, and in hindsight if we had known all the things that were going to happen, we would have made it longer in the first place. But our objective was to make it as small as we could so we could match the speed of the Skipjack, which we did.

Paul Stillwell: Well, did you then lose some speed on the 637?

Captain Jackson: Yes, because they were longer.

Paul Stillwell: And you could have about predicted that.

---

* The keel for the submarine Sturgeon (SSN-637) was laid at Electric Boat on 10 August 1963, four months after the loss of the Thresher. The Sturgeon was commissioned 3 March 1967.

Captain Jackson: Yes. Well, we did. But the Threshers turned out to be real fine ships, and it was a real tragedy that the Thresher was lost.* I knew over 100 people on her. If I hadn't transferred to Bremerton I would have been on the ship when she was lost. I would like to think that I might have prevented it, but you never know.

Paul Stillwell: How might you have prevented it?

Captain Jackson: Well, that's very difficult to answer, because first of all I don't know what happened. I think I know in pretty much detail what might have happened, but I refuse to tell anybody, particularly news type people because they put great big headlines in the newspaper, "This is what happened." And we don't know what happened.

Paul Stillwell: Yes, but I think it's useful to put on record your best hypothesis because you are so well informed on the subject.

Captain Jackson: Yes, I've done that.

Paul Stillwell: Well, please do it now.

Captain Jackson: No, I can't. No, I can't because it leads into stuff that the Navy still considers to be classified, like operating depths and so forth. They all play a part. But one thing that I can say without reservation is that whenever you have a major catastrophe like that, many things have to happen. And they all have to happen in the right sequence, because if they don't happen in the right order or they don't all happen, all you have is a near miss, and near misses go on all the time.

Paul Stillwell: Well, there must have been some concern about the silver brazing on the pipes to lead to the Subsafe Program.

---

* The Thresher was lost with all hands on 10 April 1963 while operating east of Cape Cod.

Captain Jackson: Well, that was really in the works before the Thresher was lost, particularly on the deep-diving boats. At that time when we built the Thresher we didn't have any real means of examining silbrazed joints. One of the things that most people don't know when they talk about that is that the Thresher was designed to have welded pipe in all the seawater systems. The production department guys complained about that and said, "Hey, you're killing us with cost." And cost then was just as important as it is today. They said, "If you let us silbraze, we can do it a lot cheaper."

Well, locally we took a stand that, "Hey, no, we've got something that we're venturing into much deeper depths and so forth, and what has been standard practice in the past may not be good enough, and we ought to do the best we can." Then the production department people appealed to BuShips and said, "Hey, you're letting EB silbraze. Why don't you let us silbraze?" Then BuShips instructed us to change and allow them to silbraze up through four inches. So we scrubbed off all the welding symbols and stuff and put back the silbrazed symbols. Had to order a lot of new material and so forth, so it probably cost more to go back to silver braze than it would have. But the real problem for that is that the silver braze people and the welding people work in different trades. Therefore, they have different unions, and it was a power contest of strength in the unions more than anything else.

Paul Stillwell: Yes, but didn't the Thresher incident add a lot of impact to the questioning about those joints?

Captain Jackson: Oh, yes. Of course it did, just because it was a major catastrophe, but it was happening anyway.

Paul Stillwell: Sort of like Sputnik in speeding things up?

Captain Jackson: Yes, exactly. What most people don't realize is that the Subsafe is just paperwork. It is much more demanding. You have to keep track of material from the start. You go back to the source of the ore and check it every step of the way. And when it gets put in a ship you have all kinds of procedures that you have to follow. You have to record it. Then if you have to go back in, you have to make a rip-out procedure. So it's mostly paperwork.

There were some good things that came out of it, better quality control on castings. We had X-rays, and we'd had them for a long time. The whole trade from the manufacturers of pipe fittings and the people who fabricated piping and so forth were, I think, quite lax. So we had developed such things as pentrameters. When you take an X-ray you can put that down there. A pentrameter is a piece of metal that has a hole in it, and if you can see the hole you're having a good X-ray, but if you can't see the hole you don't know what you're getting, so you can't pass the X-ray.

Paul Stillwell: Well, X-rays were not standard before then, were they?

Captain Jackson: Oh, yes.

Paul Stillwell: Oh, they were?

Captain Jackson: Oh, sure. As an example, one guy had a contract to make valves and what the spec said was that they should be 100% X-rayed. Well, his interpretation of a 100% X-ray was that he'd take a whole bunch of castings and put it on the table and shoot it all at once—100% X-rayed. He X-rayed every one of them. But it was almost meaningless when you come to read it really. So that got changed, and you once again had to X-ray small castings one at a time but all the way through.

In the big castings we just picked the parts that were the most subject to stress and X-rayed those parts. Those things were called shooting sketches. And so all the plans had to be changed to tell you where to put the film and how much, what was the power of the source, radioactive source, and take the X-ray. Very costly. Cost lots of money, and that's one reason why our submarines are so expensive. You can say it's worth it, because we haven't lost any submarines for some time. I made a study on that. Historically we have lost a submarine on the average of one every seven years. Sometimes they come quicker together, but then there's a longer space between accidents.

Paul Stillwell: You're talking about peacetime operations.

Captain Jackson: Well, yes, not the wartime because if a submarine gets lost you're not sure why. It could be from enemy action, it could be from material failure, it can be for an operational error, all kinds of things. So because of the uncertainly you just say "War loss." But in peacetime we lost on the average one every seven years. Well, Scorpion was the last one we lost in 1968, and as we're in '98 that's 30 years.* During that period statistically we should have lost four submarines, but we haven't. Why is that? Well, the Subsafe programs, just the programs of construction have gotten better, materials have gotten better, processes have gotten better. So you can't credit all of those advances to the Subsafe program, because they really would have come anyway.

Paul Stillwell: Well, another thing that people credit is Rickover's insistence on quality and safety.

Captain Jackson: Well, he didn't change that on his part at all. That's one of the things that annoy me a little bit. When people who are unknowledgeable talk about it they say, "Well, they created Subsafe, but before that there was no requirement that you make submarines safe," and that's a bunch of baloney. After the Squalus was lost, there was also a big program to review all of the standards of construction and design and so forth, and that made the submarines of World War II better. If we lose another submarine, we'll go through the same thing again, but hopefully we won't lose one.

One of the outcomes is that they reduced the operating depths of all the submarines, and I don't know if that's good or bad, because I'm not that much of an operator to know whether the deep depth is good or bad. When Thresher first went to sea she went out and operated with the Tullibee. Tullibee was a fine little submarine, but she had limited depth. When the Thresher came back from that operation, I talked to the officers on the Thresher.

---

* The submarine Scorpion (SSN-589) was lost with all hands while en route from the Mediterranean to Norfolk. She was last heard from on 21 May 1968. On 27 May she was reported overdue and on 5 June presumed lost with her entire crew of 99 officers and men. The wreckage was located on 30 October of that year. No definitive conclusion has been reached as to cause. One possible explanation is on-board torpedo explosion.

Among other things, I asked them all kinds of questions, and I said, "Hey, did you find any advantages to the deeper operating depth?"

The guy said, "No. We didn't see any."

So I said, "Well, tell me about some of the things you did." I said, "Did Tullibee ever give you any trouble?" I said, "Did they ever lock onto you?"

He said, "Oh, yeah."

I said, "Well, what did you do?"

He said, "We just went down and under them."

I said, "But you told me there was no advantage in going deep."

He says, "Well, if you think of it that way, maybe there is some advantage." I think that came as a real revelation to him that they had the ability to go down under them.

Paul Stillwell: What do you recall of Axene as a skipper?

Captain Jackson: Oh, superb. He was the right guy for that job.

Paul Stillwell: Why do you say that?

Captain Jackson: Well, just all his mental and physical characteristics. He realized he had something new, that it was a big change. He was a good thinker and a good planner. He planned everything out almost to the last detail. He was a good leader. He trained his crew well. So when I compare him to other guys that I knew in similar positions, I say he's one of the tops.

Paul Stillwell: He had been with Wilkinson in the Nautilus.

Captain Jackson: That's affirmative. He was the exec at one time.

Paul Stillwell: The skipper who was lost, Wes Harvey, was also in the Nautilus.[*] What did you know of him?

---

[*] Lieutenant Commander John Wesley Harvey, USN, was commanding officer when the Thresher was lost.

Captain Jackson: I didn't know him very well at all. I knew him by name only and reputation because he came to the Thresher after I had left up there.

Paul Stillwell: Did you get involved at all in the investigation following the loss of the Thresher?

Captain Jackson: No, I didn't, and that was a disappointment to me. I think that some of the officials thought they might be protecting me if they didn't call me for testifying. And I felt real bad about that, because I felt that I had a big responsibility in the design and development of the Thresher and that I should have been included really as a defendant, but I wasn't.

Paul Stillwell: What might you have said had you been called to the investigation?

Captain Jackson: Well, the same thing all the others said, that we didn't know what happened. But I think if they had called me I could have steered the discussion in a direction that would pinpoint the cause. I'm not sure who made the decision not to call me.

Paul Stillwell: Do you think that the investigation came to the wrong conclusion?

Captain Jackson: No. No, it was the right conclusion in which they said they didn't know what happened. They thought that in reviewing all the circumstances that it was probably caused by a failure of a piece of pipe in the saltwater system, and I concur with that. But I would go further—that I could pinpoint the point of failure and what I think is the cause for it.

Paul Stillwell: You want to say that?

Captain Jackson: No, I'll say that if anybody asks me I can't tell you, because you'll misinterpret it and say that's what happened with no qualifications. And we'll never be able to say it without qualifications.

Paul Stillwell: Well, do you want to say it with qualifications?

Captain Jackson: Well, I just said it. Yes. But not what happened. I don't think it's appropriate for me to say it in a publication that's going to get all around. One of the things that I'm in the process of doing right now, I'm taking steps to ensure that what I think happened never will happen, if it was the reason, again. But it's possible.

Paul Stillwell: Well, do you think that it was a design problem? You hinted that you might have been a defendant.

Captain Jackson: Oh, sure. I think it was a design problem as well as a production problem. And where was the design? Well, the Bureau of Ships made the contract plans that we worked to, and the ship was built like the contract plans said to build. So if it was a design fault, then where does the detail fault lie? It would be almost impossible to pinpoint a person and say, "Hey, it was his fault." It should be because there were so many guys who were involved in it. Any one of them could have changed the situation.

Paul Stillwell: What were the steps you took to prevent a recurrence?

Captain Jackson: Oh, I wrote a memorandum to the Bureau of Ships saying what I think happened and what I thought they ought to do to ensure that it wouldn't happen again.

Paul Stillwell: And those things have been implemented?

Captain Jackson: As far as I know, they have. But I'm afraid that in history they get lost, so I just have prepared another letter to remind people that there's a possibility it can happen. I haven't mailed it yet, but it's in the process of—like you do, you write something down and then you put it on the shelf, in the holding basket. Go back sometime later and read it and say, "Is that really what I want to say?"

Paul Stillwell: Well, on the other hand you were just pointing out that we have not had a submarine lost in 30 years, so people must be doing a lot right.

Captain Jackson: Oh, we are, sure. Paperwork. Sure. And other countries, particularly Russia, have lost—I have a list of their losses, but it's something like 18 in that same period.

Paul Stillwell: I didn't realize it was anywhere near that large.

Captain Jackson: Yes, it's way up. Our record is vastly superior to most other countries. That idiot that is writing papers out in the state of Washington doesn't understand what he's talking about.[*] He's making all kinds of wild suppositions which there's no basis for on the assumptions that anybody who knows about submarines is considered highly imaginative.

[Interruption for lunch]

Paul Stillwell: When we broke for lunch I asked you which was your favorite submarine of all the ones you worked on, and you said the Albacore. What would be the reasons for that?

Captain Jackson: Oh, first of all it was something new. It was perfectly obvious it was going to change the submarines of the U.S. Navy and probably the submarines of the world, which later on it did. Because it was a research submarine we didn't have the interference from DoD or OpNav and even BuShips. We were able to go ahead and do things. BuShips was calling the shots on the major things to be done, but they left us

---

[*] Ed Offley, Seattle Post-Intelligencer military reporter, published a speculative article on possible reasons for the loss of the Scorpion in his newspaper's issue of 21 May 1998.

pretty much alone. We got a task, we designed it and did it. That's pretty heady when you're making big changes and then take it out and try it. So that's one reason. But I was associated with her longer than any other ship. Barbel I was associated with over a period of about 12 years, because we started it the first time I was at Portsmouth, and we finished it when the second time I was at Portsmouth.

Paul Stillwell: You said Barbel was your second favorite and Thresher was your third.

Captain Jackson: Right.

Paul Stillwell: And Triton would probably be way down at the bottom of the list.

Captain Jackson: Well, yes. If I'd had much to do with it I would say that, but I didn't have much to do with the Triton. I was in on all the big debates on what she was going to do to justify her construction, which was very difficult because the only reason that she was built was to prove that you could put two reactors in a submarine. The reasons for which she was built all disappeared—or the alleged reasons like radar picket submarine or a troop carrier submarine. All kinds of things were dreamed up to justify it. I was a part of that because that was going on when I was in OpNav. I made a point of going to all the ship's characteristic meetings, and so I heard all those arguments.

Paul Stillwell: What else can you say about that tour at Portsmouth in the late '50s, early '60s?

Captain Jackson: Well, we had a lot of ships going then. We built two of the Skate-class submarines that were completed when I was there, Seadragon and the Swordfish. Those were the two, and they were good little ships. The people that went out and operated in the Arctic liked those ships. Waldo Lyon, who has spent probably more time in the Arctic than anybody else, thought that was the ideal submarine to take to the Arctic.[*]

---

[*] Dr. Waldo K. Lyon, a civilian employee of the Navy, was director of the Arctic Submarine Laboratory. He did pioneering development work that made possible submarine operations under the arctic icecap. His oral history is in the Naval Institute collection.

Paul Stillwell: Why?

Captain Jackson: Well, first of all he liked the twin screws. It was small, and it was maneuverable. He felt those were almost mandatory attributes to operate up there.

Paul Stillwell: Well, you told me a story yesterday when the tape recorder wasn't running about fixing the rudder stock on the Seadragon. If you would put that on the tape please.

Captain Jackson: Well, she was coming in to Portsmouth to be prepared to go through the Northwest Passage, find a route to see if you could make it all year round. They were coming in submerged at a pretty deep depth, and they came up to the continental shelf that has a very steep slope. And they were deeper than the depth of the shelf. They came up on it, and they realized that they were going to have a horrible collision, and so they put rise on the stern planes. The initial reaction of a submarine to that is that the stern goes down. They did do it in time enough so the ship could start to rise, but the lower rudder hit the continental shelf. There was not much damage, but when they got into Portsmouth we put her in dry dock to see what the damage was, and we found that the rudder stock was bent. And when we went to look at the spare parts, there were none for that rudder stock.

Paul Stillwell: How big a piece of metal is the rudder stock?

Captain Jackson: Oh, it's about 8 feet long and it's about 18 inches in diameter, and it's got tapered ends on it where it fits into the rudders. It's a big piece of metal. There was no time available to order another one through the whole chain of events that it takes to make one of those. So we're left, "What are you going to do?" Well, what we did was sit around and talk. And we said, "We'll take it over to the shipfitters' shop and put it in a big press they have over there to bend plates and straighten it out."

We did that, and the guy that operated the big press had gone home. We called him back at nighttime and on overtime and told him what we wanted to do, and he looked at it. He looked like an old man, but he was probably in his mid-60s some place. He'd been running that press for probably 30 years. He knew all the eccentricities of it. So we got it all blocked up right and put it in the press, which was hydraulically operated. It had a big lever to control the flow, and that's so you could inch it down with the big long lever.

He took a look at it, and he said, "I'd better hit it two times." So he hit it, then looked at it and said, "Well, it moved. I'd better hit another time." So he hits it again. He kept doing that until he said, "It looks pretty straight. We'd better put the straightedge on it." So he got this big long straightedge and put on it. Gee, it was almost straight. As a matter of fact, I thought it was good enough, but he said, "I'd better hit it a couple more times." So he did that. Put the straightedge on it looked real straight, and he said, "But I think maybe we'd better just touch it." So he just touched it, and I don't know whether it moved or not, but anyway it gave him satisfaction that he was really doing a good job, which he did. A real good job. So he looked at it, and he said, "I think that's pretty good, but you better take it over to the machine shop and put the dial indicator on it." That seemed prudent, so we did that. And when we measured the runout, it was about two thousandths of an inch out of line, which is not even the width of a pencil line.

Paul Stillwell: So I take it that the rudder stock fit back fine?

Captain Jackson: Yes, we put it back in and it was fine. Buttoned it up, and old George Steele went off to go through the Davis Strait.[*]

Another thing about that is there was a reserve officer came for two weeks' active duty to the yard. Before he got there, we were talking about wouldn't it be nice if we could rig up a television set that would look up so they could take TV of the underside of the ice. We knew that this guy was a TV expert, and so when we got there we said, "Hey, have we got the real job for you? One that you can make a real contribution." And we explained the job.

He looked at it, and he went down to the ship and looked at it, and he said, "Yeah, we can do that." So we went back down to New York to his place, and he got a whole

---

[*] USS Seadragon (SSN-584) was commissioned 5 December 1959 under the command of Lieutenant Commander George P. Steele II, USN. In August 1960 he took the ship on the first submerged transit of the Northwest Passage in northern Canada. The oral history of Steele, who retired as a vice admiral, is in the Naval Institute's collection.

bunch of gear, and they brought it up and we gave him a torpedo skid, and he put all the stuff in the skid, secured it real good. Put some television cameras on, ran some temporary wires down to the forward room, and tried it out. Gee, it worked fine. They were going to make a short sea trial just to check things before they left the yard, and when they turned that on and all they saw was water, but it sure looked attractive.

So they took that, and when they went under the ice they took many, many feet of TV tape under the ice, and that became a sort of a landmark for submarines operating up there, and they learned a great deal about the shape of the ice, how the keels came down and the reason why that happened, so it was good. And the amazing thing about that is it never would have happened if that reserve officer hadn't come to that two weeks' active duty.

Paul Stillwell: Was that also the Seadragon that got that TV setup?

Captain Jackson: I think it was the same TV setup, and then later on they started to make permanent installations, which are much better. But I was proud of that guy. He came and he worked like a dog, and he was a self-starter. You know, he got the gear, installed it, and got it done.

Paul Stillwell: Did you have other things that you did to submarines that were going up under the ice to prepare them?

Captain Jackson: Well, not at that time, because we really didn't know what we needed to do, and at that time the thought of breaking through the ice horrified everybody. They said, "Hey, you know, you'll lose a submarine for sure if you try that." There were lots of polynyas up there, which are thin parts in the ice, and so they always wanted to find one of those. The TV was a good instrument to find them. We really didn't need to do much else under that philosophy so we didn't do it. But later on, the 637 class had the forward planes on the sail. We made them so that you could rotate them 90 degrees, so the frontal area for going through the ice was quite small. You could break the ice with it and a number of submarines did that.*

Paul Stillwell: Was the sail itself strengthened for that?

Captain Jackson: Yes, they were made strong enough so that you could carry those big blocks of ice up there which weighed, oh, probably a thousand pounds, something like that. They were big. A lot of them hung up on top of the sail. Some of them hung up on the sailplanes. And if they got the deck out a lot of them hung up on the deck.

Another sea story about Seadragon, they were operating on the surface one night, and it was pretty dark, and they ran into a whale that was sleeping. It went up on deck forward, and it slithered off to the port side. Left a lot of blubber and meat on the deck up there, and so everybody that was on that trip got a piece of blubber in a little glass tube. I think that's the only time that a submarine's hit a whale. Okay. Well, that tells about the Seadragon and the Swordfish. Two good submarines. Had good crews too.

Paul Stillwell: Anything else about Portsmouth before we get you moved out to Puget Sound?

Captain Jackson: Well, we made the Grayback and the Growler, which were regular submarines. Had lots of problems with that because they had to take the Regulus missiles, which were very large, out of a hangar and then put it on a training device where you could train it to one side and fire the missile, the Regulus, off of the supports you rolled it up on. That was a tough job, and there were lots of problems. That was development work all the time.

Mare Island made the plans, and they felt that they had worked it all out, but when we tried to put it together it didn't quite fit. We had good people at Portsmouth. We had Project Pressure, which was to ensure that all the things that would see the deeper depth pressure would be satisfactory for installation in the ship. We also had a very extensive

---

* On 3 August 1958 the USS Skate (SSN-578), under Commander James F. Calvert, USN, became the first submarine to surface at the North Pole.

testing program for the development of noise suppression. And the name Project Pressure was not because of the sea pressure but the pressure Admiral Moore put on us all, which he did. He monitored every single thing that was going, and if it took a few hours longer than was scheduled, he asked either, "Why did that happen?" or "Why didn't you guys work harder?" But he was good. He let us do things.

The situation was that apparently Admiral Moore had confidence in me, and whenever there was a problem—whether it was on the waterfront or in the supply department or the design division—he'd call me on the telephone and say, "Get on the job."

So finally I had to say, "Hey, between you and Ben putting me on all these hot jobs, I don't have any time to be design superintendent."

Paul Stillwell: Who was Ben?

Captain Jackson: Ben Strauss, the planning officer. He was a hard guy to work for. First of all, he went to Georgia Tech but he was not an engineer, he was not a manger, but he was very energetic. To him everything was a crisis. It didn't make any difference whether it was a discussion on the color of the paint in the wardroom or something like that. It had to be a crisis that's settled right then.

Ben was killed in an automobile accident, for which I felt real bad. That's not the way to go. His wife has died since. They had a daughter and a son. The young son came to visit us, and he was a very fine young man, and it looked like he was going to be great. He was about 20 years old then.

We had other good guys there. Bob Baylis was in charge of the sound development. He was very instrumental in noise suppression at that time, did an excellent job. John Woolston was the assistant design superintendent on the detail design of things.[*] He was very intelligent, and as a result he thought he knew more about everything than anybody else could possibly know. So he was hard to work with, but he did do a good job. He was smart.

---

[*] Lieutenant Commander John Woolston, USN.

Paul Stillwell: What other individuals might you mention?

Captain Jackson: Well, among the civilians there were some engineers up there that were good. Bill Eckart was the civilian chief engineer, a great guy who was interested in all parts of the shipyard. He was very good, and he did a lot of work on the management of design and the flow of information throughout the shipyard. That's when computers were first coming out, and they mostly produced punch cards. He and I had many discussions on it and eventually wrote a paper for SNAME, which we called "A Logical Package of Work and a Common Language."[*]

As an example we used a pump that we wanted to install. But you had to have a foundation, and you had to have piping to it. It had to have electrical connections and a controller. So all those things should be designed as to be a unit, and either you have one guy that could do it all or a team of workers that could make this unit and put it in the ship all ready to go, just to pipe up and wire up. The common language was that you made all the numbering system for the plans, and that was the key for the plans.

But work orders for the shops on what to do, the procurement paper, the routing slips, everything would have that number. So that was a logical package of work, and all you had to do was to find out where it was going to be, then all this information went to that point. We actually did that work in the Dolphin, and it was quite successful.[†] We also made the plans such that you could leave the hull in sections with open ends and so you could load all of the machinery and so forth in through the ends rather than going through the top. We also did that on the Thresher.

Right now there's a lot of stuff being written—published in the paper and so forth—about the new philosophy of designing submarines, and I say that's what we did 30 years ago. Well, it's almost 40 years ago now, so it's not new. I'm sure that guys that worked on the submarines in World War II said, "Yeah, we were pretty novel, too, at that time." And they were. When I look and see what was done, they were ingenious. They

---

[*] This paper was published in 1958.
[†] USS Dolphin (AGSS-555) was an auxiliary research submarine built by the Portsmouth Naval Shipyard and commissioned on 17 August 1968.

took shortcuts that were later standard operating procedures, and John Alden's book outlines most of the things that they did in World War II.[*]

Paul Stillwell: His book on the fleet submarine.

Captain Jackson: Yes, on which he did an excellent job. Incidentally, he was one of the candidates to go to Portsmouth as design superintendent when I went there. I felt kind of bad about some of those guys, because I knew that that's the job that they wanted and they didn't get, so I know how I'd feel if I'd been nominated and didn't get it. But I didn't take any action to get that job at all. It came out of the blue. As a matter of fact, we had a nice place to live by that time down in Washington, and we were reluctant to leave it.

Paul Stillwell: But you went.

Captain Jackson: Yes, we went. Yep. "Aye, aye, sir," and we go.

Paul Stillwell: Well, are we ready to move you out to Puget Sound now?

Captain Jackson: Well, there's a heck of a lot more you can talk about what went on at Portsmouth.

Paul Stillwell: If there are other things to mention, please do.

Captain Jackson: Well, we suffered from the Harvard School of Business. We had people that had gone and taken their business course up there. Some of the precepts were beyond my comprehension in that one of them was, "You don't have to understand it to manage it. It's still just a business process, and all you have to do is look at the bottom line. If the bottom line is not right, you get somebody to correct it. But you don't have to understand it."

---

[*] John D. Alden, The Fleet Submarine in the U.S. Navy: a Design and Construction History (Annapolis: Naval Institute Press, 1979).

That was so far from my concept of how you run things it was hard to take aboard. But there some people who had taken that course, and they bought it. They also bought the philosophy that the workmen were stupid—that you had to tell them every single thing what to do. You had to give a man every single piece of material that he needed to do his work, and that if he didn't have it, he'd just sit down and wait till he got it. That was foreign to my expectations of the way things ought to work.

There's a lot to it there that I didn't agree with, but we had a production officer who was trying to put that philosophy into effect. It caused an awful lot of trouble, and I think as a result it caused some sloppy work. The unions all bought it. They thought that was great, because it relieved them of essentially any responsibility for what they were doing. It was particularly bad in the pipe shop, because they had a majority of the material that went into a submarine on the line items, but sometimes the line item was just a little elbow but it was still—as paperwork it was as big as, you know, a ten-ton piece of plate.

Accounting for all that stuff and being sure that the guy had the right piece at the right time when he came to work at 7:00 o'clock in the morning was hard. There was a lot of friction between the production department and the planning department. That was not unusual in any shipyard, but it was particularly bad at Portsmouth. I tried to be very cooperative and worry about the problems the production departments had, but they glommed the fact that the design division and the planning department were not carrying their share of the load and that they said that any problems they had were the result of lack of performance on the planning department, which was not true. But it was a good excuse for not finishing on time and things like that.

I can give you one example. Without consulting the planning department, the production officer called up the shipyard commander and said, "Hey, we have a horrible problem down here, and it's all planning's fault. They gave us the wrong plans."

Admiral Moore called me up and he said, "Hey, go fix that."

So I went down to the ship, and the first thing I did was say, "What's the problem?"

They said, "Well, when we push the stick, the plane only goes halfway."

So I said, "Let's see it." I had an aluminum locker there with a grease pencil, and I said, "Take it to five degrees, and ten degrees," and then measured the order position when it went there. It was just half. I said, "Did you guys look in the gear box that relates the position indicator to the feedback to the stick so you get a zero position?" I could see the light turn on. And the guy that made the box was there. I said, "You've got a set of gears in there with a ratio of two to one and they're in backwards." I said, "Go fix it."

I went back and told the shipyard commander, and I said, "I found out what the problem was. As far as I'm concerned, it was a production failure, not design. The design was all right." Which it was. But that was only typical of the kinds of things that went on. What they were looking for was an excuse, why it didn't work right. And those guys were smart enough to figure it out.

Paul Stillwell: You'd think the designer, the guy who had come up with it, would be a little shrewder than that.

Captain Jackson: Well, he was not involved, because Admiral Moore short-circuited him when he called me up and said, "Go get it fixed." I didn't know what the problem was, so I just went down there to find out what the problem was so I'd know who to call to fix it, but it was so obvious what the problem was. I could see the production guy that made the box when the light turned on, so I knew that he knew what I was talking about. Just an example, but it was fun. I enjoyed it, because I didn't get a chance to read the mail that I should have read when I was up there when I was down on the ship. I enjoyed very much sea trials. I never missed a chance to go to sea on a submarine.

Paul Stillwell: How many were there, would you guess?

Captain Jackson: Oh, in my whole career I made something like 250, and that included some surface ships, too, that I went on.

Paul Stillwell: Wow.

Captain Jackson: Yes. Because I was in the business where we were involved with new ships, and if I was in the bureau I would manage to go on it. If I was in OpNav I would go be OpNav representative on all the new ships. When I was in the shipyard, not only did I go on the major sea trials but all the minor ones too. I'm sure I went on many of them that weren't necessary, but I went. That was one of the gratuities you had for being in the Navy. So, a very enjoyable time.

Well, I went out to Puget Sound, and I was designated to be the planning officer, but that was back in the days when they were humping captains out early. They said there was no room for them to assign me to a more senior position. And they had one guy that that happened to. Ben Strauss was another one that it happened to.[*] But they decided that this guy should have a tour of duty as a planning officer, so they ordered us both as the planning officer. He was senior to me, so I didn't have a job.[†]

I was sent out there to help them get organized in the submarine business. They were also getting in the Polaris business, so I helped them organize there. And I helped them in nuclear power, although they had a nuclear power superintendent there, but we worked very closely together. He was a real good guy, too, Wagner. He was one of the 08 guys.[‡] So the first year there I didn't really have a responsible job other than educating everybody, which I did. I organized classes in submarine systems and operations and the Polaris system.

That got me in a little bit of trouble, because they had a weapons officer there, and he thought he ought to be in charge of Polaris, which he should have been. But since I didn't have any job, I usurped that. After the year, the other planning officer was detached, and I became the planning officer.

I was there a year when they needed a new supervisor of shipbuilding at Groton, and the personnel officer in BuShips thought that I should have that job. I was perfectly willing to stay at Bremerton a couple more years, but I came to Groton. I was there four years, and by that time Beck didn't want to move. I had subjected her to all kinds of strain, so I said, "Okay, let's stay here."

---

[*] Strauss retired as a captain in July 1963.
[†] Captain Frank A. Spencer, USN, was the shipyard's planning officer from 7 August 1962 to 12 June 1963. Captain Jackson held the billet from 13 June 1963 to 10 July 1964.
[‡] The designation for the nuclear power section within the Bureau of Ships was 08.

While I was at Puget Sound, there were two frigates that were pretty well along the line by the time I got there.* We launched them and finished them up while I was there. I made all the sea trials on those.

Tony Lilly was captain of one of them, and he was a good guy.† I thought he could have been a better ship handler, but that's only one part of the job of being captain. He was a good leader of men, and that's important.

The other guy, I thought, was very fine.‡ He had his crew really trained by the time they went in commission, and I can remember it to this day because it impressed me so much. He had all the sailors over on the pier. He had a watch on board, but everybody else was on the pier, and he passed the word, "Place the ship in commission," and, "Hoist the commission pennant," and, "Crew, take your stations." They literally ran aboard as fast as they could. He had two gangways, one forward and one aft. They went up and manned the rail all the way around. I was really impressed with that. I thought that was great. I kept in touch with him for a good many years. Sent him Christmas cards, and he sent me Christmas cards. He retired down someplace in Texas, and we've lost track with him now.

Paul Stillwell: Well, please tell me more about what was involved in getting the yard geared up to do nuclear work and handle submarines.

Captain Jackson: Oh, a lot. First of all, the yard had no experience in submarines, so first of all you had to ensure that they had the unique capabilities that the submarines need.

Paul Stillwell: What do those include?

Captain Jackson: Well, they're not many, but I'll give an example in a few minutes of what some of the problems are. But, first of all, you're working in confined spaces, and

---

* The keel for the guided missile frigate Gridley (DLG-21) was laid 15 July 1960; she was launched 31 July 1961 and commissioned 25 May 1963. The keel for the Reeves (DLG-24) was laid 1 July 1960; she was launched 12 May 1962 and commissioned 15 May 1964.
† Captain Percy A. Lilly, Jr., USN, was the first commanding officer of the Gridley.
‡ Captain Wynne A. Stevens, Jr., USN, was the first commanding officer of the Reeves.

it's very difficult to have access to all the gear. When you have to rip out in order to take something out, you have to take something else out, and pretty soon you've got everything out. If you're working on a surface ship, you don't have to do so much because you have lots more room.

Then they're unique systems—for instance, they had nobody there that really had had any experience on torpedo tubes, so we had to have drills on that. You know, what does a torpedo tube do? What kind of interlocks do you have to have? Why is it important that you watch the interlocks all the time? The electronics equipment is different, and so you need to get some electronics technicians who at least boned up on that kind of equipment. There are lots of unique problems. A lot of their work was on big ships like carriers, and there's a difference. I kept telling them, the shop masters, that there's a difference. And I could see that they really didn't understand what I was saying.

They would say, "Hey, we're good mechanics, and ships we know all about, and we can handle it." But the Kitty Hawk came in, and she tied up on the south side of the pier. Only about 20 minutes later, the Barbel came in for a major overhaul, and she tied up on the other side of the pier. So I got all the shop masters up there, and I said, "Hey, look. Your problem is you've got a 50,000 man-day job on the carrier, and you can put 50,000 men on there and theoretically you can do it in a day, because there's room enough for them to get around. Now, you've got a 50,000 man-day package on the Barbel," which was true. The package was about the same for both of them.

I said, "Look at the difference in the size of the ships. You can't put 50,000 men on that submarine, and even if you could you couldn't get them all through the hole in one day that they have to go through. Not only that, every welding lead, every gas line for cutting torches, every line for temporary lights and everything has to go through this 25-inch hatch. And then you've got to put people through it." I said, "That's your problem. It's not the skill of the mechanic. It's not the knowledge of planning your work. It's just the fact that you've got too darn many people that you have to use in too short a time." And that was a good example.

Then I used to have lunch with those guys frequently, just to get acquainted with them. I was impressed with the work ethics of the people that worked there, and so I asked some of the shop masters, I'd say, "Hey, why do your guys work so hard?"

They said, "Well, most of us came from some other place, and we don't want to go back there. We figured the only way that we can stay here is do a good job."

Paul Stillwell: Great.

Captain Jackson: Boy, that's incentive enough, and the guys really did have good work ethics.

Paul Stillwell: They had some families with multi-generations working in the yard, didn't they?

Captain Jackson: Well, not too many because they all migrated from someplace else.

Paul Stillwell: I see.

Captain Jackson: But there were some that had been there from before World War I, their families and one generation to another. It certainly was a Navy town.

Paul Stillwell: Yes.

Captain Jackson: Besides the two frigates we built a tender, the Samuel Gompers.* Gompers was a union leader and it was made a destroyer tender. And we designed and built the Sacramento.†

Paul Stillwell: Well, please tell me about the Sacramento. Admiral Shear was so proud of commanding that ship.‡

Captain Jackson: She was a wonderful ship. She really was. She was the first multi-product support ship. In other words she carried liquid fuels. She carried a whole

---

* USS Samuel Gompers (AD-37) was commissioned 1 July 1967.
† The fast combat support ship Sacramento (AOE-1) was commissioned 14 March 1964.
‡ As a captain, Shear commanded the Sacramento in 1965-66.

warehouse full of spare parts for different kinds of ships. It carried general stores like paper and anything that you need to run the ship, lubricating oil, the whole works.

Paul Stillwell: Ammunition.

Captain Jackson: Ammunition. You name it, she had everything. It was really a well-laid-out ship. One of my contemporaries, Jack Kalina, did the preliminary design on that ship, and he did an excellent job.* Times were busy there, so the people in charge at that time didn't interfere with what he was doing, so he turned out a good job in a short time.

I learned one thing on that. There's a thing known as hydro-elasticity, and that's when the hydrodynamic forces on the system match the elastic forces in the structure. I really didn't know about that. I'd heard about it, but I never had experienced it until we were on sea trials on that. The hydro-elasticity was there, and it shook the whole ship. Then that was one of the things we had to correct.

You look at it, and you say, "Well, there's two ways we can correct it, and one is to stiffen up everything, the foundations of all the machinery, the bearings and so forth. But that's a horrendous job. The other thing is we can tune the hydraulic system so that it doesn't vibrate at the same frequency as the structures. You get it out of phase, and it'll go away. Well, that sounded like a good idea, but how do you do that? That was a problem we had to correct.

We'd had similar problems on the Albacore and we stiffened. On that one we could stiffen up the support of the thrust bearing, which we did, and that was very good. That worked on Albacore. But when we were trying to noise-quiet the Thresher we had the same problem to a minor degree, and structurally and mechanically it was okay. But Baylis came up with the idea that you put a surge suppressor in the line and that we could dampen that out. So that's what we did on the Sacramento. You can imagine the transfer of information, how it went. That corrected the problem. Another thing on that, the engines for the Sacramento came out of one of the battleships that was only partially finished during World War II.

---

* Lieutenant Commander John F. Kalina, USN.

Paul Stillwell: Kentucky.*

Captain Jackson: Kentucky is right. That's right. We had some trouble fitting that machinery in the ship, and it had to be designed to take it, so there were some problems. But basically everything went along. There was a big difference between Portsmouth and Bremerton on cooperation between the planning department and the production department. Had a problem, everybody rallied around to solve it. Don't look to see whose fault it is. We're not looking for excuses. What we're looking for is to correct it.

Paul Stillwell: This is at Bremerton there was more cooperation?

Captain Jackson: Yes, much more.

Paul Stillwell: Camden, the sister ship of Sacramento, was being built at New York Ship, and that was about the last thing that that shipyard did.† Did you share information with them?

Captain Jackson: Oh, sure. We gave them all the information that they needed, but it was BuShips' responsibility to give them the information. They'd call us up if they had a problem and say, "Hey, you got any suggestions?" and we'd say, "Sure. This is how we solved it." In that area I think that the shipyard at Bremerton was most cooperative. Even though New York Ship was a commercial yard, the people at Bremerton were very cooperative. They were more cooperative than New York Ship was coming the other way. But what really put New York Ship out of business was the guy that owned it; he raped the Washington Transit.

---

* For details on the Kentucky (BB-66), which was never finished, see Gordon E. Hogg, "From Shipyard to Scrapyard," U.S. Naval Institute Proceedings, October 2001, pages 88-92. Page 92 has a short sidebar on the use of the engines from the Kentucky in the Sacramento (AOE-1) and her sister Camden (AOE-2).

† The New York Shipbuilding Corporation, Camden, New Jersey, was founded in 1899. It was liquidated in the autumn of 1967 by its parent firm, Merritt-Chapman & Scott, which was headed by Louis Wolfson. For a summary of the events surrounding the closing of the yard, see The New York Times, 3 September 1967, Section 5, page 13.

Paul Stillwell: Wolfson.

Captain Jackson: Yes, that's it. When I was at OpNav, Harry Burris had gone there to be vice president in charge of engineering. He wanted me to come to work for him, and they twisted my arm pretty hard. But particularly because Wolfson was in charge I didn't want any part of it. It was very hard to turn down the substantial increase in the compensation that would have happened if I'd taken it.

But Wolfson did the same thing to New York Ship. You know, he inflated the stock and sold it at high prices. Also, they didn't pay their bills, and eventually they went broke. But they didn't understand building submarines.* They would brag about how fast they put up the pressure hull because on a surface ship that's the big item. You get the steel up, and the job is well over half done. But in a submarine when you get the steel up the problems just begin, and so they spent all their money getting the steel up, and they didn't have enough left over to put all the wires and all the piping and all the machinery and everything else inside. So they were losing money at a rapid rate, and financially they just couldn't stand it. With Wolfson stealing all the money at the top end and the inefficiencies at the lower end, it broke them.

Paul Stillwell: When I was out there at Bremerton in the late 1960s the security was very tight. This was attributed to nuclear work. In what ways did that have to be stepped up?

Captain Jackson: Well, the biggest thing is that instead of trying to make the whole yard nuclear-secure, they put a bunch of fences around those nuclear parts, and that was really as a result of the security of the 08 people in BuShips. They got paranoid about that. I'm not so sure that they were concerned so much that their secrets would be going to Russia as they were that they'd lose control. They didn't want people to know what they were doing so that they couldn't compete with them. Since I'd worked on both sides of that, I had a feel for it.

---

* The attack submarine Pogy (SSN-647) was under construction as business dwindled at New York Shipbuilding Corporation. Soon after she was launched on 3 June 1967, her contract was cancelled and the unfinished ship was towed to Philadelphia for temporary berthing. She was subsequently assigned to Ingalls Shipbuilding, Pascagoula, Mississippi, for completion.

Paul Stillwell: So what they did was create a controlled area within the shipyard.

Captain Jackson: Right, which is pretty easy to do. They did the same thing at Portsmouth.

Paul Stillwell: Also Norfolk.

Captain Jackson: I don't know about Norfolk or Charleston, but I assume they did the same thing.

Paul Stillwell: What was that Puget Sound area like as a place to live?

Captain Jackson: Oh, great. We liked it, but both Beck and I came to the conclusion we would not like to retire there.

Paul Stillwell: Why not?

Captain Jackson: Well, we really weren't geared to that kind of life. If you were an outdoors sportsman and so forth, it was more attractive than if you were not outdoors-type people. We used to go skiing all the time. We liked it, but we had to go a long way. The only way you could go skiing was make a three-day expedition up to the mountains, and you couldn't just go for the day. The weather was much better than we anticipated. When we went there, we thought it was going to rain all the time, but when we drove up to the quarters we were going to stay in, they had the automatic sprinklers running. I said, "Gee whiz, if it rains all the time why do they have that?" I found out it doesn't rain all the time. Not far from where the shipyard is, up at Sequim, it's a desert—dryer than all get out. The people were nice. I enjoyed them, and I got to know a lot of the civilians in the yard. They invited us to their house and we invited them over to our house. It made it very good.

Paul Stillwell: Did the children enjoy it?

Captain Jackson: Oh, yes. My son went to high school for four years, and he was in three different high schools, so he had a hard time. By the time we got there at the new schools in September, all the cliques had been formatted and so forth, and he had a hard time getting in there. It was not the best thing to move around in such rapid sequence.

Paul Stillwell: Did you have any connection with the mothball fleet ships there?

Captain Jackson: Not much. I used to go down to the <u>Missouri</u> and just walk around and look at it.* When you had the shipyard duty, you had to inspect the yard twice a night, and the evenings were pretty late in the summertime, and so when I would go down and look at the reserve fleet I'd take a few minutes and walk around on the ships.

Paul Stillwell: Inside?

Captain Jackson: No, I never went inside because they were all locked up.

Paul Stillwell: I found it fascinating to see them when they were in that kind of ghostlike condition and think about how different from when they had men on board.

Captain Jackson: Yes, they sure are different.

Paul Stillwell: Almost eerie.

Captain Jackson: But I learned something from that reserve fleet. We had a captain that was in charge of the reserve fleet, and we had an admiral in charge of the shipyard. The captain was always complaining, because he said, "Here I am, I've got 30 officers and 600 enlisted men working for me, and I'm only a captain. The admiral over in the shipyard's

---

* The battleship <u>Missouri</u> (BB-63), site of the Japanese surrender that ended World War II, was in the reserve fleet at Bremerton from her decommissioning in 1955 until she was towed away in 1984 to be reactivated.

only got 27 officers and five enlisted men, who most of them are steward's mates, and he's an admiral."

So I queried him one night when he was going on and I said, "Well, what's your criteria for which rank you have?"

He said, "By the number of enlisted men you have." That was enlightening to me that that was the criteria for selecting it.

Paul Stillwell: On the other hand, the admiral had a whole lot of civil service workers working for him.

Captain Jackson: Oh, sure did, boy, and huge big responsibilities of managing that great big shipyard, which the reserve fleet was part of it.

Paul Stillwell: Well, the reserve fleet was kind of like the tail on the dog.

Captain Jackson: That's right. That was just the problem. But that was enlightening with that philosophy, and I think that permeates the Navy.

Paul Stillwell: Who was the captain?

Captain Jackson: Oh, gee. I really have forgotten his name, but that is immaterial. His son and my son were good friends, and they spent a lot of time together. I think his son was really afraid of the old man, which he shouldn't be. I mean, a son ought to be able to go to the guy with problems and say, "Hey, Dad, I've got a problem. I'd like for you to know about it, and maybe you can give me some guidance on what I ought to do." But the kid was afraid to do that.

Paul Stillwell: Some naval officers run their families like they run a ship.

Captain Jackson: Yes, exactly right. But in general all those guys at Bremerton were good people.

Paul Stillwell: My memories unfortunately are not so pleasant, because the time I was there was mostly as part of the mothballing crew on board the New Jersey in 1969 and that is truly a dreary period in the life of a ship.* Plus I think in September of that year they set a record for rainfall during the month in the Seattle area. So it was raining on our parade.

Captain Jackson: I'm sure that that was not the best time. But I used to go in and read the logs of the guys that laid up those ships. You could tell that, particularly from the engine room logs, that the guys loved that machinery, and they wrote little details on it like, "When you have this problem go adjust valve number so-and-so one-sixteenth of a turn."

Paul Stillwell: The idiosyncrasies.

Captain Jackson: Yes, they really covered the works. It was obvious that they were doing it because that was their pride and joy, those engines down there.

Paul Stillwell: In the New Jersey the captain had each department head write a letter to the person who would be his successor if the ship ever came back into commission, and I think a dozen years later when they reactivated the New Jersey those letters probably were useful.†

Captain Jackson: Oh, I'm sure they were. Yes, because little things like that, a valve adjustment, one-sixteenth of a turn, that's not much.

Paul Stillwell: That's right. Well, once you got moved from your temporary job to your real job how did your responsibilities change?

---

* The battleship New Jersey (BB-62) was decommissioned at Bremerton on 17 December 1969.
† The commanding officer during the inactivation was Captain Robert C Peniston, USN. For his recollections of the New Jersey see "The Big Ship in My Life," U.S. Naval Institute Proceedings, December 1979, pages 52-53.

Captain Jackson: Oh, in the planning organization I had the planning department, and those guys would write all the work instructions and manage all the money. Then I had the design division, and that was a big design division because we had so many surface ships there. That was a full-time responsible job.

Paul Stillwell: What does the planning department do? Do they figure out what overhauls they're going to have to do, what new construction and allocation of man-hours?

Captain Jackson: They don't plan it, because that comes from the authorities that own the ship. If it's a new ship, it's BuShips. If it's an active ship it comes from the type commander, and they provide the money. They tell the shipyard what work they want done and how much money they have to spend. Then the planning department has to make the work orders inside the ship from the planning department to the production department, and then they have to make material, ordering things which go through the supply department for them to order. Then if there's any design work, it's the responsibility of the design division to prepare the plans, which then go to the planning department to write the work orders to accomplish the work on those plans. It sounds complicated, but it's really not if it works properly. If there's cooperation between the organizations it goes smoothly. But some obstinate person can frig it all up. They can throw roadblocks into everything.

Paul Stillwell: Well, I would suspect that it's a process of negotiation, because typically the ship is going to want to get more accomplished than the shipyard has the resources or willingness to do.

Captain Jackson: Yes, and they each have levers. One, the ship wants to do as you say, just get more, and they like to get it for free. Well, the shipyard really would like to give it to them for free, but they can't do it. Legally they can't do it. So their defense is, "Sure, we'll be glad to do that, but you go get the money." It depends on the national situation whether that money comes freely or it doesn't come at all or you get some of it. But it's a big organization. The expenditure of funds is huge, so every job in the upper echelon is very, very important, that it be done and be done correctly. They had a comptroller department as well who also managed the money that gets parceled out to the various departments.

Paul Stillwell: What is the shipyard's attitude on this practice known as "cumshaw"?*

Captain Jackson: Oh, it's varied. Depends on the yard. They would be very happy to do everything the ship asks, but they realize it's illegal, and they won't do it. As I say, the defense is, "Go get the money." During World War II cumshaw was very, very liberal. That was just the state of affairs.

Paul Stillwell: Sort of an under-the-table way of getting things of done.

Captain Jackson: That's right. At the dry dock we didn't worry about money at all. If a guy wanted something, we'd say, "Well, do we have time to do it?" That was the big question.

Paul Stillwell: Well, and in the wartime the atmosphere was "Get the job done and pay for it later."

Captain Jackson: Yes.

Paul Stillwell: The money faucets were flowing.

Captain Jackson: That's right, but we didn't worry about that. Everybody got their paycheck, and that was what was important.

Paul Stillwell: Well, and another thing, I would think that just given the priority of the nuclear program that those nuclear-related jobs that came in, probably a pretty high percentage of those got done.

---

* "Cumshaw" is a slang term for a bartering system in which shipyard personnel perform work or provide equipment not officially authorized in exchange for coffee, food, or other considerations.

Captain Jackson: Oh, sure. I would say all of them. Well, the nuclear department was pretty well run.

Paul Stillwell: Who was the shipyard commander you were working for?

Captain Jackson: Floyd Schultz.* I knew him when I was an ensign. He and I went to the same junior college.

Paul Stillwell: What do you recall of him as the shipyard commander?

Captain Jackson: Well, he was a nice guy, but he certainly wasn't very forceful, and I think he rode the fence too much. He was more impressed with the fact that he was an admiral than that he was a shipyard commander, I think. Hal Shear didn't like him at all. When he had the <u>Sacramento</u>, Bremerton was her homeport, so he had a lot to do with the yard.

Paul Stillwell: Well, as Admiral Shear reminded us when we saw him this afternoon, he is a forceful person.

Captain Jackson: Yes.

Paul Stillwell: That's just the nature of his personality.

Captain Jackson: Yes. Very good.

Paul Stillwell: What else do you want to contribute about Puget Sound?

Captain Jackson: Well, we certainly enjoyed our tour of duty there, and I went away with the feeling that I had contributed something to the yard. In my courses on submarines I

---

* Rear Admiral Floyd B. Schultz, USN, commanded the Puget Sound Naval Shipyard from 29 June 1962 to 15 March 1967.

used the material that was developed for the Submarine School, so that I educated probably 600 people while I was there on submarines. Some of them were very good and very interested. For some of them it was just a way to pass the time. But they all enjoyed it, and also I think they all learned something.

Paul Stillwell: My guess is that the fact that you were wearing dolphins gave it an added degree of credibility.

Captain Jackson: I expect so. Right. And the fact that when the submarines came I knew all the officers and everything, and we were off to a good start. We were talking about Harry D. Train II today.* Well, he was captain of the Barbel at that time, so because I had known him before, I went out of my way to make him welcome and look after his crew and stuff like that, which I think he appreciated.

Paul Stillwell: I'm sure he was grateful for that.

Captain Jackson: Yes. I introduced him to all the shop masters, and when we were leaving, I'd say, "You know, this is a good guy. We're going to have lot of submarines, and he's the first one. You'd better treat him right."

Paul Stillwell: Oh, he was the first one?

Captain Jackson: Well, the Bugara was really the first one. Don Walsh was the exec on that, and I had known Don.

Paul Stillwell: Well, please tell me about him. He's a fascinating individual.

---

* Commander Train was commanding officer of the USS Barbel (SS-580) from July 1962 to July 1964. His oral history is in the Naval Institute collection.

Captain Jackson: Yes, he is that. He made a name for himself when he rode the Trieste down to the deepest part of the ocean.*

Paul Stillwell: With Piccard.

Captain Jackson: With Piccard. And from things that Don told me, I guess that relationships were not the best between Piccard and Walsh.

Paul Stillwell: I see.

Captain Jackson: Apparently Piccard thought that he didn't need a Navy officer on it, and the Navy said, "Hey, this is our submarine. We're going to have an officer, and he's going to be in charge." Piccard thought he ought to be in charge, and so Don had a hard time.

Paul Stillwell: You can understand why both of them would feel that way.

Captain Jackson: Sure I do, but that's the way it was, and there's no sense in arguing about it. We're going on this great mission by ourselves, and it's only the two of us, and we'd better learn to live with one another.

Paul Stillwell: That's right. As I remember he left the Navy early after he made captain, and he went with Scripps or somebody like that.

Captain Jackson: He did that. Then he started his own company, and he's still running that and doing a good job. I hear from him every once in a while. When I go out to the West Coast I give him a call, but I don't go to the West Coast very often anymore.

Paul Stillwell: Where had you known Harry Train before?

---

* Lieutenant Don Walsh, USN, a submariner, was officer in charge of the Navy's bathyscaphe Trieste, an underwater capsule designed by Jacques Piccard and his father Auguste. In January 1960 Walsh and Jacques Piccard submerged in the Trieste to a depth of nearly seven miles in the Pacific Ocean, 200 miles southwest of Guam.

Captain Jackson: I knew him in Portsmouth the first time I was there.

Paul Stillwell: Well, he was in the Wahoo with Wilkinson after he went to Submarine School. Later he was here as exec of Entemedor.

Captain Jackson: I knew him from the Wahoo.

Paul Stillwell: Any impressions you have of him as a person?

Captain Jackson: Oh, yes. I liked him very much. Good guy. I liked his family. His daughter was a real charmer. Old Beau Buck came to visit us at the time there, and so we had a little get-together and asked Harry and his family to come up and, you know, just have a little social hour. This young girl—I guess she was probably about 14 or 15 or something—was making eyes at old Beau Buck.

Paul Stillwell: Who's Beau Buck?

Captain Jackson: Oh, you ever hear of Beaumont Buck, the four-star general in the Army?

Paul Stillwell: No.

Captain Jackson: Well, anyway this was his grandson.

Paul Stillwell: I see.

Captain Jackson: He had the same name. He went to the Naval Academy, and he was an ED officer.* We knew him down at Portsmouth. He worked for me. Then he went to work for Hewlett-Packard, and he stayed there and he spent an awful lot of time up in the

---

* Beaumont M. Buck graduated from the Naval Academy in 1948, earned a master's degree in electrical engineering in 1954 and a master's degree in physics in 1955. He resigned from the service in 1961 as a lieutenant commander.

Arctic. Some of the stories he tells us are good. Like the time that a polar bear came into the camp, and so they had an Eskimo with them and he said, "I'm going to take some pictures of that." And he says, "I want you to take the pictures when the polar bear gets close. And if he gets too close take your gun and shoot him." So everything is all set up and the polar bear came in kind of close, and old Beau said, "Take pictures. Take pictures." Came in a little closer and he said, "Get your gun and shoot him." But the bear, I don't know if he was scared or not. Probably not because they don't scare easily, but he turned around and walked away.

Paul Stillwell: How much contact in all these years did you have with the InSurv people?*

Captain Jackson: Oh, much. I started out with that really when I was in BuShips. I made most of the InSurv trials as the Bureau of Ships representative on the DEs and the destroyers. I must have made 100 InSurv trips there.

Paul Stillwell: How would you evaluate the function that the InSurv people perform?

Captain Jackson: Well, it's great. Not so much what they do but the impact they have on getting ready.

Paul Stillwell: Just because the fact that they're coming makes you get ready.

Captain Jackson: That's right. And a lot of things get done that wouldn't get done if that hadn't happened. They were looking for incomplete work and stuff like that, and so the shipyard makes every effort to ensure that there is no incomplete work. You know, they represent a very useful thing and also in their inspections they find things that they say could be improved, and they make recommendations, say, "Hey, if you do this it would make a better ship." Because they're very experienced they generally do a good job.

---

* InSurv—the Board of Inspection and Survey.

Paul Stillwell: Well, and sometimes they can be a useful lever. If a ship's having a hard time getting something done on its own, the fact that InSurv wants it done can help get it.

Captain Jackson: Oh, if they star a card, the ship can't go to sea until it's done. And sometimes they take that action, they make a star on the card. Some guys do it in red to emphasize it.

Captain Jackson: How much contact did you have with Admiral Bulkeley in that role?[*]

Captain Jackson: Practically none because he came after I was there.

Paul Stillwell: I see.

Captain Jackson: I had some contact with him after he retired but not much. I wouldn't say I even knew him very well.

Paul Stillwell: Anything more to say about Puget Sound?

Captain Jackson: Well, I think I've told you all the highlights.

Paul Stillwell: All right.

Captain Jackson: I took the apprentice course for electronics while I was there, in the first year when I had some time, and that was good. The master of the electronics shop was my instructor, and he gave me all the requirements. I did all the studying and worked all the problems and did all the soldering and so forth that you have to do. That was a very useful thing, because I was certainly weak in electronics, and that was one way to learn it.

Paul Stillwell: Well, then you came to Groton in 1964, and you've been here ever since.

---

[*] Rear Admiral John D. Bulkeley, USN, began serving as president of the Board of Inspection and Survey in 1967, continued after his age-mandated retirement in 1974, and remained until he finally left active duty in 1988.

Captain Jackson: Yes, for four years I was a supervisor. During that time we delivered probably 25% of the Polaris fleet, either from new construction or major overhaul. I was also the supervisor of shipbuilding up at Quincy, and that made difficulty because I had to vibrate back and forth. It was a big job and a lot of politics in that too.

Paul Stillwell: What do you mean by politics?

Captain Jackson: Well, the Electric Boat Company said if you eliminated the supervisor, they could do the work a lot cheaper. We were having a conference there, and I said, "Okay. You want to do without the supervisor?"

"Yeah, sure do."

The Submarine Force and EB and BuShips all agreed to this. I said, "There's only one problem. Who's going to pay you?"

"Pay?"

On the Navy side. "What do you mean who's going to pay them."

I said, "The supervisor's not going to pay them. Are you guys going to pay them? Are you going to put the inspection to see that they're entitled to receive pay for what they do?"

"Oh, no, we hadn't thought about that."

Then I turned to EB and I said, "You want to do it for free? We'll stay out of your hair if you'll do it for free."

"Oh, no, we can't do that." That was really a fun negotiation for me because the answer was so obvious that they couldn't do away with the supervisor, and everybody went away with the agreement that, yes, the supervisor is a necessary evil.

Paul Stillwell: What is the function of a supervisor of shipbuilding?

Captain Jackson: Well, it's varied. If you ask the shipyard, their function is to be a pain in the neck. If you ask the supervisor, he says, "Well, I'm responsible for the ship that's turned out to be well built and safe." It's also his responsibility to assure that the shipyard is properly paid, not too little and certainly not too much, but to give a fair approval. And there's a horrible thing known as change orders, and you have to decide what the change order's going to say. You write the change order, and you have to assure that the work is done, and then you have to adjudicate the cost. That's a big, big problem, and it involves many, many millions of dollars.

Paul Stillwell: Can you give a few examples on how that process works?

Captain Jackson: Well, sure. You look at the plans and say, "Hey, this is supposed to be done in accordance with the plans." But when they go to do it, the plans don't match what's there.

So the contractor says, "We need a change order because the material we've been furnished is not correct."

Then the supervisor or his staff looks at it and says, "Yeah, that's a legitimate gripe," or they'll say, "It's not a legitimate gripe. Go fix it." But if it's legitimate, then they'll give him a change order to fix it. Then the shipyard fixes it, and then the inspection department of the supervisor's office has to look at it, and if there are any tests have to be run, they supervise the tests and so forth. When it's satisfactory they sign off and say, "Yeah, that's a good job." Then the next thing is the contractor submits a claim for that change order, and he justifies what he did, and he justifies also the cost that he expended on that, and then his profit.

Paul Stillwell: Because he has been asked to do something that wasn't in the original plans and contract.

Captain Jackson: That's right. And so you have to negotiate that, and I understand why the contractors always padded a little bit, because that means they get just a little more profit by padding it. Shouldn't do that, but nature being what it is, it happens. So you then negotiate with the contractor what's a fair and even price. And it is a big job. Takes a lot of time, a lot of effort. So that's one example.

Other examples are quite similar, but they just start out differently. One of them is when the plan calls for certain tolerances on the machine work, and you don't meet those tolerances for some reason. They didn't machine it right and so forth, and they request a waiver. The supervisor has authority to say, "Okay, you don't meet the requirements, but the way it doesn't meet it doesn't make much difference, and therefore we'll give you a waiver and let it go." But if it doesn't, you say, "Hey, you guys didn't make it like you're supposed to. Go fix it."

They say, "That's costs a lot of money."

And I say, "Yeah, and it comes out of your profit." There were lots of arguments like that. My philosophy was, when they come in for a waiver which you really don't agree with, don't give in: "Go back and fix it. We aren't going to talk about who pays for it, because you didn't do what you were supposed to."

I told all my people, "Be firm. And if you think you're losing the battle, bring it to me and I'll be firm." But the reason you don't give in is because if you give them a waiver for a slight defect and a similar defect comes along later but it's a little worse, they say, "Well, you gave us a waiver on that, so now why don't you give us a waiver on this?" Where are you going to draw the line? The easiest time is the first time. If you take that stand when you start, then you have a chance of enforcing it the next time without much trouble.

Paul Stillwell: Well, another case of change orders is, say, the specification calls for a certain type of equipment, whether it's electronic or whatever, and in the meantime industry has developed a better piece of gear to perform that function. Then you have the question whether to put in the new piece of gear at an increased cost and incur the cost for that change.

Captain Jackson: Yes, that's correct. But generally those change orders are settled at the bureau level, particularly if it's a big piece of equipment. Another thing is they put in a big motor generator, which is humongous, and it burns out. All right, now, whose fault is that? Is it the contractor's fault for not installing it properly or not operating it properly? Or is it the guy that manufactured that motor generator? You have to make a rendering on that.

Whoever's fault it is, you have to make a change order and say, "Take it out of the ship and fix it."

Sometimes you have to send it back to the manufacturers. I'm speaking from experience there, because that happened a couple of times on a couple of ships while I was there. One time it was the original manufacturer's fault. He didn't do a good job of insulating the windings. Another time it was the shipyard's fault because they didn't wire it up right. The supervisor shares some fault for that, because before they turn it on they're supposed to get the approval of our inspectors. It's a big legal problem. When I was a supervisor they didn't have a lawyer. Now he has a whole staff of lawyers, mostly to settle those change orders.

Paul Stillwell: Well, you sort of portrayed it as an adversary relationship. Is it that in fact, or is there also a good degree of cooperation?

Captain Jackson: Oh, it depends on who you're talking to. If you're talking to the guys who are getting the work done, there's good cooperation, very good. If you're talking to the lawyers, they'll fight for every penny. All people are not the same. There are good guys, and there are bad guys, and that's why they have white hats and black hats.

Paul Stillwell: I read this book by Patrick Tyler, Running Critical, and it just talked about an awful lot of difficulties in the workmanship at EB.[*] This is in more recent years.

Captain Jackson: Well, you can make that sound any way you want because, sure, there are lots of deficiencies, but a lot of them are minor. For instance, some guy comes along and paints some of the structure. Some guy comes along behind him and rubs his shirt against it and messes it up. All right, is that sloppy workmanship or just an accident? Surely the guy didn't run his shirt up there just to get his shirt painted.

Paul Stillwell: Right.

---

[*] Patrick Tyler, Running Critical: The Silent War, Rickover, and General Dynamics (New York: Harper & Row, 1986).

Captain Jackson: But a lot of the things come in that category. But when Veliotis was there, I guess Joe Yurso was here, and he worked for me, so we were good friends, and I used to talk to him a lot.* He and Veliotis had an awful relationship. Everybody knew that Veliotis was a crook, and there was not much the supervisor could do about it except stand his ground. And Veliotis was arrogant and very disrespectful of any human being that wasn't Greek. I've read <u>Running Critical</u>. As a matter of fact, I have a copy of it here on my bookshelf. The author makes a big point of things which most of us think are minor. He says it's a major catastrophe, but it really is a very minor incident. All he was trying to do was degrade Rickover.

Paul Stillwell: Well, he degraded Veliotis a good degree in that, and I think David Lewis was one of his targets as well.†

Captain Jackson: Yes, and guys in positions like that can be targets because they're in a no-win situation. First of all, they can't fight back, or they shouldn't fight back. Things go on that while they're responsible for which they really don't have any control over. It's awful easy to be derogatory about something you don't know anything about.

Paul Stillwell: Well, going back to the 1960s, do you have specific cases that you could cite on this business of change orders or waivers and how that played out?

Captain Jackson: Yes. When I relieved as the supervisor, the backlog on change orders was a little over $700 million, and we got some help from BuShips. They sent a team up there to give us some help, and they really taught us how to settle claims. When I left, we had the backlog down to about $20 million, which was really the pipeline. I didn't like that $20 million a month, and they weren't settled yet because you didn't have time to do it.

---

* Panagiotis Takis Veliotis was born and educated in Greece. He was with Davie Shipbuilding in Quebec, Canada, from 1953 to 1972. From 1973 to 1977 he was general manager of the General Dynamics shipbuilding yard in Quincy, Massachusetts, then became general manager of the Electric Boat Division of General Dynamics in 1977. Captain Joseph F. Yurso, USN, was supervisor of shipbuilding.
† David S. Lewis, Jr., was the chairman and chief executive officer of General Dynamics from 1970 to 1985.

Paul Stillwell: Well, that's a dramatic decrease though.

Captain Jackson: Oh, yes, it was. It was a tremendous decrease.

Paul Stillwell: What were some of those specific instances? Do you remember?

Captain Jackson: Well, they went all the way from major installation changes where we put in new equipment and so forth. They went from late delivery of government-furnished material. And they went down to damaged material, accidentally damaged material. The government is self-insured, so that depending on the accident you either had to pay for it, or you had to prove that there was negligence on the part of the contractor. I came to the conclusion that the cheapest way to settle a change order was do it fast. Even though you thought the price was a little high, it was cheaper to pay it than to let it ride because it got bigger and bigger the longer it took to figure it out, because they were adding interest on the money they didn't have and so forth. That in itself was probably illegal, but if you settle it soon, you don't pay that interest. And the contractor is entitled to have things settled quickly. He has to pay his people. He has to pay his bills for maintenance. He has to pay for materials. Certainly they pay the wages. He's entitled to it. If you go into it with that attitude and he knows that that's your attitude, he's likely to be more reasonable about his claims.

Paul Stillwell: That makes sense.

Captain Jackson: Yes.

Paul Stillwell: What was the Navy's work going on then at Quincy in that period?

Captain Jackson: Oh, big. One of the bigger things was the conversion of three T-2 tankers to range instrumentation ships, and that was a big job.* Then we built a destroyer

---

* In the conversions at Quincy the former tankers became the Vanguard (T-AGM-19) and Redstone (T-AGM-20), both of which went into service with the Military Sea Transportation Service in 1966.

tender up there. They had four submarines. Let's see, I guess that covers most of it. Had some repair work on ships that came in.

But that was funny. I had to go up there, and just as an example of some of the problems that they were facing, I went to stay at a hotel, and I went into the dining room. There was this big round table with a bunch of loud people around it. It was obvious that they'd all had too much to drink. In listening to it, I finally came to the conclusion they were the leaders of the unions, and they were having a meeting. The leader of the whole group meeting pounded on the table, and he said, "We broke Bethlehem Steel, and, by God, we'll break General Dynamics."[*]

I thought, "My God, what are these guys talking about? You put them out of business, and you have no jobs. Why do you want to do that?" But I wasn't about to enter into any argument with them, because they were all so intoxicated. But can you imagine responsible people talking like that? And say, "Hey, we've got a new shipyard here and things are going, and we'd better get on doing a good job and therefore we'll get more work, and we won't need to worry about being laid off."

Paul Stillwell: Sounds like a reasonable philosophy.

Captain Jackson: Well, it did to me. I had to chance to talk to those guys in a reasonable atmosphere, and I made that pitch. Didn't seem to make any sense because what they were worried about was how much power they had as union leaders. If all the people suffered that didn't make any difference.

Paul Stillwell: And if the company goes out of business, they do suffer.

Captain Jackson: Yes, but they would organize another union and start over.

Captain Jackson: What was involved in those range instrumentation ships? You were really converting a ship to a vastly different function than she was built for

---

[*] Bethlehem Steel had owned the Quincy yard before General Dynamics did.

Captain Jackson: Yes. First of all, we had to cut it in two and lengthen it out about 200 feet, so it made a much bigger ship. That was pretty straightforward, although we had to worry about the hull strength because it was now a longer ship. And we had to put in a bunch of very strong foundations to support the measuring devices to be sure that they didn't vibrate and so forth. They had to increase the accommodations, put in a bigger galley, more berthing, bigger supply rooms.

Paul Stillwell: Well, you had a lot of room with those oil tanks that weren't being used.

Captain Jackson: Well, that's for sure, but they weren't all usable. They had to put in a whole new bridge, because as a tanker the bridge was amidships, and now we were putting the instrumentation there so we had to build a new bridge up forward. But it was really a nice job for the shipyard. Had three of them. They were essentially all the same, but there were some minor differences particularly in the instrumentation so they could, depending on where they were, use a specific ship for that point.

Paul Stillwell: Were these for tracking missile tests?

Captain Jackson: Yes. And when I would go up there I would inspect the ship and see how they were coming. Once again, the program manager was an electronics specialist, and he knew very little about shipbuilding, so I tried to give him some guidance. I'd say, "Hey, Lou, you've got to do this and you've got to do that." It turned out that they'd done a good job, and we were getting ready for InSurv to come up. We had a minor sea trial a couple of days before InSurv, and we didn't do much real testing on the equipment. We just wanted to be sure she'd go to sea.

All the time I'd been after Lou saying, "Hey, what you want to do is be sure that the ship is clean. And by clean I mean submarine standards, and that means that everything is scrubbed, there's no loose paint, there's no dirty paint, all the decks are waxed and everything."

He said, "Oh, we can't do that. Costs a lot of money."

I said, "Lou, I won't say it's done until you do it."

So reluctantly he said, "Okay," and he got it done.

When InSurv came and it was over, the president of InSurv looked at it and inspected it very good, and then in his report he said, "This is the finest ship we've inspected ever." Old Lou took credit for it all, and I said, "Hey, Lou. It wouldn't have looked like that if I hadn't made you do it."

Paul Stillwell: Did he grudgingly agree with that?

Captain Jackson: Yes, he did.

Paul Stillwell: By then he was feeling good about it, I'm sure.

Captain Jackson: Yes, he thought it was great that he did it. On the sea trials I wanted to check it out to be sure that it was well built and so forth, and so I asked the captain if he would run with a beam sea to get some roll on the ship. He said, "Yeah, we'll do that." But he made a turn in a beam sea, and he got one roll and he came back on course. And so I said, "Hey, I thought you were going to let it roll a while."

He said, "Oh, that's enough. We see the hull rolls."

But also on the trials we had, believe it or not, hydro-elasticity in the steering system, just like we had on the Sacramento. I wanted to be sure that it would work, and I asked the company to back down as the specs required, that they should be backed down, and they refused to do it because we had this hydro-elasticity. So I put in a card and said, "Hey, it's unsat. Got to be fixed." That was about the only thing. We had a lot of minor cards, as you always do, and the shipyard cleaned them all up in a couple of days.

Hydro-elasticity was not uncommon in airplanes in the early days. They had horrible problems with that when they started using hydraulic controls. That's how the shipbuilders came to know about it. As we started getting bigger ships and so forth, we uncovered that. But if you understand the problem it's not difficult to take it out by adjusting the hydraulic circuit. Particularly from my experience on the Sacramento I knew how to do that, and I helped the company solve the problem.

Paul Stillwell: Those ships had MSTS crews, didn't they?*

Captain Jackson: Yes.

Paul Stillwell: Were they any different to work with than a naval crew?

Captain Jackson: Well, my experience would say that they're less interested in the ship. All they're interested in is running it. They don't care about any of the technical details. That's not true of everybody, but in general that's the case.

Paul Stillwell: Well, that example about the rolling would make your case.

Captain Jackson: Yes.

Paul Stillwell: Was there any concern about stability with those big antennas topside?

Captain Jackson: No because we knew what the stability was, and it was adequate. I wouldn't want to take it out in a hurricane in a beam sea, but from the kind of work they were expected to do it was perfectly adequate. The Russians had similar ships with the same kind of antennas.

Paul Stillwell: They're odd-looking ships.

Captain Jackson: They are that. One of them has gone out of commission now, and I think the other two are going to go out. I think that the reason that they're taking them out of commission is they can do the same kind of work from the satellites.

Paul Stillwell: I see.

---

* MSTS—Military Sea Transportation Service, a part of the Navy that operated ships for support functions. In some cases it chartered the ships, and it some cases it ran the ships directly with civil service mariners. In 1970 MSTS was renamed Military Sealift Command (MSC).

Captain Jackson: And the electronics of satellites have progressed to a point where they're pretty good.

Paul Stillwell: Well, you mentioned this large percentage of the Polaris fleet that you were putting out at EB during that period. What do you remember about those programs?

Captain Jackson: The pressure was on. Some of those were just major alterations so they could accommodate bigger missiles, and there were still a lot of new ships being put out also.

Paul Stillwell: Just going to Poseidon now?*

Captain Jackson: Yes. That was the move to that, and they needed bigger missile tubes, bigger compensating tanks, more electronics. The guidance system stayed about the same, although there were some minor guidance alts on those. But it was a very active time. And then we were putting out 637-class submarines at the same time. The Boat Company put me on report for being uncooperative. They went to the Secretary of the Navy and said I wasn't cooperating with them. He said, "Why?" and they said because I wouldn't agree that they could deliver seven submarines between Christmas and New Year's.

Paul Stillwell: And this is a claim they had made, that they could?

Captain Jackson: Yes. And what they were looking for was an excuse to delay the ships again, and so they said that if they could prove that I was uncooperative that that was the reason. I had to go down and talk to the Secretary of the Navy about why I was uncooperative. I explained the situation and said, "Shoot, they couldn't even deliver one

---

* The Poseidon C-3 ballistic missile, which had initially been designated Polaris B-3, was 34 feet long; 6 feet, 2 inches in diameter; and weighed about 65,000 pounds. It had a range of about 2,500 nautical miles. Flight tests began in August 1968. The first submarine to deploy with Poseidon was the James Madison (SSBN-627), which fired the first Poseidon C-3 in August 1970.

submarine between Christmas and New Year's." And that's true because they generally shut down at that time.*

Paul Stillwell: Sure. So what was the outcome of that one?

Captain Jackson: The ships were delayed. But it meant that they didn't get as much money for late delivery because they were running out of excuses why they did it.

Paul Stillwell: They were going to be delayed anyway, but they tried to blame it on you?

Captain Jackson: Sure. I was the government representative, so if they'd won the case that I caused the delay, then they could put a claim in against the government. With tongue in cheek they were saying that and they knew that they were wrong, and they knew that I knew that they were wrong.

Paul Stillwell: But they wanted to go through the drill.

Captain Jackson: Yes, on the basis that maybe it would stick.

Paul Stillwell: Well, you had been in that program from the very beginning and now coming in the late '60s is up to the end of the 41st boat, the Will Rogers.† Surely there were lessons learned and all sorts of things in the course of 41. What changes and progress did you see in that time?

Captain Jackson: Oh, the biggest change was the change in the missiles and I went from Polaris to the A-1s and then the A-2s—all that series—and then they went to Poseidons

---

* This occurred in 1967.
† USS Will Rogers (SSBN-659), the last Polaris submarine, was laid down 20 March 1965 at Electric Boat, launched 21 July 1966, and commissioned 1 April 1967.

and things.* They finally went to the last one, which were the big missiles that they were making for the Trident submarines.

Paul Stillwell: Well, just in terms of production techniques, too, I would think you had a very steep learning curve at the beginning, and after a while you mastered a lot of that.

Captain Jackson: Yes, it was, but you don't gain as much as everybody tries to make out. That's true if you have a production run where you're going to turn out a couple million units just alike, but if you've only got ten ships there'll be enough changes that come in there that you lose some of the benefit of that learning. You take advantages of it, but other things will come and cause you to delay the ship. I've got some curves that prove that and I use it in my course.

Paul Stillwell: What were the things you use in the course?

Captain Jackson: Oh, the curves showing the benefit of multi-production.

Paul Stillwell: I see. Well, one program that really took advantage of that was the Spruance destroyer program, where Ingalls built 31 of the same ship.†

Captain Jackson: Yes, but you'll find that there was a lot of difference between the 31st ship and the first one. And there's certainly difference between the first Polaris ship and the 41st.

Paul Stillwell: Any you can cite other than the change in the missiles?

---

* The first version of the submarine-launched Polaris ballistic missile, the A-1, was 28 feet long, 4 feet in diameter, and weighed about 30,000 pounds. It had a range of 1,200 nautical miles. The A-2 version was 31 feet long; 4 feet, 6 inches in diameter; and weighed about 30,000 pounds. It had a range of 1,725 nautical miles. The A-3 version was 32 feet long; 4 feet, 6 inches in diameter; and weighed about 35,000 pounds. It had a range of 2,880 nautical miles.
† USS Spruance (DD-963), lead ship of the class, was commissioned 20 September 1975.

Captain Jackson: Oh, the change in the size of the hull. And if you say the first one is the George Washington, then there are massive changes. Technology keeps running. You can't stop it. Somebody gets a good idea, and then everybody wants it.

Paul Stillwell: Still, that's a lot of ships to build in a ten-year period there.

Captain Jackson: It sure is. It sure is.

Paul Stillwell: How much was Admiral Rickover sticking his oar in at that point?

Captain Jackson: Oh, plenty. He used to come up every Friday night, particularly on the NR-1.* The boat company always had a bunch of sandwiches and stuff. He'd bring his troops in, and they'd have sandwiches while he reviewed what went on during the week. And he'd come back the next week, and I always sat in on those meetings.

Paul Stillwell: Anything to share from those meetings?

Captain Jackson: Well, they were generally pretty good. There was no question that he was running the meetings, and I think in a way they probably did some good. They would have turned out to be good ships even if he hadn't done that, or if he'd turned it over to some lower level.

Paul Stillwell: You can also compare it with what we've said about InSurv, that just the fact that he was coming probably made people do more to get ready.

Captain Jackson: Yes, that's for sure. Right.

---

* NR-1, a nuclear-powered, deep-submergence research and ocean-engineering vehicle was launched 25 January 1969 by the Electric Boat Division and delivered to the Navy on 27 October 1969. She is 140 feet long, has a beam of 12 feet, and displaces 400 tons submerged.

Paul Stillwell: One thing we were talking about at noon was the K-1 class.* Anything you would want to mention about those boats?

Captain Jackson: Well, the guy that drove that was named Benny Bass.† He was a captain on duty in OpNav, and what he was looking for was a small ship with good listening gear that he could put on station in the gap between England and Iceland and listen for any submarines coming through. While they had some defensive equipment, like torpedo tubes, it was not much. Their main purpose, if they located something coming through the gap, was they could alert the rest of the Navy to the fact that they were coming. They could do that job very well, but since they had to surface up there where it's pretty darn rough, that duty was not the best in the submarine force.

I knew a number of the captains that had them, and they were all enthusiastic about the boats, but they would have preferred to have something else. But they were good little ships. They did their job. The theory that they were going to be able to detect anything going through the gap proved false, that if you're going to do it you'd need many, many more submarines, and you'd need better sonar. So they were eventually turned into targets to train ASW forces.

Paul Stillwell: Well, please tell me as much as you're willing about the Scorpion case.

Captain Jackson: Well, I got into it because I really didn't want to retire from the Navy, and I certainly didn't want to retire from here. So I looked around to see what I could do, and I said I would like a tour of sea duty.

Paul Stillwell: What year is this, 1969?

Captain Jackson: Yes. I heard that this was going on there, and so I volunteered to go out

---

* USS K-1 (SSK-1) was commissioned 10 November 1951. On 15 December 1955 the submarine's name was changed to Barracuda and she retained her hull number. She had two sisters, K-2, renamed Bass, and K-3, renamed Bonita. They were designed for a hunter-killer antisubmarine role but were so deficient in speed, range, and endurance that they had short service lives.
† Captain Raymond H. Bass, USN.

and be an observer, and I was interested in salvage work. I was also interested to see if we could find out what happened to the Scorpion. So I was nominated to go on that expedition, and I was given an assistant to go along with me, an ED officer. Two candidates, one was Clark Sachse, and the other was Millard Firebaugh.* I didn't have much to do with the selection of it, but Clark Sachse was selected. We went out there together, and it was pretty good.

The purpose of going there was to find out what happened to the Scorpion. There was some difference of opinion between the operators and the technical people. We had some photographer people to make on-site analyses of pictures we took out there. We had an ordnance guy to look and see if the ship was sunk by ordnance. Then we had Clark and me, so there were six of us all told. We were called the on-site analysis team. I felt that we were the technical team.

So we prepared to go out there, and the Trieste was put in the White Sands and it was towed by the Apache, which was a big fleet tug. That was her permanent assignment, to tow the Trieste around. They came through the canal, stopped at Cape Canaveral, and then went on out to the Azores. Because I was going as a captain they felt that they should have a line officer captain go too. Bob Gauche was the squadron commander at that time out at Squadron One, so he went along. He and I were good friends, and he was engineer officer on the Tang when they pumped it up like a pregnant pussycat. I helped with the analysis, so that it really wasn't his fault as engineer.

Paul Stillwell: Had the Scorpion wreck been located before you went out on this expedition?

Captain Jackson: Oh, sure. We knew precisely where it was and the Mizar, which had found it, had dropped a transponder down there.† When we pinged it, we were sitting right on top of it, because we had a satellite system to locate our position. So we knew where we were, and we also knew where the Scorpion was. We sat right on top of it. That was

---

* Lieutenant Commander Clark D. Sachse, USN; Lieutenant Commander Millard S. Firebaugh, USN.
† USNS Mizar (T-AGOR-11) is an oceanographic research ship.

good. We also had all the pictures the Mizar took; there were many of them, and we tried to make some analyses from those pictures.

We did some, as it turned out, pretty good analysis on the first part. The first thing we had to do on the first trip with the Trieste was to survey the bottom. The Mizar had dropped three transponders in a triangular shape around the wreckage on the bottom. The Trieste went down and made operations where they'd pass through two buoys and measure the distance out to the others. They got in a straight line, because they got bearings; then they added up the distance between the two of them so they knew what the leg was. Then they did it on the other one. Now you've got three legs of a triangle, and you can mathematically lay out what you had. Then the next thing was to put inside that triangle where the major pieces of wreckage were.

So we had to first of all go survey that and where were they. Then we could put it in, and then we made a chart of all the known wreckage. Then the next thing was to go down and take pictures which related what you were taking on the bottom with the wreckage you had already identified so you got a better understanding of what was there. Then that took about, all told, five dives, and we only had nine dives to go through. Now we've got four.

Had a little bit of difference of opinion, because the operating crew thought it was a training exercise to train the operators. We thought that we were out there to find out what happened, so we made a great big sign, pasted it up around the ship, said, "The reason we're here is to find out what happened to the Scorpion." Some of the guys took it to heart. One of the operators became very much interested in what were doing about plotting all this stuff, and he got pretty proficient. Also the other guys said, "Well, hey, we've got to find out what's going on." So they did.

Got in real close to the ship. Got some pictures inside, which just because of the difficulty of taking pictures down there, they were incomplete. There was lots of structure and so forth that wasn't in the field of the camera so you could see something that indicated that there was something over here out of range that was very interesting. The thing that people don't realize—particularly the guy that writes derogatory reports about the Navy because they won't tell what happened to the Scorpion—don't realize that operating on the bottom of the ocean in over 10,000 feet is different than walking in the park. First of all, it's pretty damned dark down there, and you don't have much light. And what you do have is like a searchlight that you can train around, but then your field of view is very limited. Also, that the wreckage is all over the place, and it's very difficult to find the very piece that you're looking for.

Paul Stillwell: How large an area did it cover?

Captain Jackson: Oh, about three acres so it's pretty good. Also, the Trieste is a big vehicle, and it's hard to maneuver. Operating around wreckage like that is very, very dangerous. If you should bump into the wreckage and puncture the big gas tank, that's it. You're dead. So you very gingerly approach the wreckage, and you want to be damned sure you don't hit it. It's so light and it's aluminum, it doesn't take much of a bump to penetrate it.

Paul Stillwell: How did the buoyancy work on that thing? I mean, how were you able to go so deep?

Captain Jackson: Well, the buoyancy was provided by aviation gasoline, and it had big gas tanks. They'd fill it up, and so the only buoyancy you had was the difference in the weight of gasoline and the weight of seawater, which when you're at deeper depths is quite a bit. Most people think water is non-compressible, but it is compressible under extreme pressures. The normal seawater at the surface at reasonable temperatures like 50 degrees is only 64 pounds per cubic feet, but at the depth on the bottom of the Scorpion it's about 65.9. So you've got 1.9 pounds for every cubic foot increase, or decrease in buoyancy or increase in unit weight. Most people don't understand that.

Paul Stillwell: I didn't know it was possible.

Captain Jackson: So when you're going down because you're losing buoyancy you have to dump some weight, and that weight is little steel balls like BBs. They're in a big tank, and there's a magnetic clamp on the spout at the bottom of the tank. What you do is you magnetize all the steel balls, and they freeze. If you want the flow out, you take the magnet off and you dump the shot. What you want to be damned sure is that that magnet goes on and off when you want it to. Sometimes the steel balls want to rust up and make a big lump. If they get stuck in there, you've got major problems, so you do everything you can to ensure that there's no rusting.

When we started fueling the Trieste when we got out there, there was some debate whether we had aviation gasoline because aviation gasoline is colored, a bluish color, and that's so that all the mechanics and everyone knows when they're putting the right gas in the airplanes. Well, it had been in the tanks on the White Sands long enough so it wasn't blue anymore. It had all faded. The question is, "Gee, do we have aviation gasoline, or do we have regular gasoline?" It makes a big difference in the weight.

So we rigged up a little spring balance. The photographers had a little balance. We rigged that up and tried to measure the density, and then also we tried to make a given sized block of steel. We knew how much that weighed, and then we put it in to see what the difference in weight was. We did everything we could to ensure that that was good aviation gasoline, and we came to the conclusion it was. When we operated we found out it was good.

The data that we got was limited because it was such a task, and we were running out of time. The weather window had expired, and we could expect rather severe storms, and so it was deemed prudent to terminate there. So we went back into the Azores, and the Trieste prepared for the long run. They defueled the Trieste, and as soon as that was defueled they started on the way home. The rest of our task force flew home in an airplane. We made presentations to all the people who would listen or had authority to listen. We then went out to Pearl Harbor and briefed ComSubPac and the deep submergence squadron out there. So it was a lot of fun.

Paul Stillwell: How long did the project take?

Captain Jackson: Well, let's see. I reported in on it shortly after I was relieved as a supervisor, which was about the end of September. Then I stayed there until November. I was on that project till November, and I did an awful lot of traveling during that time so I was away from home a lot. Beck didn't really realize what I was doing. She thought I was just going out there to look at a bunch of wreckage, and it wasn't until I came back and told her about some of the things we did that she began to worry.

Paul Stillwell: What conclusions did you come to from all that?

Captain Jackson: Well, the conclusion I came to is that we didn't know what happened, and even at that we did an awful lot of study on the data that we brought back, all the pictures, all the sonar readings we had and so forth. There were so many things that could have happened that it was hard to sift out and say, "This is what did happen." We made all kinds of scenarios, and we got several different scenarios that would satisfy the same facts that we found.

Paul Stillwell: What were those?

Captain Jackson: Well, like where she was when she was lost. Where she broke up. How she broke up. The results of the failures. The sonar readings that we had. All of those things are related, and so you have to say, "Oh, I've got a scenario. This happened. And if it happened, would these things occur?"

People say, "Yeah, but how about this scenario, which is almost the same but some major differences?" Yeah, if all those things happened it would have been lost.

So which one do you select? You can't select either one of them. All you can say is, "Well, here's two scenarios, and anybody can take their pick." You wouldn't be any more conclusive than our pick so we say, "We don't know."

Paul Stillwell: What were the scenarios that you came up with?

Captain Jackson: Oh, well, one of them which I didn't come up with but John Craven feels absolutely certain that they had a hot run in a torpedo, and they ejected it, and it circled around and hit itself.* I don't believe that. Another scenario is that the crew just went to sleep, drove it down to collapse depth, and she sank. Doesn't sound right. Another one is that she was running heavy and had a reactor scram. That would cause you to sink. One that's been published is that they may have had flooding through the garbage ejector or trash ejector. That could have happened, but it's not completely supported by the facts that we know.

You can go throughout the ship, and you can get probably 75 or 100 different scenarios. Some of them don't fit the facts, and so you can discard them, but most of them can't be discarded on that basis because they could have happened. Highly unlikely, but it could have happened. So now these guys like the idiots that write in the big newspapers say, "Hey, you went down there, you looked, and we want you to tell exactly what happened. You guys know it, but you're just covering up and you won't tell us." That's ridiculous, absolutely ridiculous, and the unfortunate part is that the families of the people who know nothing about submarines or very little anyway believe it. They say, "Hey, you guys know exactly what happened, and you won't tell us."

Paul Stillwell: Well, now can we identify this offending person who's writing these things that get the families worked up?

Captain Jackson: Yes, Ed Offley. He was a reporter at the Norfolk—I think Norfolk Gazette. Now he's moved out west, and he's writing things out there. And all he's trying to do is make a name for himself by stirring up possibilities that are highly unlikely. They could have happened, but he's got a bug. He thinks that the Russians sank it, and there's no evidence of that whatsoever. The Navy has said that there were no Russian submarines in the vicinity, and I believe that. But it's very difficult, and any guy says that he can tell from the wreckage is perfectly welcome to go down there and take a look and find out.

Paul Stillwell: Now, what was the nature of the rejoinder you sent to the Naval Institute

---

* Craven's role with the search for the Scorpion is covered in Blind Man's Bluff. See also: John P. Craven, The Silent War: the Cold War Battle Beneath the Sea (New York: Simon & Schuster, 2001).

after we published an article on that?*

Captain Jackson: I got a nice letter back from them that said that they sent it to the review committee to see whether or not they would publish it.

Paul Stillwell: But what was the substance of what you wrote?

Captain Jackson: It was that this guy didn't know what he was talking about, and they never should have published the article. So I doubt if they'll do anything about it.

Paul Stillwell: Well, we shall see.

Captain Jackson: I wrote it directly at Hal's suggestion to the guy you were talking about that's going to retire.

Paul Stillwell: Captain Jim Barber.†

Captain Jackson: Yes, that's right. But it never got to him I know.

Paul Stillwell: No, it did. I can guarantee you because he mentioned that to me last week.

Captain Jackson: Oh, he did?

Paul Stillwell: When I told him I was coming up here, he said, "You'll probably hear about this." So I know it got to him.

Captain Jackson: Well, I was disappointed that they published that without, in my opinion,

---

* The article to which Captain Jackson objected was by Mark A. Bradley, "Why They Called Scorpion Scrapiron," U.S. Naval Institute Proceedings, July 1998, pages 30-38. Rebuttal came from Rear Admiral Robert R. Fountain in Proceedings, October 1998, pages 8, 10, 13.
† Captain James A. Barber, Jr., USN (Ret.), was chief executive officer of the U.S. Naval Institute from 1984 to 1999.

checking it out to see whether that guy knew what he was talking about. Hal was real upset.*

Paul Stillwell: That's what Captain Barber told me.

Captain Jackson: Well, he may have known about my interest and that I was going to write a letter, but I'm not sure that it got to him just from the way that the answer came back.

Paul Stillwell: I see.

Captain Jackson: I think somebody intercepted it.

Paul Stillwell: Typically things that are sent to him that fall into one of the specific areas, then he routes on to that area to provide the response.

Captain Jackson: Yes, I'm sure of that, but also I can see where it could have gone directly. The letter I got back indicated to me it was just a routine letter that they send out for things they don't want to publish.

Paul Stillwell: No, no, that's not true.

Captain Jackson: It isn't?

Paul Stillwell: Well, we'll see whether it gets printed.
    Well, anything else on that subject?

Captain Jackson: Well, yes. This guy completely ignored the fact that you had lots of energy in the ocean, and he said the only way that the damage that had been observed

---

* Admiral Shear vented his displeasure about the Scorpion article in a letter to the editor, published on page 24 of the January 1999 issue of U.S. Naval Institute Proceedings.

could be was from an explosion from the torpedo. So in my paper I made some calculations. I just used the data from a Russian submarine out of Jane's and when a submarine collapses, and the submarine I used was 4,000 tons surface condition, which is the one that counts, that there was something like 17 million foot-pounds of energy, which is the magnitude in which you measure atomic bombs. That's certainly a hell of a lot bigger than any weapon than you can shoot at a submarine. And you can't ignore that because it's there. If he goes deep enough to collapse, that's what happened, and it's obvious that he went deep enough to collapse. The big question is, "How did he get there?" and nobody knows. The Navy is not covering up anything, and I'm absolutely sure of that.

Paul Stillwell: Did you feel a sense of frustration that you weren't able to pinpoint an exact cause?

Captain Jackson: No, because I recognize the difficulties. We did come up with some clues, which sort of steered us to a scenario that probably was more likely than the others but certainly not very certain. Not enough information to say, "Yes, this is what happened."

Paul Stillwell: Are you willing to put the most likely scenario on the record?

Captain Jackson: No, and the reason for that is if it goes on the record and people read it they'll say, "Gee, there's a knowledgeable guy that says this is what happened, and that's what happened." I don't want to be put in that position, because I don't know what happened.

Paul Stillwell: I had to ask.

Captain Jackson: Okay. All right. I'm not trying to be obstinate, but—

Paul Stillwell: I understand what you're saying.

Captain Jackson: Yes. If I were like Offley with no experience and no connection, I could say, and somebody who did know would say, "He doesn't know what he's talking about."

Paul Stillwell: You had been commissioned in 1941. Why did you retire in 1969?

Captain Jackson: That's a good question. For reasons which I don't understand, I think the Navy thought that I had used all the things that I had to contribute, and that they really encouraged me to retire.

Paul Stillwell: But isn't a 30-year career standard for a captain, or wasn't it at that point?

Captain Jackson: Well, I had 34 years of service.

Paul Stillwell: Well, but commissioned service?

Captain Jackson: Yes. You can retire any time you want after 20.

Paul Stillwell: But did you have an option? Was another duty offered?

Captain Jackson: Yes, but one which I really didn't want to go to.

Paul Stillwell: What was that?

Captain Jackson: Well, it was go back to Washington and theoretically work on the design of the 688.[*]

Paul Stillwell: Why wouldn't you leap at an opportunity like that?

---

[*] USS Los Angeles (SSN-688) was commissioned on 13 November 1976 as the lead ship of a class of 39 nuclear-powered fast-attack submarines. They were followed in 1988 with the commissioning of the USS San Juan (SSN-751), lead ship of what is known as the "improved Los Angeles class."

Captain Jackson: Oh, the organization that had been created for it. I really felt we could do a better job than what had been established and already set.

Paul Stillwell: But mightn't you have had an opportunity to make a change to that if you'd stayed on active duty?

Captain Jackson: I don't think so. I don't think I had enough horsepower to do that.

Paul Stillwell: Who had the horsepower to get it set in the degree it was?

Captain Jackson: Rickover. Don Kern got killed because he proposed something different, which I think was much better.[*]

Paul Stillwell: Which was what?

Captain Jackson: Well, it came out under the name of a Conform design, but, really, what Don was talking about, was not that. That was just an example of what could be done, and Rickover took that as a threat to the design for the 688. So he crucified Don, really did. That had a big impact on me, and I said, "Gee, I don't want to put myself in the position of getting crucified like that."

Paul Stillwell: What happened to Kern?

Captain Jackson: Oh, man. He went to be shipyard commander up at Portsmouth, which if I'd stayed in the Navy, as it turned out, I would have had that job because Rickover wouldn't let Don have it, and I was an alternative. Rickover told the crews of the submarines up there, and he controlled them, to make Don's life miserable, and they did. They carried out their order to the T. That's too bad, too, because if Don had won the battle that he had with Rickover, we'd have a different Navy today and I think a better Navy.

---

[*] Captain Donald H. Kern, USN, an engineering duty officer.

Paul Stillwell: In what ways?

Captain Jackson: We'd have better submarines.

Paul Stillwell: What would be better about them?

Captain Jackson: Oh, more maneuverable, faster for the same horsepower that we had at that time, but now we've got better horsepower. The name of the game was to go fast, and Don proposed a Conform design. It was a fast submarine. Took advantage of all the things we had developed on the Albacore and the Barbel and the 637 class.

Paul Stillwell: Any specifics to mention of those characteristics?

Captain Jackson: Well, X-stern for one. A counter-rotation propeller. Used a Narwhal reactor, which was much quieter. Didn't have the big cooling pumps. The ship was smaller so it was more maneuverable. It had a better sonar, better quieting. Probably not better quieting than the 688 because she was smaller and more quiet. There's no question about that. The 688s are good if you want them to go fast in a straight line, but they're not very good if you want to maneuver.

Paul Stillwell: Was this conservatism on Rickover's part?

Captain Jackson: No. It was political.

Paul Stillwell: What do you mean political?

Captain Jackson: He didn't want to be threatened by somebody else getting credit for a good submarine. That's really what it boiled down to. And the things he did to Don just were terrible. Don's young son Bob was a lieutenant in the Navy and had been on a submarine. He was actually assigned on the ship as engineer officer, and he ran the power plant. It came time for him to go be interviewed, and he went in to go see the admiral, and the admiral said, "Your name Kern?"

"Yes, my name is Kern."

He said, "Get out of here." And that's just—and why? The kid was, he really was superb. He was outstanding.

Paul Stillwell: What happened to him?

Captain Jackson: Oh, he resigned from the Navy, and he now is a chief engineer of Raytheon's big sonar works up in Portsmouth, Rhode Island. He's doing a good job, and actually he's probably doing more good for the Navy there than he would if he'd stayed in, but he suffered because the old man had done a good job.

Paul Stillwell: Well, are you saying that if you had stayed in you would have taken Kern's place or you were likely to?

Captain Jackson: It's possible that I would have.

Paul Stillwell: Do you regret that you didn't get to command that shipyard?

Captain Jackson: No, because I would have had the same kind of problems that Don had.

Paul Stillwell: He would have been as vindictive toward you?

Captain Jackson: I think so. It's a strange atmosphere when you get up in the upper echelons.

Paul Stillwell: Well, it's unhappy to conclude a career on that kind of a note.

Captain Jackson: Well, it happened so don't dwell on it. Just get on. Tomorrow we'll talk about my career after retirement, which is every bit as exciting as my Navy career.

Paul Stillwell: Okay, I'll look forward to that.

Interview Number 3 with Captain Harry A. Jackson, U.S. Navy (Retired)

Place: Captain Jackson's home, Groton, Connecticut

Date: Thursday, 3 September 1998

Interviewer: Paul Stillwell

Paul Stillwell: Well, Captain, it's a delight to see you again today, and we're ready to resume the story of your life. I believe you wanted to go back to your high school years to add a postscript from what we've discussed about that already.

Captain Jackson: In reflecting back on the high school days and subsequent things that happened, I realized that our class and other classes of the same period had an unusual number of very successful graduates. I pondered on this as to the reasons why did it happen, and there was obviously no clear-cut answer.

    I discussed the thing with my acquaintances in the Navy that had gone to school in the same period and asked them if they had experienced the same phenomenon. There was an unusual number of people who said the same thing, and we talked about it. I finally came to the conclusion that one of the reasons that there were so many achievers is that the kids at that time had to struggle very hard—sometimes even for survival, but they certainly had to struggle to get an education. This carried on in their later life, and they used the experience of struggling to further their activities and achievements in the world. This was true of all the various occupations that these people went to. There was no one group that excelled over the others. It was sort of universal. There's not much good that comes of a Depression, but like everything else, there always is some good, and I'd like to pass that on to whoever might read it.

Paul Stillwell: That was the generation that fought World War II and brought it through to victory.[*]

---

[*] See Tom Brokaw, The Greatest Generation (New York: Random House, 1998).

Captain Jackson: Yes, sir.

Paul Stillwell: Well, anything more to catch up on your Navy career? We got just about to the point of retirement yesterday.

Captain Jackson: Well, there are lots of minor incidents that went along, and each one of them has a lesson to be learned from. In general, the lesson that I learned is that if you're going to develop and use something, if it's a component in a ship or even the ship itself, you must do the very best you can. You have to test things thoroughly. You have to take every precaution that you can to ensure that it will do its job. It's not enough to do a good job, and then when it's done walk away and forget it. You have to go back and review and observe how it's operating. That last part is frequently missed, because the job is really not done until the unit has reached its useful life and been discarded.

Paul Stillwell: What struck me as remarkable is that a lot of us take a while to find our niche in life and decide what we want to be when we grow up. And yet from your boyhood you had an interest in submarines, and even making the model of the S-4 that sank, and then years and years later you wound up your active career diving on a sunken submarine in the Scorpion, so your path was set very early.

Captain Jackson: Yes. I suppose there was some sort of connection between the two of them.

Paul Stillwell: Well, you had been involved with the Navy since your days back in Michigan, and then in 1969 it came time for you to retire. How did you start on the new phase of your life?

Captain Jackson: Well, I reflected on what I'd done and also what I wanted to do. I really wanted to put into motion something that would allow me to take advantage of all that stuff that I had learned in the Navy. And I was particularly desirous to pass that on to the younger folks coming up. But my philosophy was that I didn't want to work for anybody, and I didn't want anybody to work for me. I'd had enough problems with employees and subordinates and so forth that I said I'd just like to not have to be bothered with that aspect. It was difficult to find a job doing that. It just didn't pan out.

Paul Stillwell: Did you have in mind some sort of consulting work, for example?

Captain Jackson: Well, that's what I ended up doing, but there were a couple of trials and errors in between. I worked for a little company that was trying to develop a waste disposal organization, and their management was inadequate for what they were trying to do, and I left it shortly after. Just as I left them, I got a call from Admiral Smith, and he asked me if I would be interested in helping the Special Projects Office in the development of the Trident missile system.*

Paul Stillwell: This would be Levering Smith.†

Captain Jackson: Levering Smith, yes, sir. I said, "Sure, if you can use my talents, I'm ready."

Paul Stillwell: If you had to work for somebody, he was a good one to work with.

Captain Jackson: No one any better. But I really didn't work for him as a daily boss. I had pretty much of a free hand. What we did do was look at an alternative to the big Trident submarines, and we came up with one that was considerably smaller and would have been cheaper, but the politics in Washington was such that our study was locked up in a closet, and for all I know it may still be there.

Paul Stillwell: How far did you get on the development of it?

---

* The Trident submarine-launched ballistic missile entered the fleet in 1979; the USS Francis Scott Key (SSBN-657) began the first deterrent patrol with Trident in October of that year. The first submarines specifically designed for Trident constituted the Ohio (SSBN-726) class; the Ohio was commissioned 11 November 1981. The first version of the Trident missile, the C-4, was 34 feet long, 74 inches in diameter, and weighed about 65,000 pounds. It had a range of approximately 4,000 nautical miles.
† Rear Admiral Levering Smith, USN, Director Strategic Systems Project Office, Naval Material Command.

Captain Jackson: Well, we had what I considered a well-balanced conceptual design, and we could have departed on that to a contract design and proceeded at a good rate.

Paul Stillwell: How did it compare in size with the eventual Ohio class?

Captain Jackson: It had the same number of missiles, same size missiles, but it was pretty near 7,000 tons lighter.

Paul Stillwell: The Ohio was what, about 18,000 tons?

Captain Jackson: Eighteen thousand tons, yes.

Paul Stillwell: That's a considerable difference.

Captain Jackson: Yes, particularly when you buy them by the pound.

Paul Stillwell: How were you able to make your design so much smaller and still achieve the same function?

Captain Jackson: Ingenuity. The Polaris boats had vertical missile tubes that went from the top of the hull to the bottom of the hull, and they acted as big heavy struts. When you have a circular hull pressurized to a sea pressure all the way around, it wants to deform. If two struts are put in there, it doesn't let it deform in that direction, so it makes excessively high bending moments where you don't have struts. Therefore the structure has to be very, very heavy out there, and the penetrations of the tubes of the hull have to be very heavy. If you come up with a design that is such that the tubes don't take any stress vertically, all that bending moment is eliminated, and when you do that, lots and lots of weight is reduced. The way that was accomplished, we put a smaller diameter hull in there, and we put like a big pot down on the bottom and let the missile go into the pot. Then the tube also went into that pot, and it could go up and down with the deflection of the hull.

Later on I found out that that's what the Russians did, and when they tell me the Russians are backwards and they don't know what they're doing, I say, "Yeah, just like Timoshenko, who was the greatest structural engineer that the world has seen."* But they were pretty smart, the Russians.

Paul Stillwell: You attributed this to politics. What specifically kept your design from moving forward?

Captain Jackson: Certain philosophies had already been decided upon that they were going to have them. So there was great opposition to anything that was a threat to what had been started on the Trident.

Paul Stillwell: Who came up with the design that was actually built?

Captain Jackson: Well, that was a NavSea design.† They made the concept design, and EB did all the detail design.

Paul Stillwell: What do you remember specifically about contacts with Admiral Smith during that period?

Captain Jackson: Well, I had worked for him when we developed the Polaris system, so we knew each other pretty well. He was a great person. Admiral Raborn also was a great

---

* Stephen P. Timoshenko was born in 1878 in Russia. After being educated as an engineer he worked both in private industry and in teaching positions at the University of Michigan and Stanford University. He is considered to be as the father of engineering mechanics.
† In 1966 the material bureaus were abolished. Under the new setup the Bureau of Ships became the Naval Ship Systems Command (NavShips). In 1974 the Naval Ordnance Systems Command (NavOrd) was merged with the Naval Ship Systems Command to form the Naval Sea Systems Command (NavSea), which exists to the present.

person. He was not much of an engineer, but he was a leader of people. He could get things done. Admiral Rickover could get things done, too, but he generally achieved his things through fear. If people didn't do something right, he'd discipline them. In Rickover's case the people didn't want to be disciplined. They would do a good job. They'd work hard. But Raborn in a very mild way could say, "I want this done," and people would go charging off to do it, and there was no hollering or shouting or anything like that. It just was a way of life. You'd say, "Hey, the boss wants it. Let's go."

Paul Stillwell: What can you say about Levering Smith's personality and his managerial style?

Captain Jackson: Well, I never thought about is as being much different than Raborn's.

Paul Stillwell: I got the impression he wasn't as flashy as Raborn.

Captain Jackson: Oh, no. He was not. He was steady Eddie. And he was very thorough in his thinking and his planning. He was very intelligent, he was a hard worker, and he was a good administrator.

Paul Stillwell: Do you have any examples of his administrative style?

Captain Jackson: Well, at the time I considered it to be pretty standard. He had all of his department heads lined up, and they had meetings about once a week that we would go to. Everybody had an opportunity to speak up and express their opinions, and he considered them all. After he had considered them to the extent that he wanted to, he would make a decision and say, "Okay, we'll do it this way."

Paul Stillwell: Was he the kind of man who inspired a great deal of loyalty?

Captain Jackson: Oh, yes. Absolutely. People loved him. Same way with Raborn. Very loyal.

Paul Stillwell: I've heard Levering Smith described as a scientist in uniform.

Captain Jackson: Oh. Well, there's lots of those and depends on what you imagine a scientist is. But you can say there are lots of engineers in uniform. You can say there are lots of businessmen in uniform, the Supply Corps guys. Yes, you could say that about anyone. Admiral Smith did fit that description. There's no question about it.

Paul Stillwell: Did you feel a sense of frustration that you had what you considered a superior product that just got shunted aside?

Captain Jackson: No, I accepted it as a fact of life. I had the benefit that what we came up with was a good job, and the Trident was a good submarine too. You can't fault it because it was built. We built 20 Tridents, and they have been all successful, so how can you fault it? The Trident program built its foundation on Polaris. There's a lot of similarity between the two ships, a lot of the same philosophy. The reason that we looked at something different was mostly for economy. You know, could we make it cheaper?

Paul Stillwell: Because they are very expensive submarines.

Captain Jackson: Oh, yes. If you can save a few million dollars on each submarine, it mounts up to a big number.

Paul Stillwell: Sure.

Captain Jackson: The guys that were working on that called the design "Captain Jackson's Neat Ship."

Paul Stillwell: One thing that's interesting to contemplate, of course, is that there was a great motivator when Polaris was being developed in that that was the height of the Cold

War, and now the Cold War has gone away. I wonder what motivates the submariners to go out on those long patrols month after month.

Captain Jackson: Well, one thing it does, and it's hard for people who have never tried it to understand, is the guys like it. It's a good way of life. They like the homecomings that they come back to and the relationships that they have when they are off duty or off patrol. They also realize that they are a barrier to future attack and so forth. They stand out there and know that if anybody should attack the United States, they're ready to defend it, and they're right on the firing line. So I personally understand why they do it, and if I were younger and had the opportunity I would so the same thing.

Paul Stillwell: You talk about the relationships when they're off patrol. They must develop good relationships when they're on patrol as well and enjoy those.

Captain Jackson: Oh, sure. The relationships on the ship or any ship you're on, you get attached to your shipmates, and particularly in the submarine business, because you know that your life might depend on the action of your shipmates. Everybody has the same feeling and says, "You know, gee, I've got to do the very best I can, because I might be the guy they call on for the heroic action."

Paul Stillwell: The basing of those Tridents is at Kings Bay and Bangor.* What can you say about the development of those bases and of the qualities they bring?

Captain Jackson: Well, it's part of a massive change in management of the armed forces. It's certainly good, because those two bases turned out to be new facilities with all new equipment and so forth. They were built for the primary purpose of supporting the Trident submarines. Most people think the facilities they have there are superb, and I do too. As a matter of fact, I think it some cases they went overboard.

---

* The East Coast base for the Trident submarines is at Kings Bay, Georgia. For a description of the West Coast SSBN base at Bangor, Washington, see Jim Davis, "Building the Tridents' Home," U.S. Naval Institute Proceedings, March 1979, pages 62-73.

Paul Stillwell: In what ways?

Captain Jackson: Well, they made them too fancy, and some of the things are better than necessary, I think, the quarters and the barracks and so forth. But they have superb capability, and that capability is directed right at the maintenance of those big ships.

Paul Stillwell: But you could argue that those ancillary things contribute to what we were talking about, about men enjoying the job.

Captain Jackson: Yes, I guess you can.

Paul Stillwell: From the hindsight of the years since then, what would be your assessment of Admiral Rickover's overall legacy?

Captain Jackson: Well, the legacy takes many forms. Some of them are very good and others are not so good. He certainly established the rules that are carried out which have ensured that there's been adequate safety in the operation of the biggest collection of nuclear reactors in the world. It's been 50 years since we've started, and we've never had a major incident. Other navies have, and the commercial world is notorious for the ones that they have. That particularly in the beginning took a very strong will to say we've got to ensure that we will never have an incident because you just couldn't stand it. If you did, there'd be such a hue and cry they'd say do away with nuclear power in the Navy.

Paul Stillwell: Imagine if there had been a U.S. Navy equivalent of Chernobyl, for example.[*]

Captain Jackson: Yes, they would shut it down right away, quickly. You couldn't operate in any port worldwide, and if you couldn't come to port you wouldn't be much good. But

---

[*] On 24 April 1986 the power station at Chernobyl, near Kiev in the Soviet Union, suffered an explosion and fire in the graphite core of one of its four nuclear reactors. The accident released radioactivity that spread over the Soviet Union, Europe, and Scandinavia.

I think that's one legacy and it's a very good one. Some of his management methods have left some legacies, which the Navy is suffering from right now, which are bad.

Captain Jackson: What would you cite in that regard?

Captain Jackson: Well, the absolute control that the nuclear power people have over the submarines: in the development, building, the operations, and now the demobilization of them. That's a big problem.

Paul Stillwell: How do you see it being done differently and better in other ways?

Captain Jackson: Oh, I'm not sure there is any better way. I know that there's been a great deal of thought put into what we're going to do, and there's also a lot of thought of what we can do in the future, but it doesn't look like there's any quick solution. In the meantime, they're just storing the spent fuel in the desert, waiting till they can develop a way for disposal, but that's a tough problem.

Paul Stillwell: Do you see any negative effects from the fact that Admiral Rickover stayed on active duty as long as he did?

Captain Jackson: I had a close association with him through most of my naval career, and in the early days he was pretty good. He was eccentric, he was demanding, and all those things, but he still had a sense of humor. He was, I felt, a really likable person, although he did have some enemies. But as time passed and he got more and more popularity, the mystical description or the general opinion of people was that he was an outstanding individual but also somebody superhuman. In my opinion he got drunk with power.

Paul Stillwell: He certainly got entrenched.

Captain Jackson: He did that, and I think that was bad. Now, whether he stayed too long or not depends on how you look at his achievements. I think that if he had left after the first developments of the nuclear submarines and rested on his laurels, he'd be a very, very famous person and I think rightfully so. But some of the things he did when he was in his later years I couldn't condone at all.

Paul Stillwell: Such as?

Captain Jackson: Well, when he would throw tirades. He was very, very vindictive to people that he felt had crossed him, and his idea of being crossed was when the guys didn't have the same idea he had, and he wouldn't debate it. He just said, "Hey, that's the way it is. Get out of here." At any rate, to answer your question, there is no answer to it. My personal opinion is that the Navy would have been better off had he left at a normal time, at the end of 30 years' service or so.

Paul Stillwell: One downside that comes with that is that you don't know what possibilities might have been in the alternatives. For example, if Admiral Moore had been able to take over the program, maybe he would have been able to bring some innovation to it that Admiral Rickover would have probably stifled.

Captain Jackson: Yes. I think that's a possibility, but you'll never know.

Paul Stillwell: You'll never know.

Captain Jackson: And certainly Rickover blocked the advancement of a lot of very capable and good people.

Paul Stillwell: Well, and even some of the early ones that were in the program, such as Miles Libbey, Roddis, and Dunford.

Captain Jackson: Yes.

Paul Stillwell: They had to get out to achieve their destiny.

Captain Jackson: Yes, they did. And too bad too.

Paul Stillwell: You talked about the alternative to the Trident. What other things were you involved in as you embarked on your post-retirement career?

Captain Jackson: Well, Admiral Raborn got to be, quote, a consultant as well. He did it right. When he reached retirement for admirals, he retired, but he didn't want to really give up either. He was young or relatively young and energetic and so forth, and so he went around to several of the companies and said, "Hey, if there's any way I can help I'll be willing to."* And because of his stature a lot of people took him aboard as a consultant.

Admiral Smith had asked Raborn to come back and be a consultant at Special Projects. So I came back to help Admiral Smith, and Admiral Raborn and I shared an office down there, and so I got to know him even better than I had known him before. After a while, as he was consulting for these companies, he said they ought to hire me as a consultant, which they did. So I consulted with Lockheed and Hughes Tool in the electronics division with the big things. I'd have to go through the list of them, because he was very active, and so I had more consulting work than I almost could handle. Very lucrative. I made more money consulting like that than I could have made working for anybody.

Paul Stillwell: And certainly more than if you'd stayed on active duty.

Captain Jackson: Oh. Active duty wouldn't even have paid the taxes.

Paul Stillwell: You said you got to know him better. What observations do you have from that period?

Captain Jackson: Oh, a very human person.

---

* Vice Admiral William F. Raborn, Jr., USN, retired from active duty in September 1963 at the age of 58. He subsequently returned to active duty and served as Director of the Central Intelligence Agency from 28 April 1965 to 30 June 1966.

Paul Stillwell: What examples do you remember?

Captain Jackson: Well, we traveled a lot together, just the two of us, and we stayed in the same hotel and ate our meals together and all that. He was in some respects a surrogate father to me. He was some guy I could look up to, you know, and associate with. And I think he was genuinely fond of me—at least he appeared to be. One evening when we were having dinner I asked him about the PERT system, and one of the questions I asked him was, "Why didn't we use the PERT system as it was developed?"

He said, "Well, I wanted to run the SP program, and I didn't want a lot of help. I needed something that I could point to and say, 'Hey, I'm managing this thing very well.'" He said, "I just wanted a management system that I could demonstrate."

So he started out, and we actually used it a little bit to start with, and so that helped development. But all the shipyards and the missile concerns and everyone had their own way of doing business, and they had their own way of keeping track of their progress and their expenses and everything. I don't know whether they actually resisted using the PERT system or not, but they at least paralleled it with their regular system, and that's the one they used. Admiral Raborn had a meeting generally once a week, but sometimes some weeks were missed, in which he brought representatives from all the activities together to report on what they were doing and discuss what was happening.

I went to quite a few of those meetings, and PERT was one of the things that was discussed. Well, in order to assure everybody that he was managing the system okay he made a great show of PERT, and particularly to McNamara, who was the Secretary of Defense at that time. Mr. McNamara observed and looked at this thing, and he said, "Boy, that's great. It's not only great for SP, but it ought to be great for everything." So McNamara started trying to sell it to the Air Force and the Army and the Marine Corps and stuff like that.

PERT really didn't fit in everything. If you had a big project like SP, it would fit all right, but you couldn't run the whole Army with PERT. Anyway, they kept up the PERT for several years, but it got less and less attention as time passed, and they fell back to what you might call the standard ways of running business. Anyway, that was his story.

He says it was not a scam, but it was—the reason it was built was not to manage the SP but to demonstrate to other people that it was under control.

Paul Stillwell: What other kinds of things did he tell you when he let his hair down?

Captain Jackson: Well, he told me a lot about his family and his growing up. He told me about one thing when he was learning to fly. In those days the airplanes had retractable wheels, and there were retracted by cranking a big lever and manually lifting the wheels up or extending them. One day that he was up there flying and making practice landings he landed all right, but the plane didn't behave right, and it tipped over and it was upside down. And when the rescue people went out there, the wheels were slowly being cranked up.

Paul Stillwell: From inside?

Captain Jackson: From inside. And he told that on himself, you know, not as a good sea story.

Paul Stillwell: Well, I guess what I'm asking is what was his personality like when he wasn't putting on a show in public as he did throughout Polaris?

Captain Jackson: Oh, when it was just the two of us, as I say, it was sort of like a father-and-son relationship. And he gave me a lot of good advice on what to do.

Paul Stillwell: Well, it sounds like he took good care of you, too, helping you get these consulting jobs.

Captain Jackson: Oh, he did, no question about it.

Paul Stillwell: What do you remember from working for some of these specific companies? What projects were you involved in?

Captain Jackson: Well, the Neat Ship was done out at Lockheed, so that was one of my consulting jobs.

Paul Stillwell: Well, please tell me about that.

Captain Jackson: Oh, I did. That's the one that, the small Trident.

Paul Stillwell: Oh, okay, that's what it was called. All right.

Captain Jackson: Yes, Captain Jackson's Neat Ship.

Paul Stillwell: What were some of the others?

Captain Jackson: Well, Hughes was working on a lot of electronic stuff to put on a submarine, and I worked on the interface of that and the submarine. That was a good job. They had big antennas. But, like most of those things, they do a lot of development work, and then it's never used. I think that's one of the big deficiencies of our Defense Department. They waste an awful lot of money like that.

Paul Stillwell: Well, but this was kind of a standard way of doing business—like with airplane companies there'd be two or three competitors and then a fly-off to decide which one was the best.

Captain Jackson: Yes. And that's being forced on the Navy right now too. It just shows my elderly status in life that I have reservations about what's going on in that regard. We're being forced to build submarines like they build airplanes, and they're vastly different.

Paul Stillwell: Any specifics you want to mention in that regard?

Captain Jackson: Well, there now is coming into use that a prototype submarine is built and taken out to sea and modify any deficiencies or something and correct it. Then you could build a whole big production line, like 30 or 40 of them. And what was proposed is that on the new SSN they would build one what they call prototype. And once that's settled down, then they would build 30 of them at the rate of one a year. So for 30 years you don't make any changes and technology's moving too darn fast, because take 30 years ago, we put out good ships like that, but you'd never build one like that today because we know how to do it so much better. But that's the Air Force philosophy. In my opinion it doesn't match. It doesn't match with the problem. If you're going to say you're going to build several prototypes and go through them and then build 50,000 airplanes or 50,000 submarines, great. But they're so big and expensive that we're really only building them one at a time.

Paul Stillwell: What is your assessment of the SSN-21, the Seawolf?*

Captain Jackson: Well, it's a superb submarine. There's no question about that. It really is. But you ask yourself, "What is it supposed to do?" The operators are greatly thrilled about the fact that it will go fast and quiet in a straight line, and that's good if you want to go in a straight line. But as soon as you start maneuvering, you find that because it's such a big ship it doesn't maneuver like, let's take the 637 class, which are considerably smaller.

So everything is a compromise in submarine design. Sometimes you have to give up something in order to improve something else. So someplace along you've got to make up your mind what you want it to do. A few years ago they had as the philosophy for the submarine force that everything was they called "from the sea", and to come "from the sea" to the land. That says that you've got to take these ships to run them in shallow water in hazardous conditions, and on paper it sounds pretty good. But if you have a ship that's

---

* USS Seawolf (SSN-21), the first of a two-ship class of nuclear-powered attack submarines, was commissioned 19 July 1997. She displaces 7,460 tons surfaced and 9,137 tons submerged. The ship is 353 feet long, 40 feet in the beam, and has a maximum draft of 36 feet. Her top speed on the surface is 15 knots; top speed submerged is 35 knots. The submarine is armed with Tomahawk missiles and has eight 26½-inch torpedo tubes.

not very maneuverable and you go in shallow water, there's a chance of running around, chance of running into things. It's another world.

So you have to think about how you want to use your equipment before you really start to lay it out. That's very important. My feeling is—and I should probably acknowledge that I really don't know what's going on these days—that if you're really going inshore, the last thing you want to do is to send your most expensive vehicle in harm's way. You ought to have quote expendable submarines. Take the landing craft of World War II. We built millions of them because they were expendable. They were built cheap. They did their job, but it was recognized that the attrition rate was going to be terrific, and it was. If you're going to have submarines fighting in the same environment, do you want your most expensive submarines to do it? I don't know. That's for the DoD or the Congress or somebody to decide that. But in my opinion that's not the way I'd do it.

Paul Stillwell: Your way of doing it, I take it, would be to have a larger number of smaller, less expensive submarines.

Captain Jackson: In general. But there's a place for those big submarines, and the place changes with the world conditions. When the Russians had a huge big submarine fleet, and it operated in the open ocean, then the big submarine's high speed and stealth was very important. But right now the Russians don't have a big fleet. Whether they ever will again I don't know, and I don't think anybody knows, particularly our lawmakers.

But I look at what's happening in Russia right now, and I liken that to what happened to Germany, that they pulled themselves out by becoming warmongers, and we ended up with the most horrible war that the world ever saw. I hope it doesn't happen with Russia or some other European countries, but it could. There's certainly more war going on now in the whole world than at any other peacetime if you can call it peacetime. Africa, Central Europe, Mideast, China, Asia, all over the world people fighting each other and developing weapons of mass destruction. So if you're prudent you'll keep all your bases covered, but I don't think we're doing that.

Captain Jackson: How would you do things differently?

Captain Jackson: Well, if you don't have any responsibility, it's easy. You can suggest all kinds of things whether they're practical or not. But I would look at some smaller alternative submarines. I would re-look at some of the air-independent submarines that the foreigners have developed. They're pretty good.

Paul Stillwell: By that you mean diesel submarines?

Captain Jackson: Well, no, they all have a diesel engine as a primary source, but they have other ways of operating so they can stay submerged for two weeks and things like that. They're pretty good little submarines, and they'd be effective. They're also relatively cheap. Wouldn't put them in the expendable category unless the situation demanded it, but I would at least consider those and take a look at it. There was an article in the New London Day this morning that said that the Navy needs more and larger nuclear submarines. I would challenge that. We've got lots of good submarines that we're scrapping, cutting them up in little pieces. If we need more, that's one place to get them pretty cheap.

Paul Stillwell: Not cut them up.

Captain Jackson: Yes. You save all that money.

Paul Stillwell: Well, I think the 688s are already going that way. Have done.

Captain Jackson: Right. And the 637 class, only two left, and both of them are excellent ships. I went down to the decommissioning of one just about two or three weeks ago and I went through the ship. It was beautiful. All cleaned up, polished and everything worked. I asked them what their out-of-commission list was and they said, "We don't have one."

Paul Stillwell: What ship was that?

Captain Jackson: That's what I'm trying to think. It was one of the later 637s—a good ship.

Paul Stillwell: Well, it would be interesting if the United States got into a new family of nonnuclear submarines in developing a training program, because we don't now have crews to run such ships.

Captain Jackson: Yes, but that wouldn't be hard. You could train them up pretty fast, I think. Did in World War II. We were training crews in three months at a steady rate. As a matter of fact, we were training crews faster than they could build submarines, which was a terrific rate. People that are in charge now, some of them weren't even born in World War II, and so it's very difficult for them to visualize what was done. When the war started—oh, back in '39, even before it—they asked Portsmouth Navy Yard if they could increase their rate of production, and they were turning out one submarine a year, in that order. Not every year did they turn out one but in that order.

After great deliberation they said, "Well, we could probably gear up, and we could perhaps make two a year." It was only about three years later when they delivered 52 submarines in one year. That's one a week. So when the chips were down, they measured up and they did all kinds of things to ensure that they could do that. And, of course, one of the things is that they increased their manpower supply by letting women work. And the women of the world, or at least the United States, did a really superb job during the war, and unfortunately I don't think they get the proper credit. They keep talking about Rosie the Riveter, I guess, just because that's a nice slogan.* But there were so many others that made the system go. There were welders. There were shipfitters. There were carpenters. There were pipe fitters. And obviously there were office workers. That almost doubled our manpower supply overnight when they just said, "We'll let the women work." Not ask them to work, just let them.

---

* Redd Evans and John Jacob Loeb created the popular song "Rosie the Riveter" (New York: Paramount Music Corp., 1942) to celebrate the contributions of women in the wartime work force.

Paul Stillwell: For many years I thought that Rosie the Riveter was kind of a hypothetical artificial term, but I think it was last year I saw in the newspaper the obituary for the woman who actually was Rosie the Riveter. Some photographer had been going around taking shots of women war workers, and he found the riveter and her name was Rosie. Another observation is that blacks were able to enter the work force in that era where they were denied previously.

Captain Jackson: Yes.

Captain Jackson: Well, in your consulting work was Electric Boat also one of the firms you were working for?

Captain Jackson: No, I was by law prohibited from working for them because I had been the supervisor of shipbuilding. They said, "You can't go there." As a matter of fact, I felt that was a pretty good law. It has been changed by now. There are so many people who got assigned to jobs like the supervisor's office with the idea that they would get a good job from the company, and therefore they weren't as strict as they should have been. So I felt it was wrong.

Paul Stillwell: How long did that prohibition last? Is that a lifetime ban on you working with them?

Captain Jackson: No, it was relieved. As a matter of fact, a couple of guys that were supervisors went to work directly for Electric Boat Company, right after retiring from the Navy.

Paul Stillwell: But I mean was there some period of time in your case that you would have been allowed to go back had you wanted to?

Captain Jackson: Oh, I guess so. By that time, though, I was getting pretty old, and I'm sure EB wouldn't have any interest. Well, to get on with the story, when the Jennifer

Project—that name's been declassified now—went into effect I was asked if I wanted to work on that, and the reason that they asked me is my experience on the Scorpion. I sort of jumped at the chance, because it certainly sounded like an interesting project.

Paul Stillwell: In this case we're talking about a Soviet Golf-class submarine that was lost in the Pacific.*

Captain Jackson: Yes, that's right. But the cover story also was very interesting. The cover story was that you're going to develop a system to mine the manganese nodules from the bottom of the ocean. And it so happened that Hughes had already invested a lot of money in that, and also Tenneco was investigating the possibility of mining the ocean.

Paul Stillwell: When did this first come to you as a project?

Captain Jackson: About '71, end of '71. So there was a lot of secrecy on that, and the Hughes Company had—under the direction, I guess, of Howard Hughes—had their own security, which was in my opinion tighter than the government's. And the people that I contacted in there were really paranoid about everything. When I was associated with it there had been some studies made, preliminary studies and so forth, but I got there in time to influence some of the design on the big ship. And one of the areas, specific areas, that I was working on was on the stability of the ship, which was a tough problem.

Paul Stillwell: You're talking about the Glomar Explorer.

Captain Jackson: The Glomar Explorer, right. And then the hull compensating system. I was able to make some contributions on that. Eventually it turned out that the method we

---

* The Glomar Explorer, a ship with a large concealed opening in the bottom, was built for operation by the Central Intelligence Agency for the purpose of recovering a Soviet submarine. The Golf-class diesel-powered ballistic missile submarine sank 750 miles northwest of Oahu, Hawaii, in 1968. In August 1974 CIA technicians raised the submarine about halfway to the surface from a depth of three miles. The submarine then broke apart and fell back to the ocean floor. Word of the operation became public in February and March 1975 as a result of news media reports.

used to compensate the rise and fall of the big tower was the same one we used in submarines as a resonance changer, so I understood that one pretty well.

Paul Stillwell: What does that mean, a resonance changer?

Captain Jackson: Well, as the propeller goes around, it goes through a varying wake, and so there is a varying thrust on the propeller. Depending on the frequency of that, it can excite the vibrations in the hull. So if you want to change that relation to a frequency, the speed of the propeller can be changed, which in turn changes the speed of the ship. Or you can filter out the impulses, and the resonance changer is the system that does that. It's built into the thrust bearing, and they have little hydraulic cylinders that take the thrust from the propeller shaft and lead it into the foundation and to push the ship.

If you take that hydraulic oil and pipe it up so that there is what in electronics is known as a RC circuit, which stands for resistance and capacitors, you can change the frequency by changing either the resistance or the capacitance. You can do that hydraulically by putting a little throttle valve in it and an accumulator with which you can change the air pressure on it, and so that changes the capacitance. And if you change the little throttle valve you can change the resistance, so you can tune it to the offensive frequency, and the offensive frequency will be eliminated, so that's called a resonance changer.

Well, there was the same kind of thing with the big derrick going up and down. Their throttle valves were huge. They were big because the flows were so much greater. And then the air bank for the capacitance, there were two of them and they were fantastic. They were about 24 feet long, and they were 18 inches in diameter and we had a 10x10 unit on either side of the ship so that's 200 of these big flasks full of high-pressure air.

Paul Stillwell: Now, wasn't there some kind of a chamber in the Glomar Explorer that was big enough to take the Soviet submarine? Was that the intent to pull it up inside the ship?

Captain Jackson: Yes, it had a moon pool.

Paul Stillwell: What does that term "moon pool" mean?

Captain Jackson: Well, that comes from the roughnecks that work on the big oil drilling ships, and it's a hole through the ship in which they put the pipe down through. On those kinds of ships the moon pool is only about 20 feet square. But ours was somewhat larger.

Paul Stillwell: Well, how much larger was it?

Captain Jackson: Much.

Paul Stillwell: Longer than the submarine?

Captain Jackson: Can't say.

Paul Stillwell: How did you have room with that large moon pool then to have space to store manganese nodules?

Captain Jackson: Well, manganese nodules are generally pretty small. They are the houses of little critters that live on the bottom of the deep ocean, and they're primarily silicates, but they have a reasonably high percentage of copper and manganese, nickel, so those things are very desirable. The world's running out of the supply of that stuff, so if you can mine these off the bottom of the ocean you'll have enough supply to carry us for maybe a couple thousand years. Lots of it.

They are at deep water. I think they did find some, but a small field of it, at about 7,000 feet. The usual places are maybe at 15,000 to 25,000 feet. So no matter where you go, it's deep water, so you've got to have a lot of gear that will go down there. Both Hughes and Tenneco built ships to develop a system that they could mine these deep depths, and actually Hughes picked up 7,000 tons of them. Not all at once, but they go out and try a scheme, pull them up, and then they find out what they did wrong, and they go back and do it again. So they probably pick up maybe 200 or 300 tons at a time.

Paul Stillwell: What was the technique of picking them up?

Captain Jackson: Well, there were several techniques. They all involved a thing like a big vacuum cleaner, and it's very simple to make. It's just a big pipe, and it has a fitting just like a big vacuum cleaner. And then you pump air into pretty near the top of the pipe up there so that now you have a head difference of water, and that causes a flow through there. And then you have a place where the pipe comes up on the ship, it's got an arc in it and then a big tank in which you catch manganese nodules. And, boy, they really come barreling out of there.

Paul Stillwell: Do you have a 7,000-foot long hose that they come up through?

Captain Jackson: If you're only working at 7,000 feet, that's all that is needed.

Paul Stillwell: They're even longer hoses than that.

Captain Jackson: Yes, and those are really big pipes.

Paul Stillwell: How big around?

Captain Jackson: Well, it's tapered and that's for strength, but the biggest part of that's about 30 inches in diameter and the smallest part's about 15 inches.

Paul Stillwell: I would think you'd have to have a lot of storage space on the ship just for that long a pipe.

Captain Jackson: They do, indeed. I have a picture of the Glomar Explorer's pipe lying on the dock waiting to go on board the ship. Took up the whole parking lot.

Paul Stillwell: Who did the design of the overall ship?

Captain Jackson: Global Marine. They were good, and they had a lot of experience developing ships in the oil industry.

Paul Stillwell: And where was it built?

Captain Jackson: Built at Sun Ship, which went out of business.

Paul Stillwell: Chester, Pennsylvania.

Captain Jackson: Yes. Here's a hypothetical thing is that Brezhnev was the wheel in Russia when all this happened, and he calls in his Chief of Naval Operations and he says, "Comrade, I understand you lost a submarine."[*]

"Yes, Comrade, that's correct."

"And I understand you sent a whole fleet out there to look for it."

"Yeah, Comrade, that's right."

"And I also understand that you couldn't find it."

"Unfortunately, Comrade, that's correct. We looked and looked and looked for the damned thing and we couldn't find it."

"Okay. Dismissed. You're gone."

Then he calls in his head of security and he said, "Comrade, I understand that the Americans found our submarine."

"Apparently so, Comrade."

"And I also understand that they designed and built a whole ship to go pick it up."

"Yes, Comrade, that's unfortunately correct."

"And also I understand that it was successful."

"That's what I understand, too, Comrade."

"And I understand that you had some ships out there watching them do it."

"Yes, Comrade, that's so right."

"And I understand those ships left just before they finished."

---

[*] Leonid I. Brezhnev served as general secretary of the Central Committee of the Soviet Union's Communist Party from 1964 until his death in 1982.

"Yes, Comrade, that's right."

And he says, "What in the hell am I paying you for?"

Paul Stillwell: Well, you said you were hired for this because of your expertise and involvement from the Scorpion experience. How were you able to use that knowledge in the project?

Captain Jackson: Well, it's sort of difficult to say specifically, but there weren't very many people who had operated on the bottom of the ocean at deep depths. There were others who could have done the job just as well as I did, but I was selected to do it. The problems of working and developing systems to work on there were equally transferable because it was a deep-ocean project. I made, I guess, a lot of suggestions on the ways to do things. I think my biggest contribution to the whole project is that when we had problems I worked diligently to solve the problems in an expeditious manner, and most of the time we were successful.

Paul Stillwell: Were you on board the ship when she was operating?

Captain Jackson: Yes, I made the maiden voyage on it.

Paul Stillwell: Any details you can share from that?

Captain Jackson: Well, yes. We had a lot of instrumentation on the ship, and one of the fascinating things was a wave rider, which was a buoy that would go up and down with the waves. And it had accelerometers in it and using the technology for the SINS measurements, they were in the rider.[*] They would measure the accelerations up and down, and they could convert that into velocity and distance. So we knew exactly how high the waves were, and I spent a lot of time going out on deck and looking at the waves and trying to estimate how high they were. Then I'd go in and look at the wave rider and see how close I came.

---

[*] SINS—Ship's inertial navigation system.

I found that for the little waves I was overestimating the height regularly, but on the big waves I was underestimating them, that the waves were actually higher than I thought they were. I still haven't rationalized why that happened, on the why about that, but it's a fact. The biggest waves we ever measured were 45 feet from trough to crest, which is a pretty big wave.

Paul Stillwell: Yes.

Captain Jackson: But the ship behaved very well.

Paul Stillwell: What was the displacement of that ship?

Captain Jackson: I think it was 58,000 tons fully loaded.

Paul Stillwell: That's as big as a battleship.

Captain Jackson: Yes, it's pretty good.

Paul Stillwell: Well, that would enhance the stability right there I would think, just the size.

Captain Jackson: Yes, but push that ship around, you know the waves are pretty darned strong. We had lots of thrilling experiences. As a matter of fact, we weren't supposed to keep logs, but I kept little notes in code. Seemed like we had a thrilling experience at least once a day.

Paul Stillwell: Any examples of those thrilling experiences?

Captain Jackson: Well, we got a big piece of pipe loose hanging in the big derrick, so it was like a pendulum. So we had this 20-ton piece of pipe swinging around trying to lasso it. That's pretty exciting. And if you don't believe that, try it.

Paul Stillwell: How was it accomplished?

Captain Jackson: Well, we finally got some big steel cables, and it wasn't swinging continually like this. It was going all around like that, and sometimes it was going pretty slow, and we had it all ready. Then, when it got in the right place, we had a whole gang of guys around it, and they pulled it up and snatched it. One of the guys was a bullfighter, he liked to fight the bulls, and he was up there and he said, "Gee, this is great. This is just like a bullfight."

Paul Stillwell: How large was the crew?

Captain Jackson: I think it was 120, around 125. Food was superb. Everybody gained weight.

Paul Stillwell: A hundred and twenty is not many for a 58,000-ton ship.

Captain Jackson: Well, yes. Commercial standards.

Paul Stillwell: Well, that's true. How had the submarine been located?

Captain Jackson: I'll have to say I don't know.

Paul Stillwell: It's interesting that the U. S. found it and the Soviets weren't able to.

Captain Jackson: Yes.

Paul Stillwell: What more can you say about being on board the Glomar Explorer?

Captain Jackson: Well, we had a good group of guys. A lot of them were Mormons. That was really my first association with Mormons, and they turned out to be very, very good.

They were reliable and worked hard, and they were intelligent. As I was growing up I knew there were such things as Mormons, but I hadn't the slightest idea what they were. And that's like where I grew up. It was in a Republican community, and there was a lot of talk about the Democrats. I didn't know what they were, except I knew they were bad.

Paul Stillwell: I told you the other night that I had interviewed John McCrea, who grew up in Marlette, Michigan, certainly a Republican community. His mother was just appalled when he became the naval aide to President Franklin Roosevelt, who was a Democrat.* He had to explain to her that this was not a political job.

    Well, this was a project conducted in great secrecy, and then the whole world found out about it. How did that happen?

Captain Jackson: I don't know the details, but obviously the thing had to be reported to the Congress, and from things that people told me it appeared that the leaks came through Congress. When it was first announced on the radio, it was early in the morning, and Beck and I were eating breakfast, and she said, "Did you hear what I heard?"

    I said, "Yes."

    She said, "Were you there?"

    I said, "I don't know," because I was still—and I'm still under wraps on what I can say about the whole project.

Paul Stillwell: She had known you were on the Glomar Explorer, I take it.

Captain Jackson: Yes, she knew that.

Paul Stillwell: But she didn't know what the mission was.

Captain Jackson: No. Well, I'll tell you. We were out there, and we were running pipe. We got a message from a British ship, the Belle Hudson, and said that they had a guy that

---

* Captain John L. McCrea, USN, served as President Franklin D. Roosevelt's naval aide, 1942-43. The oral history of McCrea, who retired as a vice admiral, is in the Naval Institute collection.

had a heart attack. They called any ship that had a doctor aboard, and we did have a doctor. Big question. Should we let him on, or should we just ignore it? They said, "Well, we're out here on a legitimate mining expedition. We're trying to do this. It's customary at sea if somebody has a problem, you help them." So we decided that we could help. So we radioed back, and we said, "We have a doctor. We can't move, but if you want to come this way and deliver a guy on board, we'll look at him."

But when they got there, we said, "Well, we'll send the doctor over to look at him first and see if it's possible to move him." So the doc goes over there, and the guy is complaining of horrible pains in his chest, and the captain of the ship and other officers were sure that the guy had a heart attack.

The doc looked at this fellow, took his blood pressure and all the other things that they do, and he couldn't find anything wrong with him. So he said, "Gee, what we need is an X-ray, but the only X-ray machine around here is over on our ship." So he called back, and he said, "I want to bring the guy back and put him in our hospital." Another big debate. Going to let the guy on board? So we generally kept everything pretty well closed up, and we said we had to close up a few things, which we did.

So they put their boat in the water and brought him over, and, of course, now we had the boat crew to worry about. So we left half the boat crew there. We took the other half, marched them right up to the mess room, and gave them a good meal. The doc took the guy into the hospital and took an X-ray. Gee, he had three broken ribs. "Well, how'd you get those broken ribs?"

"I don't know." He said, "I woke up and I had this horrible pain."

So we asked the second mate who was in the charge of the boat that brought him over. "Hey, Mr. Mate, what do you know about this?"

And he said, "Well, all I know is that this guy was the messman on the ship, and he and the captain got drunk, and it ended up in a fight. When the fight started, I got the girls out of the wardroom, and so I didn't see the fight. But when I came back this guy was out cold laying on the deck, and when he woke up he complained about this horrible pain in his chest." So apparently the captain hit the guy in the chest and broke his ribs.

Paul Stillwell: Or maybe he fell and hurt it on something.

Captain Jackson: Well, I don't know what the story is.

Paul Stillwell: But I take it you managed to get them off without compromising the mission.

Captain Jackson: We did that. Yes, did that.

Paul Stillwell: Did the doctor patch him up once he found out what the problem was.

Captain Jackson: He taped him all up, and he said, "Hey, it's going to be sore for three or four weeks, but don't let anybody hit you again." I guess some of those ships are pretty lax about some of things they do.

Paul Stillwell: Well, it's interesting you say, "Get the girls out of the wardroom." They must have had a mixed crew.

Captain Jackson: Or something.

Paul Stillwell: What kind of ship was the British ship?

Captain Jackson: She was a general cargo ship. They were on their way to Seattle, and so we asked them if they would take mail for us and they said, "Sure." So we passed the word that if anybody wanted to post a letter, that the Belle Hudson would take it for us.

Paul Stillwell: How long were you out on this mission?

Captain Jackson: We were on station for 62 days, a little over two months.

Paul Stillwell: There's one more thing that fits in that category of questions I have to ask, and that is were you on board when the Glomar Explorer grasped the submarine?

Captain Jackson: I made the maiden voyage on it.

Paul Stillwell: Well, I don't know whether that happened on the maiden voyage or not.

Captain Jackson: It only made one voyage.

Paul Stillwell: Oh, okay. Well, that does answer that question. Can you tell me any more about that experience?

Captain Jackson: No, no, I've already told you more than I should.

On another subject, the thing that I'm most proud about is that I—my friend Dean Horn was the professor of naval science up at MIT, and I used to go up there, and he had to go off on temporary duty on the Scorpion investigation. He asked me if I would come up there and sit in for him while he went off, and I said, "Sure," so I went up there. And I gave a course in submarine design.

Paul Stillwell: When did that start?

Captain Jackson: That was in early 1970. I had just retired. The guys liked it, so Bill Porter relieved Dean and came up there. That was when the Vietnam War was on, and there was a lot of agitation against teaching war things at the university, any university. I knew a lot of professors as well as the students who were demonstrating against having the war courses at MIT. So Bill Porter said, "We will go over to the Draper Lab," which had spun off from MIT for the same reason.* Now this was a semi-private organization. They could demonstrate against it, but they didn't have the same clout.

So they asked me if I would teach that course, and so I said, "Sure." It was successful, so it just got perpetuated, and it still goes on. From that I got a lot of opportunity to be a consultant on different kinds of projects, mostly with the Navy, and

---

* Named for Dr. Stark Draper of the Massachusetts Institute of Technology, who had an important role in the development of the inertial navigation systems used in Polaris missiles and later in the space missions sent to the moon.

that has continued up till today. And it's expanded, and first of all I just talked to Navy people, but gradually I picked up regular students from MIT and act as their advisor on theses and so forth. So it's been very, very rewarding, and in all the teaching I've done, like at Portsmouth and MIT and Bremerton and then short courses at the shipyards and so forth, I've taught that course probably to almost a couple thousand students, so I have students all over.

Paul Stillwell: What can you say about the caliber of the students at MIT that you taught?

Captain Jackson: Most of them are very good, as you would expect, because they are especially selected to go there. They go through a very rigorous screening process. They all stand pretty high in their college class, and they come from nowadays all kinds of universities, all over.

Paul Stillwell: Was this a graduate-level course?

Captain Jackson: Yes. There are really two parts to it. One group goes to get a master's degree, and that takes about three years. Then, depending on their performance there, if they're selected and they pass the qualifiers, they can go on to a Ph.D. They generally have two Ph.D. candidates every year. I'm a thesis reader for most of those, and so a reader has the responsibility to do some sort of guidance for the students and be available for consultation all the time.

Paul Stillwell: What are some of the subjects of the theses they worked on?

Captain Jackson: Oh, design of innovative electric motors. The guy that's there right now is working on the development of new propulsors for submarines, which is going to change submarine design. It won't happen right away, but it will happen gradually over a long time. And that's great. I've enjoyed working with those guys, and I've had to work very, very hard myself just to keep up with them. I think that's probably as rewarding as anything I've ever done.

Paul Stillwell: It's a legacy to the future too.

Captain Jackson: Yes. Well, the guys that came to see me last night, two of them had been my students, and they're doing real well. They've gotten good jobs. One of them was a Ph.D. candidate, and the other one got an engineer's degree, which is about halfway between a master's and a doctorate. The big difference is that to get a professional degree you don't need to write a thesis. You write a thesis for your master's, but you don't have to write a special one for engineer.

Paul Stillwell: What percentage of these students you've taught were naval officers?

Captain Jackson: At MIT about 90% are naval officers. Some of them are from foreign countries.

Paul Stillwell: So do they become EDOs then on completion of the course there at MIT?

Captain Jackson: Well, some of them are already EDs.

Paul Stillwell: I see. And they're just going for an upgrade or—?

Captain Jackson: Well, no, when they sign up to be an ED it's assumed that they will take that course.

Paul Stillwell: I see. And that is part of their overall curriculum?

Captain Jackson: That's right. It's a good program, and it's been going since 1908. And Dr. Hunsaker was one of the naval officers that was ordered up there as an instructor.[*] He

---

[*] Jerome Clarke Hunsaker was the number-one man in the Naval Academy class of 1908. He made substantial contributions in the field of aeronautical engineering.

was so good that the university hired him to develop the department of aeronautics up there.

Paul Stillwell: Well, one thing that's useful to put on the record is that you and Hunsaker were high-school classmates. If you could explain that please.

Captain Jackson: Well, after I told you that the other day I began to review it in my memory, and I'm not sure that we're classmates. He may have been one or two years earlier. But Saginaw High School had a program like many high schools of every year designating some person as a distinguished alumnus. When I was a senior they decided that they would designate Dr. Hunsaker as a distinguished alumnus who certainly deserved it. But when they looked at his record, they found that he hadn't graduated. He hadn't graduated because he had gotten an appointment to the Naval Academy, and he had to report down there on the first of June. His graduating class didn't graduate until the end of June, so he missed his graduation. It was a quandary, and they said, "How do we handle this?"

The administration said, "Well, that's easy. We'll make him an honorary member of the senior class."

Paul Stillwell: So this was like the class of '32 or '33, somewhere in there?

Captain Jackson: Or it might have been '34 and I always thought it was '34, but the only way I can check it is go back to my high school, which has changed, and find out. But it really doesn't make too much difference. But they made him an honorary graduate of the class, and then they made him a distinguished alumnus.

Paul Stillwell: [Laughter] Simultaneously

Captain Jackson: In my class there were three people who were designated distinguished alumni, and that was the largest number of any class in the history of the school. Fortunately, I was one of those.

Paul Stillwell: Who were the other two?

Captain Jackson: Well, Bill Birewaltz who was one of my very best friends, and he was the guy that went on to be the famous doctor of nuclear radiation for goiters. The other guy was George Kendall. He was real good. He didn't go on to college, but he did go to work for the Wicks Boiler Company, and he changed it to be like a Home Depot, and so he was very successful. Margaret Curry, who was the first female lawyer to be admitted to the bar, had been nominated, but the year she was nominated somebody from another class was selected, but she should have been there.

Paul Stillwell: So she was the first woman lawyer admitted in Michigan?

Captain Jackson: Yes. Once again, our class had some outstanding people.

Paul Stillwell: Well, one of the famous people that you encountered at MIT was Dr. Stark Draper. What do you recall about him?

Captain Jackson: Oh, he was a character, a unique character, and very likable, very intelligent and very practical. If anybody made the Polaris system go, it was Dr. Draper.

Paul Stillwell: The guidance part of it.

Captain Jackson: Yes, but that was necessary. If there wasn't guidance, there wasn't any system. So he developed that over a lot of years, and he tried to sell it to the Navy, and they really didn't believe it would work. So he put it in a big truck body, a semi-trailer, and he set it at Cambridge and drove it all the way down to Washington. Then he invited all the guys that were interested in it to come at look at it. So he made a big ceremony of taking the padlock off the doors and opening it up there. They put it in there, and so they looked at the instrumentation and checked the latitude and longitude. It was right on.

Paul Stillwell: Now, this is the inertial navigation system he was demonstrating?

Captain Jackson: Yes.

Paul Stillwell: What year would that have been?

Captain Jackson: It was shortly after the war, so let's say '48.

Paul Stillwell: That early?

Captain Jackson: Yes. That was pretty crude, and it really did fill up the whole trailer, and from then on it was just developing it and making it smaller and packaging it. He also did a lot of work on the guidance for the missile itself. Now he had the SINS, the navigation system for the ship, and the missile, and it only remained to tie them together.

Paul Stillwell: Would you describe him as a down-to-earth individual?

Captain Jackson: Yes. If he wanted to make something, he didn't go get a workman to do it. He'd get the material, and if it was something on a metal lathe or something he'd cut it up.

Paul Stillwell: Sort of like you would do.

Captain Jackson: Well, I don't know about that. Those are things to highlight what I did after I retired from the Navy. As I look back at it, it's been a fabulous career. If I had to do it all over again there are some things I'd do differently. But at any rate I guess that completes the story of my life.

Paul Stillwell: Well, do you want to mention any of those things you might have done differently?

Captain Jackson: Well, no, I guess probably not. I haven't thought enough about it.

Paul Stillwell: Are there any overall lessons you want to do by way of summing up on this enlightening exploration we've had over the last few days?

Captain Jackson: Well, with all my students I try to pass on to them the lessons that I have had the opportunity to learn, those that are the way to do things and also the way to not do them. I feel very strongly about that because it's an opportunity that some of the young fellows wouldn't get if people like me didn't take the trouble to tell them. So I make an effort of that like last night when I had a group of people here. I related some of the things I had done to what they're trying to do now, and they seem to appreciate that. I would recommend that all people as they get older make a conscious attempt to pass on to the younger people the benefit of the things that they did during their careers.

Paul Stillwell: In a way that's what we're doing right now.

Captain Jackson: Well, perhaps so. But it's important. I talked about Admiral Paul Lee and Admiral McKee. I can include Dr. Sawyer from the University of Michigan in with that lot of people. They had a big influence on my life, and they were the types of persons that I said, "That's what I'd like to be," and so I did. I tried to be like them, both McKee and Lee. And as I said in there that I had a leg up, because they're both small, so I like them. Young people, I would recommend you do the same thing. Pick out somebody you admire and decide why you admire them and then use them as a role model and try to be like them. It helps.

Paul Stillwell: Well, judging by number of your former students who recommended you for an oral history, you must have succeeded in that.

Captain Jackson: Well, I don't know. They're all good guys.

Paul Stillwell: Well, one thing you mentioned to me when the machine wasn't running is that the students are very receptive to what you're teaching, but NavSea is posing some objections. Why is that?

Captain Jackson: I really don't know, and I've thought about that a long time. Why do they take me to task? My action was—instead of getting mad and starting to fight with them or something, I politely invited them to come up to my course and see for themselves what we're doing. And they did change their opinion. They went away, and when they did they said, "Hey, you're doing a good job." I think at one time they were jealous of the recognition I was getting as a submarine designer, and they thought that they should be getting that recognition. That's the only way I can explain it.

Paul Stillwell: Please tell me about the Saunders and the Taylor Awards.

Captain Jackson: Well, those were both complete surprises. I never expected that I'd get either one of them, because both of them are very prestigious awards. I got the Saunders Award because my friend Dean Horn nominated me. He also rounded up a lot of the students that I had had up to that time to write letters for me and so forth, and so I think that's what carried the day, that they had a number of good recommendations. Then, when the Taylor Award came up, Dick Couch, who would have been—first he worked back in BuShips and at the Model Basin, and then he went to the University of Michigan as a professor so I'd known him a long time.

Unbeknownst to me he nominated me for that Taylor Medal. But I wasn't selected at that time, and I mentioned it to Francis Ogilvie up at MIT, who was the head of the department. It was just a fact. I said it was great that he nominated me, but I didn't make it. Well, that's okay. Not everybody does make it. So, anyway, he took it upon himself to re-nominate me, and then he got all the local students up there and all the former students to write letters in support of it. I wasn't supposed to know this, but the secretary showed me a stack of letters, and it was about that thick.

Paul Stillwell: Inch and a half?

Captain Jackson: Oh, at least. But I felt very humble in getting it. To be included with the great people who got that medal is just fantastic. There's only one other guy, John Niedermair, who was a long-term Navy civilian employee in the ship design. He was a member of the team that supervised the salvage on the S-4 and the S-51. John and I are the only two that got both medals.

Paul Stillwell: And we have his oral history also.

Captain Jackson: Yes.

Paul Stillwell: So now we've got both.

Captain Jackson: Yes. He was considerably older than I was, so he was one of the guys that I looked up to as certainly technically I wanted to be like him. At any rate, I got those two medals. Also while I was in the Navy I got two Legions of Merit for my work on submarines. I got one when the Thresher was completed and the other was when I retired. Then I get the Meritorious Service Award for the work I did on the Scorpion. And I got an award that most everybody got at the end of World War II for their work.

Paul Stillwell: The Victory Medal?

Captain Jackson: No, no, not a Victory Medal. It was higher than the Victory Medal. I got three Victory Medals. World War II, Vietnam War, and the Korean War.

Paul Stillwell: Well, please tell me about life here in Groton since retirement.

Captain Jackson: Oh, it's been good. When we moved here we had moved a great number of times, and my wife said, "This is it. I'm never going to move again." And she's held fast, so we haven't moved. I had a number of opportunities to go work other places, but it would mean pulling up stakes and going someplace else, and she didn't absolutely refuse, but she made it known that she didn't want to.

Paul Stillwell: Well, this is a very pleasant place to settle, I must say.

Captain Jackson: Yes, it is.

Paul Stillwell: And, as she said, you built this building we're in which is a combination of a workshop and an office, and now that this is here you can't move.

Captain Jackson: Well, I had a lot of fun building it as well as using it.

Paul Stillwell: You told me you did every part of it yourself except pouring the concrete foundation.

Captain Jackson: That's a fact.

Paul Stillwell: Please tell me about your sailing.

Captain Jackson: Oh, I've been a lifelong sailor. A lot of people have been involved. My first experience was sailing with Bill Birewaltz, who had an 8-foot pram, and we used to sail that quite extensively, day in and day out, practically all day. We took a cruise. We sailed from one beach to another, which was eight miles, when we were only eight years old. Our parents were waiting for us at the other beach, but it was pretty near a whole day's sail.

  Also Charlie Christy, who I've mentioned several times had a boat, and he also had a nice dinghy. He built both of them. He used to take us from Saginaw to Bay City out through the bay and let us sail his dinghy. Then I bought a little sailboat. Sailed it in Saginaw River. And when I needed a car I traded the sailboat for a car. Sailed an awful lot with Fred Klein. He built a little 18-foot sloop under Christy's guidance, and I helped him, and then I learned how to use woodworking tools and so forth. Later, after about two years, he sold that to Bill Birewaltz and then built a 25-foot yawl, which we used to go sailing all over on it. Drove our mothers frantic, because we would go sailing and lose the wind or something and not show up and things like that. So I've been sailing ever since. Every place I go I get a boat and sail it.

Paul Stillwell: Yesterday you showed me the green boat that's not far from here and very convenient for you.*

Captain Jackson: Yes, it's only about a quarter mile. One of the advantages of living here because I walk down there frequently. And, for some reason or other, I got to be a good sailor, but that paid off a lot because I was able to transfer the lessons of sailing to the big ships. When I was in college we had yearlong design projects, and two other guys and I designed a big passenger ship that was like the America.† It was designed to carry passengers across the Pacific. I still have those drawings, and I get them out and look at them every once in a while, and I say, "You know, hey, that wasn't so bad."

Paul Stillwell: Well, anything else you want to say on any subject?

Captain Jackson: No. I've already talked too much.

Paul Stillwell: No, you haven't. I have certainly learned a lot in visiting with you these last three days, and I'm most grateful for the contributions you've now made to history to supplement those that you've made to your Navy before that, so thank you very much.

Captain Jackson: Well, thank you for your time and trouble. I appreciate it very much.

*   *   *

---

* The boat is a fiddlehead-friendship sloop.
† The 35,400-ton passenger liner America began her maiden voyage on 22 August 1940 as flagship of the United States Lines. She was 723 feet long, 93 feet in the beam, had a maximum draft of nearly 33 feet and a top speed of 17.5 knots. She was acquired by the U.S. Navy for conversion to a troopship and commissioned as the USS West Point (AP-23) on 15 June 1941. During World War II she carried more than 350,000 troops. She was struck from the Navy list on 12 March 1946, converted back to a commercial ship, and resumed service as the America.

Supplement to the oral history of Captain Harry A. Jackson, USN (Ret.):

During my review of the transcripts, I noted the omission of many contemporaries and coworkers. Some of the best that were omitted were Ralph Lacy, a superb naval architect and submarine designer, from whom I learned much. Others of the same stature were Owen Oakley, Phil Mandel, Pete Palermo, Captain Bob Baylis, and a host of others. The list goes on and on. I can earnestly state that I never met a person from whom I did not learn something. Any omission of worthy contribution is not intentional but an indication of my failing memory.

United States Pacific Fleet
Flagship of the Commander-in-Chief

The Commander in Chief, United States Pacific Fleet, takes pleasure in commending

LIEUTENANT COMMANDER HARRY ALLEN JACKSON
UNITED STATES NAVAL RESERVE

for service as set forth in the following

CITATION:

"For meritorious service in the line of his profession as Docking Officer and Hull Repair Officer of Advance Base Sectional Drydock THREE, during its erection and operation from 5 January to 2 September 1945. By his outstanding initiative, proficiency and capable supervision, Lieutenant Commander Jackson performed valuable repairs to major ships of the United States Pacific Fleet which had been damaged in action against the enemy. His professional skill, experience and devotion to duty were material contributing factors to the successful prosecution of the war against the Japanese Empire and were at all times in keeping with the highest traditions of the United States Naval Service."

Commendation Ribbon Authorized

J. H. TOWERS,
Admiral, U.S. Navy.

THE SECRETARY OF THE NAVY
WASHINGTON

The President of the United States takes pleasure in presenting the LEGION OF MERIT to

**CAPTAIN HARRY A. JACKSON
UNITED STATES NAVY**

for service as set forth in the following

CITATION:

"For exceptionally meritorious conduct in the performance of outstanding services from June 1958 to July 1961 as Design Superintendent, Portsmouth Naval Shipyard. During this period, Captain Jackson made important contributions in the field of submarine design and development, including both overall design and that of components. His contributions in this field have resulted in significant improvements in submarine capabilities. His leadership, professional skill, and devotion to duty were in keeping with the highest traditions of the United States Naval Service."

For the President,

Fred Korth
Secretary of the Navy

CHIEF OF NAVAL OPERATIONS

The President of the United States takes pleasure in presenting the LEGION OF MERIT (Gold Star in lieu of the Second Award) to

CAPTAIN HARRY A. JACKSON
UNITED STATES NAVY

for service as set forth in the following

CITATION:

For exceptionally meritorious service from August 1964 to November 1968 while serving as the Supervisor of Shipbuilding, Conversion and Repair, USN, Groton, Connecticut. During this period, Captain Jackson reorganized and consolidated the shipbuilding and repair functions of his commands into a single command, and supervised the detail design and construction of the last group of POLARIS Submarines, two classes of nuclear attack submarines, a prototype nuclear attack submarine, and a prototype nuclear-propelled oceanographic research submarine at the Electric Boat Division. Concurrently, at the Quincy (Massachusetts) Division, he also supervised the detail design and construction of the APOLLO tracking ships, a new class of ammunition ships, a new class of replenishment oilers, and a new class of submarine tenders. Through firm insistence on quality workmanship, Captain Jackson contributed substantially to the Submarine Safety Program and to overall Fleet readiness. These accomplishments, which represent major segments of both the submarine and surface new construction, were made possible by Captain Jackson's careful attention to details, his superb technical skill, and his sound organizational talent. His outstanding performance was in keeping with the highest traditions of the United States Naval Service.

For the President,

T. H. Moorer
Admiral, United States Navy
Chief of Naval Operations

THE SECRETARY OF THE NAVY
WASHINGTON

The Secretary of the Navy takes pleasure in commending

USS APACHE (ATF-67), USS WHITE SANDS (ARD-20), and TRIESTE II

for service as set forth in the following

CITATION:

For exceptionally meritorious service during the period 3 February to 7 October 1969 as an Integral Operating Unit for SCORPION Phase II operations. During this period, USS APACHE towed USS WHITE SANDS, support ship of the Bathyscaphe TRIESTE II, over 14,000 miles, in addition to providing communications, small-boat, and rigging services. WHITE SANDS provided the vital support of TRIESTE II, her crew, and the special equipment required for deep-ocean search technology. As the only operational deep-submergence vehicle in the Navy, TRIESTE II was piloted to unprecedented working depths on nine occasions, thus ensuring the complete success of an operation of great significance to the United States. The officers and men of this Integral Operating Unit, through their superb teamwork, untiring efforts, and dedication, merged their diverse elements into a unit which provided a deep-ocean search capability for the United States. Their inspiring performance of duty reflected great credit upon themselves, and was in keeping with the highest traditions of the United States Naval Service.

All personnel attached to and serving on board any of the three vessels listed above during the period of this citation, are hereby authorized to wear the Navy Unit Commendation Ribbon.

Secretary of the Navy
(Acting)

The National Aeronautics and Space Administration

presents the

Apollo Achievement Award

to

Capt. K. A. Jackson, USN

In appreciation of dedicated service to the nation as a member of the team which has advanced the nation's capabilities in aeronautics and space and demonstrated them in many outstanding accomplishments culminating in Apollo 11's successful achievement of man's first landing on the moon, July 20, 1969.

Signed at Washington, D.C.

ADMINISTRATOR, NASA

DEPARTMENT OF THE NAVY
NAVAL SHIP SYSTEMS COMMAND
WASHINGTON, D.C. 20360

6 November 1970

Captain H. A. Jackson, USN
17 Birch Lane
Groton, Connecticut

Dear Captain Jackson:

Your meritorious performance as a member of the NAVSHIPS team which converted five ships for the APOLLO program has earned the APOLLO Achievement Award for you. A lapel pin and a certificate from the National Aeronautics and Space Administration is forwarded herewith on behalf of the Goddard Space Flight Center Director, Dr. John F. Clark, and the Director of the Manned Space Flight Network, Mr. Ozro M. Covington. I am happy to pass the award along to you with my personal appreciation for your performance which contributed greatly to the success of the APOLLO program.

A copy of this letter will be placed in your official personnel record.

With warmest regards, I am

Sincerely yours,

Bob

R. C. GOODING
Rear Admiral, USN

Encl:
(1) Lapel Pin and Certificate

Copy to:
NASA/GSFC (Code 802)

THE UNITED STATES OF AMERICA

THIS IS TO CERTIFY THAT
THE PRESIDENT OF THE UNITED STATES OF AMERICA
HAS AWARDED THE

MERITORIOUS SERVICE MEDAL

TO

CAPTAIN HARRY A. JACKSON, UNITED STATES NAVY

FOR

OUTSTANDING MERITORIOUS SERVICE FROM 21 MAY TO 6 AUGUST 1969

GIVEN THIS 12TH DAY OF MAR 1970

SECRETARY OF THE NAVY

The American Society of Naval Engineers

takes pleasure in presenting

The Harold E. Saunders Award for 1979

to

Capt. Harry A. Jackson, USN (Ret.)

*for his significant contribution to Naval Engineering
as set forth in the following*

Citation:

In recognition of his outstanding leadership and singular contributions in every phase of submarine design, engineering, development, and construction over the past thirty-five years.

Combining his experience in the nuclear power program with the success of the single-screw Attack Submarine, Captain Jackson led the design and development of the deep diving SSN 594 Class Submarines. This stands as the greatest advancement in performance and capability yet achieved in a single new class design. His design and engineering expertise were crucial factors in the successful development of the Fleet Ballistic Missile Submarine that currently is one of the Nation's primary strategic defense systems.

In his post-active duty career, Captain Jackson continues to direct his talents and expertise toward improving submarine design and engineering: as an advisor and counselor to Navy management; as an engineering consultant; and most importantly, as a teacher, passing on his expertise and experience to future Engineering Duty Officers and civilian engineers. The soundness of his personal contributions have stood well the test of time, and his continuing service and teaching of those who will follow him augur well for the future.

The Society therefore considers him most worthy of being recognized and is honored to present him with its Harold E. Saunders Award for 1979.

THE DAVID W. TAYLOR MEDAL
FOR 1993

*for notable achievement in naval architecture
and/or marine engineering*

HARRY A. JACKSON

The career of Captain Harry A. Jackson, USN (Ret.) has spanned the entire development of the modern nuclear submarine. As an active duty naval officer, he made crucial contributions to the redesign of the ALBACORE, predecessor of the BARBELL, the first modern single-crew submarine. He proposed the air-pressure vertical-launch system for the Polaris submarines, and he supervised construction of one-fourth of the entire Polaris fleet. He was a leader in establishing both Portsmouth and Bremerton Naval Shipyards in the nuclear-power field. He supervised much of the detail design of the THRESHER, which represented a major step forward in submarine development.

In later years, Captain Jackson taught literally an entire generation of U.S. Navy officers and civilian engineers the art of submarine concept design. For over 20 years he has offered a two-week course at the Massachusetts Institute of Technology, in which students progress from the most basic principles to carrying out actual design projects. At the Society's Annual Meeting in 1992, he presented a landmark paper that was effectively a highly abridged version of this course. In addition, Captain Jackson takes an active role in guiding design projects of students in the Naval Construction and Engineering Course at MIT.

Captain Jackson is a 50-year member and Fellow of the Society. He has served as Section Chairman of the New England Section and was a member of its Executive Committee for ten years. He has contributed over twenty papers to Sections of the Society. He is also a Fellow of the Royal Institution of Naval Architects, United Kingdom.

Index to the Oral History of Captain Harry A. Jackson, U.S. Navy (Retired)

ABSD-1, USS
Floating dry dock that suffered a casualty at Espiritu Santo during World War II when one section capsized, 49, 51-52, 63

ABSD-3, USS
Floating dry dock that was used in Guam during World War II, 48-74; docking procedures, 50-51; repair job on the battleship South Dakota (BB-57), 53-54; repair job in September 1945 on the battleship Pennsylvania (BB-38) after she had been torpedoed the previous month at Okinawa, 55-57; construction of a temporary bow for the heavy cruiser Pittsburgh (CA-72) in 1945 after she lost her bow in a storm, 57-60; repairs to the escort carrier Wake Island (CVE-65), 57, 62; construction and delivery of the separate sections of the dry dock, 60-61, 63-64, 69-71; a young sailor from the battleship New Mexico (BB-40) was killed when he fell into the dry dock, 61-62; work on merchant ships, 64-65; living conditions for the crew of the dry dock, 67-68; command arrangements, 69; size of the crew, 71-72; letdown in the motivation of the crew in August 1945 when the war ended, 72-73

Abraham Lincoln, USS (SSBN-602)
Ballistic missile submarine that was built in the late 1950s and early 1960s at Portsmouth Naval Shipyard, 164-165

Air Force, U.S.
In the early 1950s Pease Air Force base in New Hampshire supplied the Navy with a B-47 parachute for use in tests involving the experimental submarine Albacore (AGSS-569)

Albacore, USS (AGSS-569)
Experimental submarine developed in the early 1950s to test the feasibility of the teardrop-shaped hull, 97-106, 136-139, 141, 184-185; the submarine is now on display at the Portsmouth Naval Shipyard, 103; in the 1950s CNO Arleigh Burke hosted British Admiral Lord Louis Mountbatten's visit on board the Albacore, 123-125; similarity in hull shape to blimps, 135-136, 141-142; correction of problems with hydro-elasticity, 199

Antisubmarine Warfare
Role of the Bureau of Ships during World War II in the design and construction of ASW ships, 28-35, 40-41

Arco, Idaho
Site of a prototype nuclear power plant for Navy ships, 90-92

Arctic
In the early 1960s U.S. nuclear submarines conducted under-ice operations, 185-188

Axene, Commander Dean L., USN (USNA, 1945)
In 1961 was the first commanding officer when the submarine Thresher (SSN-593) went into commission and made sea trials, 161-162, 175, 181

Bangor, Washington, Submarine Base
Well-developed site that is used as a base for Ohio (SSBN-726)-class Trident missile submarines, 250-251

Barbel, USS (SS-580)
Diesel submarine that in the early 1960s was overhauled by the Puget Sound Naval Shipyard, 197, 209-211

Barbel (SS-580)-Class Submarines
When this class of diesel boats was designed in the 1950s, it took advantage of some of the concepts of the teardrop-shaped hull, 101-102, 138-139, 141-142, 185; problems with silver-brazed pipe joints, 109; built in several shipyards, 140

Bass, Captain Raymond H., USN (USNA, 1931)
Role in the late 1940s in the development of the K-1 (SSK-1)-class submarines, 228

Baylis, Lieutenant Commander John Robert, USN (USNA, 1946)
In the late 1950s did an excellent job in submarine programs while stationed at the Portsmouth Naval Shipyard, 172, 190, 199

Bikini Atoll, Marshall Islands
In the summer of 1946 was the site of U.S. testing of nuclear weapons, 75-79

Blimps
During World War II Jackson made a round trip in blimps between Moffett Field, California, and San Diego, 134-135; similarity in shape to submarines, 135-136, 141-142

Boats
In the late 1920s, while in school in Michigan, Jackson became interested in building model boats, 5-6; Jackson was involved for many years in sailing, 5-6, 134, 283-284

Boston Navy Yard
In 1941 the yard was involved in a variety of ship construction and repair projects, 18-26; work on the British battleship Rodney, 19-20; storage site for large pontoons used in ship salvage work, 23-25; construction of a sludge barge, 25-26

Buck, Lieutenant Commander Beaumont M., USN (USNA, 1948)
Engineering duty officer who in the 1950s was assigned to the Portsmouth Naval Shipyard, 211-212

Budgetary Considerations
In the 1950s the Regulus missile program was cancelled to provide funding for the Polaris ballistic missile submarine program, 130

Bureau of Construction and Repair
In the period shortly before the United States got into World War II, the bureau sent out representatives to recruit young officers as naval constructors, 14-15

Bureau of Ships
Role in the design, construction, and trials of new warships during World War II, 27-48; relationship during the war with the U.S. Maritime Commission, 27-30; role of Rear Admiral Edward Cochrane as wartime bureau chief, 42-44, 46-47; role in the early 1950s in developing the teardrop hull shape for the experimental submarine Albacore (AGSS-569), 98-99, 184-185; insisted on being informed in the late 1950s on the development of the Polaris submarines, 155; in the late 1950s did preliminary design for the Thresher (SSN-593)-class submarines, 160-161; in the late 1950s allowed shipyards to silver braze pipe joints in submarines rather than welding them, 178

Burke, Admiral Arleigh A., USN (USNA, 1923)
In the 1950s, as Chief of Naval Operations, hosted British Admiral Lord Louis Mountbatten's visit on board the experimental submarine Albacore (AGSS-569), 123-125; decision in the 1950s to cancel the Regulus missile program in order to provide funding for Polaris, 130; aggressively pushed the completion of the Polaris program, 151

Burris, Captain Harry, USN (USNA, 1924)
During his service with the Bureau of Ships in World War II, did not get along with Captain Hyman Rickover, 38; shortly after World War II had medical problems that diminished his effectiveness, 86; in the 1950s, after retiring from the Navy, was a vice president for the New York Shipbuilding Corporation, 201

Cochrane, Rear Admiral Edward L., USN (USNA, 1914)
During World War II demonstrated both great professional knowledge and people skills as Chief of the Bureau of Ships, 42-44, 46-47

Commercial Ships
During World War II the ABSD-3, a floating dry dock based at Guam, got quite proficient on making repairs to Liberty ships, 64-65; in the mid-1970s a doctor from the Glomar Explorer provided medical assistance to a seaman from the British merchant ship Belle Hudson after the man had suffered broken ribs, 271-273

Communications
Development in the late 1950s of a retractable whip antenna for Thresher (SSN-593)-class submarines to use for radio communications, 143-144

Conform
Alternative nuclear submarine design that was proposed in the late 1960s by Captain Don Kern but shot down by Vice Admiral Hyman Rickover, 239-241

Conrad, Lieutenant Commander Edward E., USN (USNA, 1938)
In the late 1940s got involved in the nuclear power program at the General Electric Company in Schenectady, New York, 81; as commanding officer of the Halfbeak (SS-352), enabled Jackson to qualify in submarines, 92-93

Construction Corps, U.S. Navy
In the period shortly before the United States got into World War II, the Bureau of Construction and Repair sent out representatives to recruit young officers as naval constructors, 14-15; was abolished in the early 1940s, and its members became engineering duty only officers in the restricted line, 44-46

Craig, Captain Edward C., USN (USNA, 1922)
In the early 1950s commanded the Portsmouth Naval Shipyard when it was building Tang (SS-563)-class fast-attack submarines, 110-112

Craven, John P.
Civilian engineer who developed scenarios to try to explain the 1968 loss of the submarine Scorpion (SSN-589), 233-234

David Taylor Model Basin, Carderock, Maryland
Role in the early 1950s in developing the teardrop hull shape for the experimental submarine Albacore (AGSS-569), 98-99, 102-103

Draper, Dr. Stark
Role of this MIT professor in the late 1950s in developing the guidance system for Polaris missiles, 278-279

Dubuque, USS (IX-9)
Gunboat that was used in the 1930s for Naval Reserve training cruises on the Great Lakes, 15-16; Jackson served with one of his Dubuque shipmates in World War II, 69, 72

Education
Jackson's experiences in Michigan schools in the 1930s, 2-3, 5, 8-10, 13-14, 244, 277-278; from 1970 onward Jackson taught classes in submarine design at MIT, 274-276, 280-281

Ela, Captain Dennett K., USN (USNA, 1938)
Engineering duty officer who in the late 1950s scoffed at a proposed method for launching Polaris missiles from a submerged submarine, 144

Electric Boat Division, General Dynamics Corporation
In the early 1950s built some of the fast-attack submarines of the Tang (SS-563) class, 108, 113-114; in the late 1950s did the detail design and then built the first Polaris ballistic missile submarine, George Washington (SSBN-598), 149, 155-156, 158-159; relationship in the mid-1960s between the commercial shipyard and the Navy supervisor of shipbuilding, 214-219, 224-225; role in the 1970s of P. Takis Veliotis as general manager of the shipyard, 218; shipyard claims on change orders, 218-219; construction of submarines in the mid-1960s, 224-225

Ellsberg, Captain Edward, USNR
Relationship during World War II with Commodore William Sullivan, 61

Engineering Corps, U.S. Navy
Was abolished in the early 1940s, and its members became engineering duty only officers in the restricted line, 44-46

Espiritu Santo, New Hebrides
During World War II the floating dry dock ABSD-1 suffered a casualty when one section capsized, 49, 51-52

Ethan Allen (SSBN-608)-Class Submarines
Design of in the late 1950s to include parts originally intended for attack submarines, 150; these ships were built in the early 1960s on an accelerated schedule, 159

Evans, Lieutenant Robert L., USN (USNA, 1932)
In the late 1930s served as ship superintendent during the construction of the submarine Squalus (SS-192) at Portsmouth Navy Yard, 12; after World War II made a technical survey in Japan, 74

Fletcher, USS (DD-445)
New destroyer that had capable officers when she went into commission in June 1942, 32

Fletcher (DD-445)-Class Destroyers
Design, construction, and trials of these ships that were built during World War II, 28, 31-33

General Dynamics Corporation
See: Electric Boat Division; Quincy Division

General Electric Company, Schenectady, New York
Role in the late 1940s and early 1950s in the Navy's development of nuclear propulsion for ships, 79-80, 83-84, 88-91

George Washington, USS (SSBN-598)
As the first of the Polaris submarines, used some long-lead items of material originally intended for the attack submarine Scorpion (SSN-589), 149; was built in a short time, 150, 153-154, 159

Gibbs, William Francis
During World War II headed the naval architecture firm Gibbs & Cox, 36-37

Gibbs & Cox, Inc.
Role of this firm during World War II in designing Navy ships, 32, 36-37

Glomar Explorer
In the mid-1970s the United States used this large ship as part of Project Jennifer, an attempt to raise a Soviet Golf-class submarine that had been lost in 1968 northwest of Hawaii, 262-274; a doctor from the Glomar Explorer provided medical assistance to a seaman from the British merchant ship Belle Hudson after the man had suffered broken ribs, 271-273

Grayback, USS (SSG-574)
Regulus-armed submarine built in the late 1950s at the Portsmouth Naval Shipyard, 189-190

Great Lakes
Site of Naval Reserve training cruises during the 1930s on board the gunboats Dubuque (IX-9) and Wilmette, 15-16

Gridley, USS (DLG-21)
Guided missile frigate built in the early 1960s by the Puget Sound Naval Shipyard, 196

Growler, USS (SSG-577)
Regulus-armed submarine built in the late 1950s at the Portsmouth Naval Shipyard, 132, 189-190

Grumman Corporation
In the mid-1950s Grumman built the experimental submarine X-1, 166-170

Guam
During the latter part of World War II provided a great deal of ship repair and logistic support to the Navy's operating forces, 49-67

Gummerson, Commander Kenneth C., USN (USNA, 1944)
Role as first commanding officer in 1953 of the experimental submarine Albacore (AGSS-569), 100, 105

Guppy Program
In the early 1950s the Portsmouth Naval Shipyard did the Guppy modification to the submarine Sea Robin (SS-407), 92, 115-116

Harvard University, Cambridge, Massachusetts
Application in the late 1950s and early 1960s of Harvard Business School techniques to the management of naval shipyards, 192-193

Harvey, Lieutenant Commander John Wesley, USN (USNA, 1950)
In April 1963 was commanding officer of the submarine Thresher (SSN-593) when she was lost on trials, 181-182

Huey, Commander Enders P., USN (USNA, 1941)
In 1951 was the first commanding officer of the submarine Tang (SS-563) when she went into commission, 113

Hunsaker, Jerome C.
After graduating from the Naval Academy in 1908, he got into aeronautical engineering and for many years taught at the Massachusetts Institute of Technology, 276-277

Hyman Rickover, USS (SSN-709)
At the ship's commissioning in 1984, the man for whom she was named, Hyman Rickover, made what Jackson considered inappropriate remarks, 40

Idaho, USS (BB-42)
In World War II was dry-docked at Guam to have the bottom painted and check alignment of the rudder, 54-55

Inspection and Survey, Board of (InSurv)
Role of in improving the material condition of Navy ships, 212-213, 221-222

Jackson, Captain Harry A., USN (Ret.)
Boyhood in Michigan in the 1910s and 1920s, 1-8, 134, 244; parents of, 1-4, 9-10, 17, 136; brother of, 1-3, 8-9, 17; education of, 2-3, 5, 8-10, 13-14, 244, 277-278; in 1935 began serving duty as a Naval Reservist, 10, 15-16; in 1941, as a newly commissioned officer, served as ship superintendent at the Boston Navy Yard, 18-26; service from 1941 to 1943 in the Bureau of Ships, 27-48; wife of, 40, 47-48, 202, 233, 271, 282; from 1943 to 1945 was assigned to ABSD-3, a floating dry dock in the Western Pacific, 48-74; involvement in the 1946 tests of nuclear weapons at Bikini Atoll, 75-79; service from 1946 to 1951 at General Electric in Schenectady, New York, as part of the Navy's nuclear power program, 79-97; duty in 1951-54 at

the Portsmouth Naval Shipyard, 97-120, 166-170; children of, 118-119, 203-204; served 1954-56 in the nuclear power section of the OpNav staff, 120-163; duty from 1958 to 1962 at Portsmouth Naval Shipyard, 163-165, 170-195; served 1962-64 at the Puget Sound Naval Shipyard, 195-213; had duty from 1964 to 1968 as supervisor of shipbuilding in Groton, Connecticut, with additional duty to Quincy, Massachusetts, 213-228; in 1969 served as technical adviser in the examination of the remains of the submarine Scorpion (SSN-589), 228-238; retirement in 1969 from active naval service, 238-241; post-retirement jobs included consulting work and teaching, 244-249, 254-257, 262-262, 274-276, 280-281; involvement in the mid-1970s in Project Jennifer, the attempt to raise a lost Soviet submarine, 262-274; received the prestigious Saunders and Taylor awards, 281-282

Jennifer, Project
In the mid-1970s the United States ran this operation in an attempt to raise a Soviet Golf-class submarine that had been lost in 1968 northwest of Hawaii, 262-274

K-1 (SSK-1)-Class Submarines
Development of in the late 1940s and early 1950s as picket-type submarines, 228

Kalina, Lieutenant Commander John F., USN (USNA, 1945)
In the early 1960s did an excellent job on the preliminary design of the Sacramento (AOE-1)-class fast combat support ships, 199

Kaplan, Captain Leonard, USN (USNA, 1922)
Was subject to prejudice while at the Naval Academy in the early 1920s because he was Jewish, 38-39

Kentucky (BB-66)
Unfinished battleship that in the early 1960s supplied main engines for two fast combat support ships, 200

Kern, Captain Donald H., USN
Engineering duty officer who had difficulties with Vice Admiral Hyman Rickover in the 1960s when he advanced a Conform design for a new class of nuclear submarines, 239-241; his son was turned down for the nuclear power program by Rickover, 240-241

Kingdon, Dr. Kenneth H.
In the late 1940s was technical director of the General Electric Laboratory working to develop nuclear power for the Navy, 88

Kings Bay, Georgia, Submarine Base
Well-developed site that is used as a base for Ohio (SSBN-726)-class Trident missile submarines, 250-251

Kitty Hawk, USS (CVA-63)
Aircraft carrier that in the early 1960s was overhauled by the Puget Sound Naval Shipyard, 197

Klein, Captain Fred M., Jr., USN (Ret.)
While growing up in Michigan in the 1920s and 1930s had a strong interest in sailboats, 134; varied naval career that included being a blimp pilot, 134-136

Kniskern, Lieutenant Commander Leslie A., USN (USNA, 1922)
In 1941 went out on behalf of the Bureau of Construction and repair to recruit young officers, 14-15, 17

Laning, Commander Richard B., USN (USNA, 1940)
In the mid-1950s was the first skipper of the nuclear-powered submarine Seawolf (SSN-576), 82-83, 85

Lee, Rear Admiral Paul. F., USN (Ret.) (USNA, 1919)
Service in the Bureau of Ships shortly after World War II, 75; work in the early 1950s in developing the teardrop hull shape for the experimental submarine Albacore (AGSS-569), 98; value as a role model, 280

Lilly, Captain Percy A., Jr., USN (USNA, 1941)
In 1963 was the first commanding officer when the guided missile frigate Gridley (DLG-21) was commissioned, 196

Lindbergh, Charles A.
Aviator who flew over Saginaw, Michigan, shortly after his solo flight in 1927 from New York to Paris, 7

Los Angeles (SSN-688)-Class Submarines
Contending issues in the late 1960s and early 1970s over the design of this class, 238-240

Mandelkorn, Captain Richard S., USN (USNA, 1932)
In the mid-1950s served as production officer of the Portsmouth Naval Shipyard, 167-169

Maritime Commission, U.S.
Relationship during World War II with the Navy's Bureau of Ships, 27-30

Marshall Islands
In the summer of 1946 Bikini Atoll was the site of U.S. testing of nuclear weapons, 75-79

Massachusetts, USS (BB-59)
In September 1941 was launched at a commercial yard in Quincy, Massachusetts, 22-23

Massachusetts Institute of Technology, Cambridge, Massachusetts
From 1970 onward Jackson taught classes in submarine design at MIT, 274-276, 280-281; for many years Dr. Jerome C. Hunsaker, a Naval Academy graduate, taught aeronautics at the school, 276-277; role of Dr. Stark Draper in the late 1950s in developing the guidance system for Polaris missiles, 278-279

McCann Chamber
Device used in the spring of 1939 for recovery of crew members who had been trapped in the submarine Squalus (SS-192) off Portsmouth, New Hampshire, 11-12

McElroy, Rear Admiral Rhodam Yarrott, Jr., USN (USNA, 1935)
His sister married Jackson, 122; on duty in the 1950s in OpNav, 122, 125

McKee, Rear Admiral Andrew I., USN (Ret.), (USNA, 1917)
In the early 1950s did a preliminary design sketch for what proved to be the nuclear-powered submarine Nautilus (SSN-571), 93-94; philosophy on submarine test depth, 94-95; work in the early 1950s in developing the teardrop hull shape for the experimental submarine Albacore (AGSS-569), 98-99; pre-World War II work in submarine design, 141; did limited consulting work after retiring from his post-Navy job with the Electric Boat Division, 158-159; value as a role model, 280

McNamara, Robert S.
As Secretary of Defense in the early 1960s, was impressed by the PERT system for tracking progress of the Polaris program, 162-164, 254-255

Medical Problems
During World War II, while on board the floating dry dock ABSD-3, Jackson measured susceptibility to seasickness as it related to vertical acceleration, 70-71; shortly after World War II Commander Harry Burris had medical problems that diminished his effectiveness within the Bureau of Ships, 86; in the mid-1970s a doctor from the Glomar Explorer provided medical assistance to a seaman from the British merchant ship Belle Hudson after the man had suffered broken ribs, 271-273

Merrill, Captain Grayson, USN (USNA, 1934)
In the mid-1950s served a the first technical director of the Polaris missile program, 131, 152, 163

Michigan, University of
In the 1930s Jackson studied engineering at this school, 9-10, 13-14

Mills, Rear Admiral Earle W., USN (USNA, 1918)
During World War II served as Assistant Chief of the Bureau of Ships, 44; shortly after World War II selected Captain Hyman Rickover to run the nuclear power program, 86

Missiles
Development in the 1940s and 1950s of submarines armed with Regulus I, 129-130; the Regulus program was cancelled to provide funding for Polaris, 130-131; the Polaris program initially considered but then rejected liquid-fueled missiles in favor of solid-fueled, 142-143, 147; development in the late 1950s of the guidance system for Polaris missiles, 155; firing dummy Polaris missiles at San Francisco Naval Shipyard, 156-157; possibility of using Polaris missiles in other ships besides submarines, 157-158; in the late 1950s and early 1960s Polaris missiles were replaced by the more capable Poseidon missiles, 224-226; in the early 1970s Rear Admiral Levering Smith asked Jackson to work in the Special Projects Office on the development of the Trident missile system, 245-246; role of Dr. Stark Draper in the late 1950s in developing the guidance system for Polaris missiles, 278-279

Mizar, USNS (T-AGOR-11)
Oceanographic research ship used in 1969 in the examination of the remains of the submarine Scorpion (SSN-589), 229-230

Moffett Field Naval Air Station, Sunnyvale, California
During World War II was used as a base for blimps, 134-135

Momsen, Captain Charles B., USN (USNA, 1920)
Submarine rescue specialist who in 1945 commanded the battleship South Dakota (BB-57), 11

Moore, Rear Admiral Robert L., USN (USNA, 1930)
In the early 1960s, as Deputy Chief of the Bureau of Ships, went on sea trials of the submarine Thresher (SSN-593) and had strained communications with Vice Admiral Hyman Rickover, 161-162, 175; in 1958 concurred in the assignment of Jackson to Portsmouth Naval Shipyard, 163-164, 171; in the late 1950s commanded the shipyard at Portsmouth, 170-171, 189-190, 193-194; would have been a logical successor if Rickover had retired at the end of a normal career span, 253

Morgan, Rear Admiral Armand M., USN (USNA, 1924)
In the early 1950s chaired a conference leading to the design of the first nuclear-power submarine, 93; in 1958 concurred in the assignment of Jackson to Portsmouth Naval Shipyard, 163-164, 171

Mountbatten, Admiral of the Fleet, Lord Louis, Royal Navy
In the 1950s, during a visit to the United States, went aboard the experimental submarine Albacore (AGSS-569), 123-125

Mumma, Captain Alfred G., USN (USNA, 1926)
Service in the Bureau of Ships shortly after World War II, 75, 86; opposed the choice of Captain Hyman Rickover to run the nuclear power program, 86; in the mid-1950s sent Jackson to work on the design of the Polaris submarines, 115, 128

Nautilus, USS (SSN-571)
Development in the early 1950s of the Navy's first nuclear-powered submarine, 86, 88, 91; Captain Andrew McKee did an early design drawing of the ship, 93-94; debates over whether she should have a weapon system, 95-96; InSurv trials in the mid-1950s, 96-97; in the late 1950s had a periscope problem that was solved by the Portsmouth Naval Shipyard, 116-117

Naval Academy, Annapolis, Maryland
Anti-Semitism was an issue in the early 1920s, 38-39

Naval Reserve, U.S.
In the 1930s Jackson was a reservist while attending the University of Michigan, 10; training cruises on the Great Lakes in the 1930s on board the gunboats Dubuque (IX-9) and Wilmette, 15-16

Naval Sea Systems Command
In the 1990s objected to some of the things that Jackson taught to his students at the Massachusetts Institute of Technology, 281

New Jersey, USS (BB-62)
Battleship that was inactivated in 1969 by the Puget Sound Naval Shipyard, 205

New Mexico, USS (BB-40)
A sailor from the ship was killed during World War II when he fell onto the floor of a floating dry dock at Guam, 61-62

New York Shipbuilding Corporation, Camden, New Jersey
In 1967 the shipyard went out of business because of financial problems, 200-201; problems building submarines, 201

Niedermair, John
Navy civilian engineer who was involved in ship salvage work, 8, 24; role during World War II in designing tank landing ships, 41-42; in the mid-1950s backed Jackson to design the Polaris submarines, 128-129; received the prestigious Saunders and Taylor awards, 281-282

Nimitz, Fleet Admiral Chester W., USN (USNA, 1905)
Had a heavy workload as Chief of Naval Operations shortly after World War II, 125-126

Nuclear Power Program
Role of the General Electric Company in the late 1940s and early 1950s in the Navy's development of nuclear propulsion for ships, 79-80, 83-84, 88-91; earliest officers who were assigned to the program, 81-82; development work at Oak Ridge, Tennessee, 81-82; tests to fit nuclear power in a destroyer escort were not successful because of liquid sodium, 82; use of a sodium-cooled plant in the submarine Seawolf (SSN-576), 82-83; work of the Westinghouse Corporation, 84-85; role of Admiral Hyman Rickover included a strong emphasis on safety, 85-87, 95, 251-253; prototype plant at Arco, Idaho, 90-92; in the mid-1950s the Navy was designing the Triton (SSN-586) as a two-reactor submarine, 120-121, 185; disposition of nuclear reactors after ships go out of service, 121-122; new submarine classes considered in the mid-1950s, 126-127; in the early 1960s the Puget Sound Naval Shipyard got into work on nuclear-powered submarines, 195-197, 201; disposition of spent nuclear fuel, 252

Nuclear Weapons
In the summer of 1946 Bikini Atoll in the Marshall Islands was the site of U.S. testing of nuclear weapons, 75-79; concern about radioactivity during the Bikini tests, 77-78
See also: Polaris Program

Oak Ridge, Tennessee
In the late 1940s was the site of development work in the Navy's nuclear propulsion program, 81-82

Observation Island, USS (EAG-154)
Test ship that fired dummy Polaris missiles in the late 1950s, 157

Offley, Ed
Newspaperman who has written about possible causes of the 1968 loss of the submarine Scorpion (SSN-589), 184, 234, 238

Ohio (SSBN-726)-Class Submarines
In the early 1970s Jackson designed a Trident missile submarine that was a smaller alternative to the Ohio class that was actually built, 246-247, 249-250; fancy bases for the ships at Kings Bay, Georgia, and Bangor, Maine, 250-251

Okinawa
Repair job in September 1945 on the battleship Pennsylvania (BB-38) after she had been torpedoed the previous month at Okinawa, 55-57

Pennsylvania, USS (BB-38)
Was dry-docked for repairs at Guam in September 1945 after having been torpedoed at Okinawa the previous month, 55-57; in 1946 was used as a target for nuclear weapons tests at Bikini Atoll in the Marshall Islands, 77

PERT
See: Program Evaluation Review Technique (PERT)

Pittsburgh, USS (CA-72)
Heavy cruiser that received a temporary bow at Guam in 1945 after her original bow was torn loose in a storm and subsequently salvaged, 57-60, 67

Polaris Program
In the late 1950s Rear Admiral William Raborn demonstrated excellent leadership qualities while running the program, 87, 130, 142, 147-149, 151, 155, 247-248; in the mid-1950s Jackson took on the job of designing the Polaris submarines, 128-129, 132-133, 142-150, 159; initially considered but then rejected liquid-fueled missiles in favor of solid-fueled, 142, 147; decisions concerning the number of missiles to be carried by each submarine, 146-147; the Soviets' launch of the Sputnik satellite in 1957 dramatically sped up the timetable for the Polaris program, 148-151, 158; PERT charts were used primarily as a public relations gimmick, 151-153, 255-256; the first Polaris-armed submarine, George Washington (SSBN-598), went into commission in December 1959 and fired missiles for the first time the following year, 150, 153-154; development in the late 1950s of the guidance system for Polaris missiles, 155; limited role for Rear Admiral Hyman Rickover, 155-156; difficulty getting sufficient trained personnel to man the submarines, 156; firing dummy Polaris missiles at San Francisco Naval Shipyard, 156-157; possibility of using Polaris missiles in other ships besides submarines, 157-158; in the late 1950s and early 1960s Polaris missiles were replaced by the more capable Poseidon missiles, 224-226; evolution and improvement in the submarines from the late 1950s to the late 1960s, 226-227; role of Dr. Stark Draper in the late 1950s in developing the guidance system for the missiles, 278-279

Portsmouth Navy Yard/Naval Shipyard, Kittery, Maine
In the early 1950s did the Guppy modification to the submarine Sea Robin (SS-407), 92, 115-116; design work in the early 1950s on the teardrop-shaped submarine Albacore (AGSS-569), 97-106, 136-139, 141; design and development of the Tang (SS-563)-class submarines in the early 1950s, 99, 106-114; design and development of the Barbel (SS-563)-class submarines in the 1950s, 101-102, 138-139. 141-142, 185; the Albacore is now on display at the shipyard, 103; in the late 1950s Jackson solved a periscope problem on the submarine Nautilus (SSN-571), 116-117; in the 1950s the yard was operated by good people, 117-118; in the late 1950s built the missile-armed submarine Growler (SSG-577), 132; in the late 1950s Jackson had a fine relationship with the families of many shipyard employees, 164; construction of the ballistic missile submarine Abraham Lincoln (SSBN-602), 164-165; experiments in the mid-1950s in preparation for nuclear power work, 166-168; in the late 1950s Rear Admiral Robert Moore commanded the shipyard, 170-171; construction in the late 1950s-early 1960s of the submarine Thresher (SSN-593), 172-176, 191; construction and repair of Skate (SSN-578)-class submarines, 185-189; top-notch individuals assigned to the command in the late 1950s and early 1960s, 190-191; application of managerial techniques from Harvard Business School, 192-193;

internal friction between departments within the shipyard, 193-194; dramatic increase in the rate of building submarines by the Portsmouth Navy Yard as World War II approached, 261

Poseidon Missiles
In the late 1950s and early 1960s Polaris missiles were replaced in submarines by the more capable Poseidon missiles, 224-226

Program Evaluation Review Technique (PERT)
Was used in the Polaris program in the late 1950s and early 1960s primarily as a public relations gimmick, 151-153, 255-256

Propulsion Plants
Reciprocating engine operated in the 1930s on board the Naval Reserve training ship Wilmette, 16-17; in the 1930s, ship propulsion machinery was getting lighter in weight, 33; the destroyer escorts built in World War II had a wide variety of engineering plants, 40-41; role of the General Electric Company in the late 1940s and early 1950s in the Navy's development of nuclear propulsion for ships, 79-80, 83-84, 88-91; in the early 1950s the Tang (SS-563)-class submarines experienced lots of problems with pancake-type diesel engines, which were later replaced, 106-114; in the mid-1950s the U.S. Navy was designing the Triton (SSN-586) as its first two-reactor submarine, 120-121, 185; disposition of nuclear reactors after ships go out of service, 121-122

Puget Sound Naval Shipyard, Bremerton, Washington
Work in the early 1960s on nuclear-powered submarines, 195-197, 201; construction in the early 1960s of the guided missile frigates Gridley (DLG-21) and Reeves (DLG-24), 196; overhaul work on different types of ships, 197-198, 209; construction in the early 1960s of the fast combat support ship Sacramento (AOE-1), 198-199; in the early 1960s a number of mothballed ships were preserved by the shipyard, 203-204; inactivation in 1969 of the battleship New Jersey (BB-62), 205; role of the planning department in the early 1960s, 206-208; training for shipyard workers, 208-209

Pyne, Captain Schuyler N., USN (USNA, 1925)
In 1941 went out on behalf of the Bureau of Construction and repair to recruit young officers, 14-15, 17; in 1945-46 served as industrial manager for the Naval Operating Base Guam, 49-50

Quincy Division, General Dynamics Corporation
In the mid 1950s converted two tankers to become range instrumentation ships, 219-223; labor union problems in the 1960s, 220

Raborn, Rear Admiral William F., Jr., USN (USNA, 1928)
Leadership qualities in the late 1950s while running the Polaris missile program, 87, 130, 142, 147-149, 151, 155, 247-248; used the PERT system primarily as a public

relations gesture, 151-154, 255-256; post-retirement activities as a consultant, 254-256; aviation experience, 256

Radio
Development in the late 1950s of a retractable whip antenna for Thresher (SSN-593)-class submarines to use for radio communications, 143-144

Reeves, USS (DLG-24)
Guided missile frigate built in the early 1960s by the Puget Sound Naval Shipyard, 196

Regulus Missile
Development in the 1940s and 1950s of submarines armed with Regulus I, 129-130, 189-190; the program was cancelled to provide funding for Polaris, 130-131

Religion
Admiral Hyman Rickover misused the Anti-Semitism issue, claiming it was the reason people opposed him, 38-40; Anti-Semitism was an issue in the early 1920s at the Naval Academy, 38-39

Rescue at Sea
Recovery in the spring of 1939 of crew members who had been trapped in the submarine Squalus (SS-192) off Portsmouth, New Hampshire, 10-12

Reserve Fleet
In the early 1960s a number of mothballed ships were preserved by the Puget Sound Naval Shipyard, 203-205

Rickover, Captain Hyman G., USN (USNA, 1922)
During World War II headed the electrical section in the Bureau of Ships, 37-38; misused the Anti-Semitism issue, claiming it was the reason people opposed him, 38-40; personality, 40, 248, 253; shortly after World War II got involved in the Navy's nuclear power program, 85-87, 95; in the mid-1950s had a number of contacts with Jackson, 127-128; concerns in the late 1950s about the development of the Polaris ballistic missile submarine program, 155-156; in the early 1960s went on sea trials of the submarine Thresher (SSN-593) and had strained communications with Rear Admiral Robert Moore, 161-162, 175; involvement in the submarine program in the mid-to-late 1960s, 227, 239-241; varied legacy includes a strong emphasis on safety, 251-252; stayed too long on active duty, 252-253

Roddis, Lieutenant Commander Louis H., USN (USNA, 1939)
In 1946 was involved with nuclear weapons tests at Bikini Atoll in the Marshall Islands, 75-76; shortly after World War II became one of the first U.S. Navy officers involved in the development of nuclear propulsion, 81-82

Rodney, HMS
  British battleship that was repaired by the Boston Navy Yard in 1941 after sustaining battle damage, 19-20

Roseborough, Commander William D., Jr., USN (USNA, 1940)
  In the mid-1950s was one of the finalists to work on the design of Polaris submarines, 128-129; in the early 1960s was planning officer at the Portsmouth Naval Shipyard, 171

Royal Navy
  The British battleship Rodney was repaired by the Boston Navy Yard in 1941 after sustaining battle damage, 19-20; in September 1941 acquired the U.S. destroyer Welles (DD-257), which became HMS Cameron, 20-21; Corps of Naval Constructors, 21; during World War II supplied the U.S. Navy with plans for antisubmarine ships, 28; had a role in designing tank landing ships (LSTs) during World War II, 42; in the 1950s incorporated into British submarines lessons learned from the U.S. experimental submarine Albacore (AGSS-569), 101; in the 1950s Lord Louis Mountbatten went on board the Albacore during a visit to the United States, 123-125

Russian Navy
  Decline of its submarine capability in the 1990s following the demise of the Soviet Union, 259

S-4, USS (SS-109)
  After this submarine sank in 1927, Jackson made a model of it and practiced salvaging the model, 4-5, 244

Sachse, Lieutenant Commander Clark D, USN
  Engineering duty officer who assisted Jackson in 1969 during the examination of the remains of the submarine Scorpion (SSN-589), 229

Sacramento (AOE-1)
  Fast combat support ship that was built in the early 1960s by the Puget Sound Naval Shipyard, 198-200; correction of problems with hydro-elasticity in the steering system, 199, 222; the ship's engines came from the unfinished battleship Kentucky (BB-66), 200; was home-ported in Bremerton, Washington, after being commissioned, 208

Safety
  Accidents on board the floating dry dock ABSD-3 took place during World War II because safety precautions were not followed, 61-62; Admiral Hyman Rickover's varied legacy includes a strong emphasis on safety, 251-252;

Sailing
  Jackson was involved for many years in sailboats and sailing, 5-6, 134, 283-284

Salvage
   In the early 1940s large pontoons for ship salvage were stored at the Boston Navy Yard, 23-25; recovery of the bow of the heavy cruiser Pittsburgh (CA-72) in June 1945 after the bow was torn off in a typhoon, 58-60; in the mid-1970s the United States ran Project Jennifer, an attempt to raise a Soviet Golf-class submarine that had been lost in 1968 northwest of Hawaii, 262-274

San Francisco Naval Shipyard
   In the late 1950s the yard fired dummy Polaris missiles as part of the submarine-launched ballistic missile program, 156-157

Saratoga, USS (CV-3)
   Aircraft carrier that sank at Bikini Atoll in the Marshall Islands after being a target for nuclear weapons tests, 76, 78

Schultz, Rear Admiral Floyd B., USN (USNA, 1932)
   In the mid-1960s commanded the Puget Sound Naval Shipyard, 208

Scorpion, USS (SSN-589)
   Submarine that was lost in the spring of 1968 while en route to Norfolk, 180, 184; mission in 1969 to examine the remains of the ship in the Atlantic, near the Azores, to determine what had caused her sinking, 228-233; possible conclusions on the cause of the loss, 233-238

Seadragon, USS (SSN-584)
   Submarine that in the early 1960s did arctic under-ice operations, 185-188; received repairs at the Portsmouth Naval Shipyard, 186-187; collision with a whale, 189

Sea Robin, USS (SS-407)
   Submarine that in the early 1950s received the Guppy modification at Portsmouth Naval Shipyard, 92, 115-116

Seawolf, USS (SSN-21)
   New submarine developed in the 1990s for the U.S. Navy, 258-259

Seawolf, USS (SSN-576)
   Submarine that went into service in the mid-1950s equipped with a sodium-cooled nuclear reactor, 82-83, 85, 88

Shear, Admiral Harold E., USN (Ret.) (USNA, 1942)
   In his oral history he complained about the diesel engines in Tang (SS-563)–class submarines, 106; in the mid-1960s commanded the fast combat support ship Sacramento (AOE-1), 198, 208; personality of, 208; expressed displeasure about a magazine article that offered conjecture on causes of the 1968 loss of the submarine Scorpion (SSN-589), 236-237

Shipbuilding
In 1941 the Boston Navy Yard was involved in a variety of ship construction and repair projects, 18-26; submarine construction in the 1950s by the Electric Boat Division of General Dynamics, 108, 113-114, 149, 155-156, 158-159, 214-219, 224-225; submarine construction in the 1950s and 1960s by the Portsmouth Naval Shipyard, 113-114, 132, 164-165, 172-176, 185-189, 191; building of various types in the early 1960s by the Puget Sound Naval Shipyard, 195-199, 201; dramatic increase in the rate of building submarines by the Portsmouth Navy Yard as World War II approached, 261; in the early 1970s the United States developed a large ship called the Glomar Explorer for use in an attempt to raise a Soviet Golf-class submarine that had been lost in 1968 northwest of Hawaii, 262-267

Ship Design
Role of the Bureau of Ships during World War II in designing various classes of ships, 31-36, 40-42; detail designs by Gibbs & Cox, Inc., 32, 36; early designs in the late 1940s and early 1950s for nuclear-powered submarines, 90, 93; Andrew McKee's philosophy on submarine test depth, 94-95; design in the early 1950s of the teardrop-shaped submarine Albacore (AGSS-569), 97-106, 136-139, 141, 184-185; design and development of the Tang (SS-563)-class submarines in the early 1950s, 99, 106-113; design and development of the Barbel (SS-580)-class submarines in the 1950s, 101-102, 138-139, 141-142, 185; benefits of having counter-rotating propellers in submarines, 102; the Skipjack (SSN-585) class was the first to apply the teardrop hull to nuclear-powered submarines, 103-104, 139; selection of a nuclear power plant and then design of a submarine to house it, 127; in the mid-1950s Jackson took on the job of designing the Polaris submarines, 128-129, 132-133, 142-150, 158-159; submarine design experiments in the pre-World War II period, 141; design in the late 1950s of Ethan Allen (SSBN-608)-class ballistic missile submarines, 150; design work in the late 1950s for the Thresher (SSN-593)-class submarines, 160-161, 172, 182-184; design of the Sturgeon (SSN-637)-class submarines as a lengthened version of the Thresher class, 176-177; philosophy of submarine design, 191-192; design in the early 1960s of the Sacramento (AOE-1)-class fast combat support ships, 198-199; contenders in the late 1960s for a new submarine design, which turned out to be the Los Angeles (SSN-688) class, 238-240; in the early 1970s Jackson designed a Trident missile submarine that was a smaller alternative to the Ohio (SSBN-726) class that was actually built, 246-247, 249-250; in the early 1970s the United States developed a large ship called the Glomar Explorer for use in an attempt to raise a Soviet Golf-class submarine that had been lost in 1968 northwest of Hawaii, 262-267; from 1970 onward Jackson taught classes in submarine design at MIT, 274-276, 280-281

Shugg, Carleton (USNA, 1921)
In the late 1950s was president of the Electric Boat Division of the General Dynamics Corporation during the building of the first Polaris submarines, 149, 155-156

Skipjack (SS-585)-Class Submarines
Designed in the 1950s as the first U.S. nuclear-powered submarines to have teardrop-shaped hulls, 103-104, 139; parts for the planned Scorpion (SSN-589) were used for the first Polaris submarine, George Washington (SSBN-598), 149-150; the Thresher (SSN-593) class was designed as an improvement over the Skipjack class, 160-161

Smith, Rear Admiral Levering, USN (USNA, 1932)
Universally admired officer who took over in the late 1950s as technical director of the Polaris program, 131-132; in the early 1970s asked Jackson to work in the Special Projects Office on the development of the Trident missile system, 245-246, 254; personality and leadership style, 247-249

South Dakota, USS (BB-57)
In the summer of 1945 this battleship was dry-docked at Guam for repairs, 11, 53-54

Soviet Navy
In the mid-1970s the United States ran Project Jennifer, an attempt to raise a Soviet Golf-class submarine that had been lost in 1968 northwest of Hawaii, 262-274

Soviet Union
The launch of the Sputnik satellite in 1957 dramatically sped up the timetable for the Polaris program, 148-150

Special Projects Office
Established in the late 1950s to oversee the development of the Polaris program, 142-143; development in the late 1950s of the guidance system for Polaris missiles, 155; in the early 1970s Rear Admiral Levering Smith asked Jackson to work in the Special Projects Office on the development of the Trident missile system, 245-246, 254

Spence, USS (DD-512)
Destroyer that capsized in a typhoon off the Philippines in December 1944 as the result of not being properly ballasted, 33-35

Sputnik
The Soviets' launch of the Sputnik earth satellite in 1957 dramatically sped up the timetable for the Polaris ballistic missile program, 148-149

Squalus, USS (SS-192)
Submarine that sank in May 1939 while doing practice dives off Portsmouth, New Hampshire, 10-13

Steele, Commander George P. II, USN (USNA, 1945)
Commanded the submarine Seadragon (SSN-584) in 1960 during under-ice operations in the Arctic, 187-188

Stevens, Captain Wynne A., Jr., USN
In 1964 was the first commanding officer when the guided missile frigate Reeves (DLG-24) was commissioned, 196

Strauss, Commander Ben A., USN
Was planning officer in the late 1950s for the Portsmouth Naval Shipyard, 116-117, 190; family of, 190; in 1963 had to retire from the Navy, 195

Sturgeon (SSN-637)-Class Submarines
Designed in the early 1960s as a lengthened version of the Thresher (SSN-593) class, 176-177; conducted under-ice operations in the Arctic, 188-189; construction of in the 1960s by the Electric Boat Division, 224-225; the submarines were still in fine shape when decommissioned in the 1990s, 260

Submarine Force Atlantic Fleet
In the early 1950s tried to stifle maneuvers by the experimental submarine Albacore (AGSS-569) that were well beyond the previous norms, 101, 139

Submarine Rescue
Recovery in the spring of 1939 of crew members who had been trapped in the submarine Squalus (SS-192) off Portsmouth, New Hampshire, 10-12

SubSafe Program
Was initiated in the early 1960s and then sped up after the April 1963 loss of the submarine Thresher (SSN-593), 177-180

Sullivan, Commodore William A., USN
Supervised the recovery of the bow of the heavy cruiser Pittsburgh (CA-72) in June 1945 after the bow was torn off in a typhoon, 58-60; relationship with Captain Edward Ellsberg, 61

Tang, USS (SS-563)
Problems that developed on sea trials in the early 1950s with overheating in the stern diving section, 110-112; Enders Huey was the first skipper of the boat, 113; problems during construction with hydraulic systems, 165

Tang (SS-563)-Class Submarines
Design and development of the first class of post-World War II in the early 1950s, 99, 106-113; lots of problems with pancake-type diesel engines, 106-109; in later years the submarines were lengthened and given new engines, 107-108; problems that developed on sea trials with heating in the stern diving section, 110-112; Commander Enders Huey was the first skipper of the Tang, 113

Teller, Dr. Edward
Role in the mid-1960s in pushing the Polaris missile program forward, 148

Thresher, USS (SSN-593)

In the early 1960s this submarine went on sea trials out of the Portsmouth Naval Shipyard, 6-7, 161-162, 175-176, 180; construction of in the late 1950s-early 1960s, 172-176, 191; in July 1960 the submarine was launched, 172-174; in April 1963 the submarine was lost because of internal flooding, 177-179; investigation following the loss into the causes of the sinking, 182-184

Thresher (SSN-593)-Class Submarines

Problems with silver-brazed pipe joints, 109; development of a retractable whip antenna for radio communications, 143-144; in the late 1950s the Bureau of Ships preliminary design work on the class, designed as an improvement over the Skipjack (SSN-585) class, 160-161, 172

Train, Commander Harry D. II, USN (USNA, 1949)

In the early 1960s commanded the diesel submarine Barbel (SS-580), when she was overhauled by the Puget Sound Naval Shipyard, 209-211

Trident Program

In the early 1970s Rear Admiral Levering Smith asked Jackson to work in the Special Projects Office on the development of the Trident missile system, 245-246; in the early 1970s Jackson designed a Trident missile submarine that was a smaller alternative to the Ohio (SSBN-726) class that was actually built, 246-247, 249-250; fancy bases for the ships at Kings Bay, Georgia, and Bangor, Maine, 250-251

Trieste

Navy bathyscaphe that in 1960 made a dive to the deepest part of the ocean, 209-210; in 1969 was used in the search for the remains of the submarine Scorpion (SSN-589), 229-232

Triton, USS (SSN-586)

Was designed in the mid-1950s as the U.S. Navy's first two-reactor submarine, 120-121, 185; search for a mission for the ship, 121; in 1969 she became the first nuclear submarine to be taken out of service, 121-122

Trout, USS (SS-566)

Submarine that was used in the late 1950s for heavy-weather tests connected with the design of Polaris submarines, 145-146

Tullibee, USS ((SSN-597)

Nuclear submarine that in the early 1960 operated with the new submarine Thresher (SSN-593), 180-181

Veliotis, P. Takis

In the 1970s was controversial as general manager of the Electric Boat Division of General Dynamics, 218

Wadsworth, Lieutenant Commander Frank A., USN (USNA, 1944)
In the early 1950s, as a submarine division commander, was told by his type commander, ComSubLant, to inhibit the trials performed by the experimental submarine Albacore (AGSS-569), 101

Wahoo, USS (SS-565)
Submarine built in the early 1950s by the Portsmouth Naval Shipyard had some initial engine problems, 113-114, 210-211

Wake Island, USS (CVE-65)
Escort carrier that received repairs at Guam in World War II after being hit by a bomb, 57, 62

Walsh, Lieutenant Don, USN (USNA, 1954)
In January 1960 he and Jacques Piccard set a depth record in by bathyscaphe Trieste, 209-210

Washington, D.C.
Housing was scarce in the city during World War II, 27

Weather
In December 1944 three destroyers were lost during a typhoon near the Philippines, 33-35; in June 1945 the bow of the heavy cruiser Pittsburgh (CA-72) was torn off in a typhoon, 57-60; in the late 1950s the submarine Trout (SS-566) was used for heavy-weather tests connected with the design of Polaris submarines, 145-146

Welles, USS (DD-257)
U.S. destroyer that was turned over to the Royal Navy in September 1941, 20-21

Westinghouse Corporation
In the late 1940s was involved in the development of nuclear propulsion plants for Navy ships, 84-85

Wharton, USS (AP-7)
Transport that was used in the summer of 1946 as a barracks ship during nuclear weapons tests at Bikini Atoll in the Marshall Islands, 75, 77

Wilkinson, Commander Eugene P., USN
In the late 1940s was one of the earliest officers involved in the Navy's development of nuclear propulsion for ships, 81, 84; in the mid-1950s was the first commanding officer of the submarine Nautilus (SSN-571), 85, 95-97; in 1952 was the first commanding officer of the submarine Wahoo (SS-565) when she went into commission, 113-114

Wilmette, USS
Gunboat that was used in the 1930s for Naval Reserve training cruises on the Great Lakes, 16-17

Wolfson, Louis
In 1967 liquidated the New York Shipbuilding Corporation because of financial problems, 200-201

Wylie, Lieutenant Commander Joseph C., USN (USNA, 1932)
Capable officer who served during World War II as first executive officer of the destroyer Fletcher (DD-445), 32

X-1, USS
This midget submarine, built in the mid-1950s, carried bags of hydrogen peroxide in her ballast tanks, 166; the ship, which was designed to carry commandos, had a short career, 169-170